Room at the Inn

Historic Hotels of British Columbia's Southern Interior

Room at the Inn

Glen A. Mofford

FOREWORD BY GREG NESTEROFF

Copyright © 2023 Glen A. Mofford;
Foreword copyright © 2023 Greg Nesteroff

All rights reserved. No part of this publication may be reproduced, stored in a retrieval system, or transmitted in any form or by any means—electronic, mechanical, audio recording, or otherwise—without the written permission of the publisher or a licence from Access Copyright, Toronto, Canada.

Heritage House Publishing Company Ltd.
heritagehouse.ca

*Cataloguing information available from
Library and Archives Canada*
978-1-77203-423-3 (paperback)
978-1-77203-424-0 (e-book)

Edited by Karla Decker
Proofread by Nandini Thaker
Cover and interior design by Setareh Ashrafologhalai
Cover image: The Kalamalka Hotel, ca. 1935.
Image F-02471 courtesy of the Royal BC Museum.
All best efforts were made to confirm and reconcile source material and references in the text as well as to track down the original sources of all the images included.

The interior of this book was produced on FSC®-certified, acid-free paper, processed chlorine free, and printed with vegetable-based inks.

Heritage House gratefully acknowledges that the land on which we live and work is within the traditional territories of the Lkwungen (Esquimalt and Songhees), Malahat, Pacheedaht, Scia'new, T'Sou-ke, and W̱SÁNEĆ (Pauquachin, Tsartlip, Tsawout, Tseycum) Peoples.

We acknowledge the financial support of the Government of Canada through the Canada Book Fund (CBF) and the Canada Council for the Arts, and the Province of British Columbia through the British Columbia Arts Council and the Book Publishing Tax Credit.

27 26 25 24 23   1 2 3 4 5

Printed in Canada

This book is dedicated to my brother, David Mofford, and my sister-in-law, Evelyn Mofford. And to my lifelong friend, Selene Higgins

CONTENTS

PUBLISHER'S NOTE
xi

FOREWORD
1

CHAPTER ONE
Similkameen, Nicola, Thompson, and Shuswap
5

CHAPTER TWO
The Okanagan
67

CHAPTER THREE
Boundary Country
143

CHAPTER FOUR
West Kootenay
Part One
173

CHAPTER FIVE
West Kootenay
Part Two
211

CHAPTER SIX
East Kootenay
257

AFTERWORD
285

ENDNOTES
287

SELECTED BIBLIOGRAPHY
321

Forty Historic Hotels of BC's Southern Interior

○ **Similkameen, Nicola, Thompson, Shuswap:**
1) Keremeos Hotel
2) Princeton Hotel
3) Coalmont Hotel
4) Driard Hotel
5) Spences Bridge Hotel
6) Ashcroft Hotel
7) Walhachin Hotel
8) Montreal / Leland Hotel
9) Montebello Hotel

◇ **Okanagan:**
10) King Edward Hotel
11) Armstrong Hotel
12) Kalamalka Hotel
13) Eldorado Arms
14) Lakeview / Mayfair Hotel
15) Palace / Royal Anne Hotel
16) Summerland Hotel
17) BC Hotel
18) Incola Hotel
19) Oliver Hotel
20) Reopel Hotel
21) Rialto Hotel

✕ **Boundary Country:**
22) Bridesville Hotel
23) Riverside Hotel
24) Beaverdell Hotel
25) Winnipeg Hotel

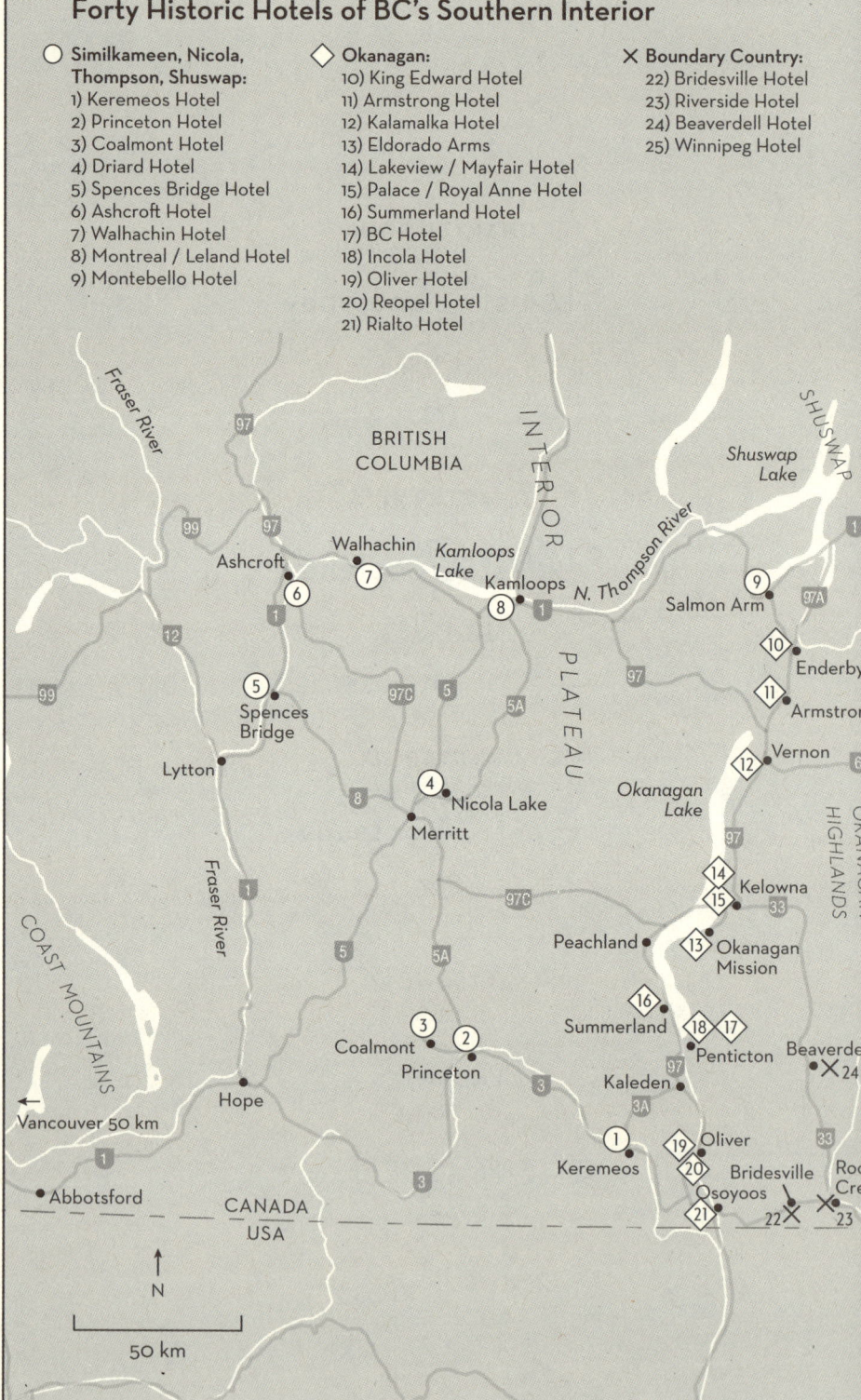

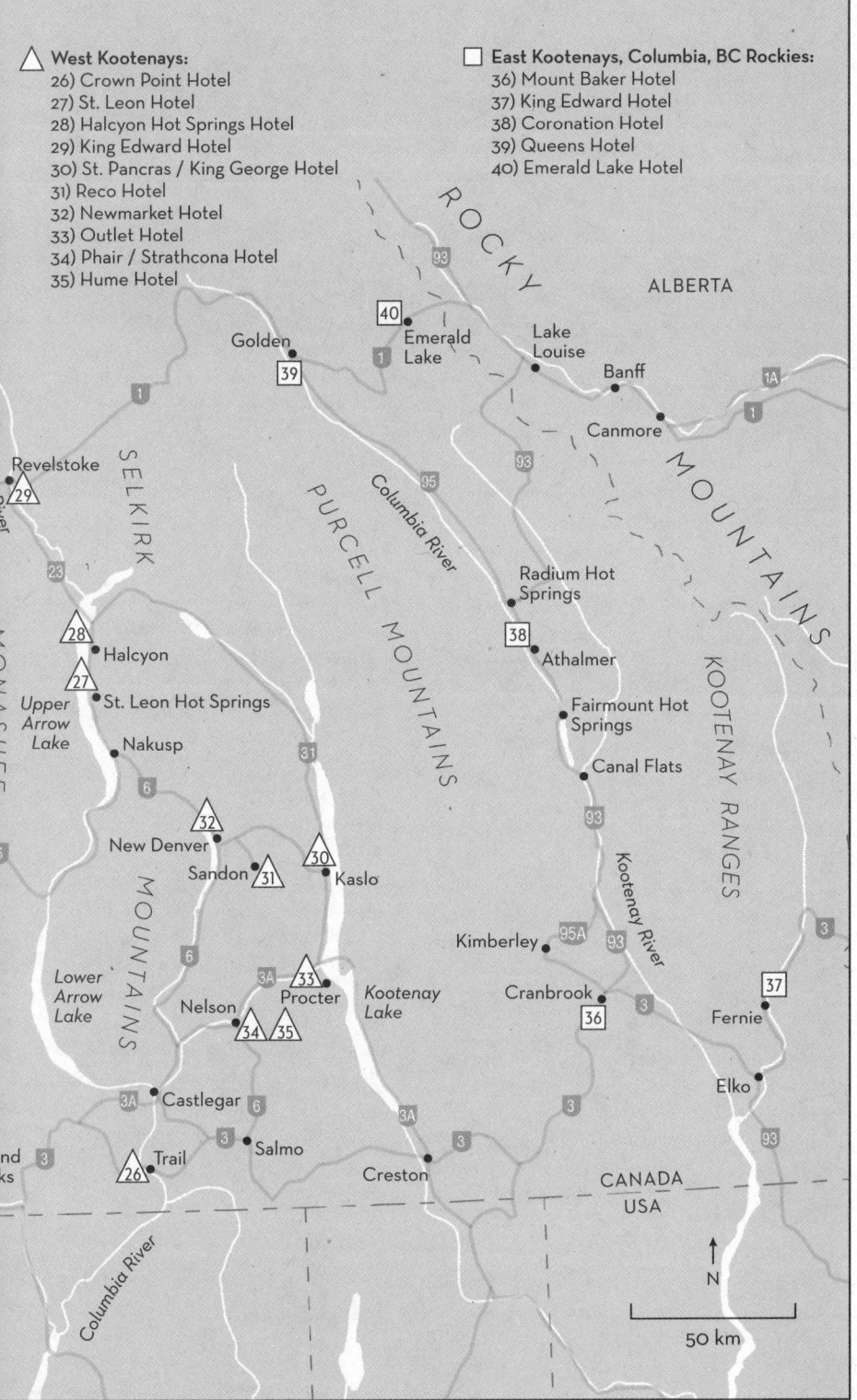

PUBLISHER'S NOTE

It is important to acknowledge the hotels described in this book operated on the unceded traditional and ancestral territories of a number of Indigenous Peoples, including the Ktunaxa, Nlaka'pamux, Secwépemc, Sinixt, St'át'imc, and Syilx Peoples, who have lived on and been stewards of the land for millennia. Many of the trails and transport routes that connect the different towns and cities mentioned in this book were, and still are, used by Indigenous Peoples as seasonal travel and trade routes. As many of the hotels described were built and operated during times of colonial expansion across the British Columbia, Indigenous Peoples were frequently squeezed into shrinking territories or pushed out entirely to instead provide land for white settlers and homesteaders, mining claims, new towns, and the Canadian Pacific Railway.

Until around the First World War, it was common for many social institutions and businesses to openly adopt policies to only serve white patrons. Even though many of them employed Indigenous, Black, and Asian people among their staff, some hotels and pubs remained inaccessible by people of colour for years, even after the 1920s, until attitudes and social policies changed and became more open and equitable.

FOREWORD

COMMUNITIES IN BC are sometimes measured in hotels. A long-standing habit in popular history is to evaluate a town's importance by the number and quality of its hostelries. A fledgling city that boasted many places to stay, dine, and drink must have been very prosperous and significant indeed, or so we are invited to conclude.

They may not have all been palatial, but pioneer hotels were and are a beloved part of our province's heritage. Aside from their architectural, economic, and historic significance, they contributed to our well being.

They were a welcome respite for weary or thirsty travellers looking to spend the night, particularly in the days when travel was much more difficult and time-consuming. They were local landmarks. They served as community centres before the concept existed. Some may have been very modest, no more than glorified log cabins, while others were lavish, built by owners who spared no expense.

Some survived to the present and continue to function much as they originally did. Many more, however, live on only in memory.

It's the good times we associate with them, I believe, that makes their histories so compelling.

Glen Mofford, the pre-eminent authority on BC's frontier hotels and pubs, having written two earlier books about them, chose forty such establishments from the southern interior to profile in these pages. They're a mix of well-known and obscure. He could have easily picked forty different ones, yet in some ways the overall story would be the same.

Many hotels followed a similar trajectory, beginning with their construction around the turn of the twentieth century by someone hoping to cash in on a mining or railway boom (or enjoying success from that boom).

For a while, the hotel reverberates with dances, banquets, and parties. But it falls on hard times with the outbreak of the First World War and enactment of Prohibition. The long-time proprietor decides to sell.

Business rebounds during the beer parlour era, but a series of additions and modernizations robs the hotel of much of its original charm. During the mid-twentieth century, a dizzying number of owners and managers come and go, each leaving their mark, though not always for the better.

Then one day, perhaps to no one's surprise, fire claims the building. There may have been numerous close calls leading up to the final big blaze. Overnight, all that community capital goes up in smoke.

A distressing number of pioneer hotels met this fate—a result of a combination of wooden construction, lack of fire codes and standards, and ever-present lit cigarettes—and each year it seems like we lose another.

Some were rebuilt, but many more were not, leaving gaping holes in their towns, physically and psychically. Today they are remembered fondly and wistfully.

Of course, many variations exist on this basic outline, and many stories can be told from within their walls

In addition to the stories of the buildings are the stories of the people who built and ran them. While the proprietors were usually men, you'll find a few notable exceptions, including a Chinese Canadian woman who ran a hotel in Ashcroft.

Many of these stories have never been told, which is sometimes surprising given how important the hotels were and are to their communities.

This book is a tribute to them. It's also a tribute to Glen Mofford himself, who died suddenly in February 2022 at the age of sixty-eight, only a few days after completing the manuscript.

It came as a horrible shock to his family and all who knew him. But I'm certain he would have been very pleased to see the book come to fruition.

We're all better for the efforts he invested in chronicling BC's historic hotels and pubs. The next time you spend the night or raise a glass in one, you can thank him.

GREG NESTEROFF
January 2023

CHAPTER ONE

Similkameen, Nicola, Thompson, and Shuswap

KEREMEOS HOTEL

(1907–60)
Keremeos, BC

IN 1892, George and Ada Frances Kirby, with their daughters in tow (Violet, aged two, and infant Louise May), emigrated from England to Victoria, British Columbia. Shortly after arriving, they decided to move to Vancouver, into a house they rented on Granville Street. George Kirby had a difficult time finding suitable employment, and after three months of fruitless searches, he accepted the advice of his brother Stanley and moved the family to Okanagan Mission, a small town just south of Kelowna. The Kirbys lived there from 1893 to 1896, adding two more girls to their brood: Marguerite ("Rita"), born in 1893, and Mildred, in 1895. The following year, George Kirby landed a well-paying job as a bookkeeper for the Stemwinder Mine Company in the bustling Okanagan mining community of Fairview, today a ghost town located just west of Oliver.[1]

In 1899, the Kirbys pre-empted land west of Fairview at Shuttleworth Creek in what was later called "Upper" Keremeos, signifying that the community was located at a higher elevation compared to subsequent settlements that sprang up nearby. The Kirbys built their home there, and, nearby, George planted an apricot tree in 1901. They also built a general store that contained the post office.[2] Over the next few years a community grew up around Kirby's store, including new businesses such as a livery stable, butcher shop, real estate office, blacksmith's shop, and bakery. The growing town's future seemed assured until fate stepped in and dealt a blow to the fledgling community and to the Kirby family personally.

Keremeos Hotel, ca. 1930. IMAGE E-03831 COURTESY OF THE ROYAL BC MUSEUM

The newest member of the Kirby family was a healthy boy they named George Donavan ("Donny"). When he was two years old, curious little Donny found some matches and crawled under the front stairs of the Kirby store and began playing with them, starting a fire that soon burned down the family business—but not before little Donny safely escaped. The loss was financially devastating for the Kirbys; as luck would have it, their business insurance had lapsed only a week earlier.[3] With the loss of the store and all their merchandise, the Kirbys' finances were in a desperate state, so they quickly came up with a plan to rebound. They decided to go into the hotel business and scrambled to add a second storey to their home that would operate as a hotel.[4]

George Kirby, an astute businessman and now the postmaster of Upper Keremeos, caught news that the Victoria, Vancouver and Eastern Railway (VV&E), an arm of the Great Northern Railroad, was planning to build a line through from Oroville, Washington, to Hedley, BC, and that the line would pass on the level ground close to the Similkameen River. Kirby wisely purchased a lot at the newest townsite near the railway right-of-way and built the Keremeos Hotel. In 1905, the Kirbys moved to the new location, named Keremeos Centre, only two miles away from Upper Keremeos. Both towns were constructed on the arid flats to the northeast of present-day Keremeos. Keremeos Centre quickly became a mining supply depot and stagecoach stop.[5] In 1906, the town shifted for the last time by about a half mile to where it is situated today. The VV&E Railway promised a stable future for the town's inhabitants from the flow of commerce and travellers passing through. As long as the mines continued to produce, there was optimism that the years ahead would be prosperous. By 1906, Upper Keremeos was totally abandoned as the population had moved closer to the railway station. George Kirby was pleased and thankful that his new hotel was located across the street from the new train station and that the struggles of the past few years were over. In fact, business at the hotel over the next seven years would prove excellent as Keremeos came into its own.

The Keremeos Hotel became one of a handful of social centres in town where clubs and businesses held their meetings and where dances and other social functions took place. On one occasion, the Ladies Guild of Keremeos put on a dinner and charity dance at the hotel. A highlight of the evening was when the participants were treated to a comic song sung by their gracious host, George Kirby. Fifty dollars was raised that evening that went to "deserving cases."[6] These were the days before the social safety net protected people, before Old Age pensions, employment insurance, and social assistance. People had to rely on help from charities, trade unions, and organizations like the Salvation Army. George Kirby was very active in community affairs, becoming president of the Keremeos Board of Trade and sitting on the public school board.[7]

In March 1910, a fire broke out in the nearby Alcazar Hotel. The flames travelled down the stovepipe into the bar below, where the fire spread quickly throughout the wood structure and gave only the briefest of time for the staff and guests to grab what they could and flee. By the time the Alcazar was fully engulfed in flames, a water-bucket line had been formed as citizens frantically fought to stop the flames that threatened nearby buildings such as the Innis Brothers stables.[8]

The threat of fire was one thing, but the loss of a child was the worst fear that a parent could endure. On September 12, 1910, the Kirbys' nineteen-year-old daughter, Louise ("Lulu") May, died from diabetes. She left behind her husband, Henry ("Mannie") Barcelo, and two sons, aged two years and three months.[9] Ada Kirby kept busy, trying to keep her mind off the tragic loss of her daughter. She began taking a more active role in the management of the Keremeos Hotel. When George Kirby went away on business, Ada ran the hotel. In the fall of 1912, George Kirby applied to have the hotel licence transferred from his name to Ada's.

There is some discrepancy as to what happened to George Kirby after that. In May 1913, George and Ada spent about a week at beautiful Banff on a well-deserved holiday. On their return to Keremeos on May 8, they were interviewed by the Hedley newspaper. As George had not been seen in town in weeks, rumour had it he was in the Okanagan drumming up business. The newspaper reporter commented that Mr. George Kirby was, "looking fine and as young as ever."[10] Some contemporary articles written about the history of the Keremeos Hotel mention that George Kirby died on May 18, 1913, in Vancouver, BC. But I found this was not the case. The George Kirby who died in Vancouver and the George Kirby that opened and operated the Keremeos Hotel were two different people. Our George Kirby lived a long life and died at his home in Spokane, Washington, in August 1960, at the ripe old age of ninety-three.[11] I had wondered why I couldn't find anything about George Kirby after 1913 and speculated that he and his wife Ada had a falling-out and separated. This is supported by the fact that George left for Oroville, Washington, in 1917 and never returned. Ada Kirby became the sole owner of the Keremeos Hotel. Keremeos resident and former mayor Francis Peck recalls having tea at the Keremeos Hotel: "I remember Mrs. Kirby, walking down the street in high boots and old fashioned clothing, with her dogs. My mother and I had many teas with Mrs. Kirby." Peck's recollections are from the era when the hotel's main entrance was at the corner of Seventh Street and Veterans Avenue.[12] Ada continued as proprietress of the Keremeos Hotel for the next thirty years. After George had left, around 1917, Ada advertised for a woman to assist in the general duties at the Keremeos Hotel.[13]

In the summer of 1926, a fire destroyed a handful of buildings in Keremeos, including the liquor store. A new location, either in a new building or another existing structure, was needed to house the replacement. Ada suggested that the liquor board lease her spacious pool room in the hotel, and on February 28, 1928, the new liquor outlet in Keremeos opened inside the Keremeos Hotel, to the delight of local and American customers.[14] After the prohibition of alcohol had been repealed in British Columbia in 1920 and the first liquor outlets opened in Victoria and Vancouver in June 1921, service expanded throughout the province. The situation was quite different in the US, where Prohibition was in effect from January 1, 1920, until it was repealed in 1933. But Prohibition didn't stop the Americans living just across the border from Keremeos from purchasing their fill at the new liquor store.

Having a liquor store inside the hotel was helpful for the bottom line, and with the café and beer parlour (beverage room), business at the Keremeos Hotel was very good. Ada ran simple but effective advertisements on a regular basis in newspapers from the Similkameen to the BC coast that read, "Hotel Keremeos—well furnished, comfortable."[15]

On the eve of the Second World War in 1939, Ada was in her mid-seventies and, having successfully run the Keremeos Hotel for thirty-two mostly wonderful years, she decided to retire. She put the hotel up for lease, retaining ownership of the only business and home she had known since she and her family had moved from Upper Keremeos in 1906. A parade of proprietors followed from 1940 to 1945: Mr. and Mrs. W.A. Phillips, Mrs. K. Matthews, Mrs. P. Matvonko, and J. Morra.

Ada Frances Kirby passed away in the Penticton Hospital in early September 1944.[16] Her will divided her assets between her three surviving daughters and her son. The Keremeos Hotel was owned by the family until Marguerite Kirby-Coleman sold it in 1946.[17]

In February 1946, the town of Keremeos finally received twenty-four-hour telephone service, which was first set up in the lobby of the Keremeos Hotel.[18] Also that month, the hotel had a new owner, Mr. Albert Neilson of Vancouver. It was during Neilson's tenure that the exterior of the hotel was stuccoed over, giving the hotel a considerably different look.[19] Stucco was very popular from the 1940s to the 1960s. This was the first of many changes that the old hostelry was to go through from 1947 through to the mid-1960s; its facade changed many times. The Keremeos Hotel Ltd. renovated the old hotel in 1951 and put it on the market as a new, modern twenty-nine-room hotel, complete with a large beer parlour with seating for 240 thirsty patrons, a banquet room, dining room, and lunch counter.[20] If Ada Kirby were to visit, she wouldn't recognize the place. Gone was the distinctive tower, and with the clapboard siding stuccoed over back in 1946, the appearance of the hotel was totally changed.

The Keremeos Hotel was no longer a railway hotel but, rather, catered to the car-driving public, a difference that would soon be reflected in the name change to the Keremeos Motor Inn. The business would continue to change over time in both appearance and name until 2014, when a fire put an end to its long and remarkable journey.

PRINCETON HOTEL

(1896–1911, 1912–2006)
Princeton, BC

FROM KEREMEOS, we head northwest past the mining town of Hedley, following the Similkameen River west until it meets with the Tulameen River at Princeton. Today it is about a thirty-minute drive between the two communities along BC Highway 3. On the banks of the Tulameen is an outcropping of red ochre, prized by the local Smelqmix People for face paint, which prompted the early white settlement to be called Vermillion Forks.[21] It was also known as Allison, named for J.F. Allison, who owned a large ranch a mile out of town. Forbes George Vernon reserved an area of land, about a square mile below the forks of the river, on the trail that is now Old Hedley Road, and called it Princeton.[22]

Prospector and all-around colourful character James ("Jim") Wallace had visited Princeton regularly from his modest saloon at Granite Creek (also known as Granite City), a new community approximately eighteen kilometres west along the Tulameen River from Princeton, near present-day Coalmont, that saw a gold rush take place in 1885. Wallace was one of the first to build a makeshift saloon at Granite Creek during the madness of that gold rush. Gold was first discovered on Granite Creek by prospector Johnny Chance, who stumbled across placer gold nuggets on the bedrock of the Tulameen. As word got out of the find, a stampede of men poured into the valley with dreams of striking it big.[23] By the spring of 1886, five hundred men, a mix of European and Chinese ethnicities, turned the once-quiet creek into a hive of activity. A gold-mining town was erected that included nine general stores and fourteen hotels, along with other businesses.[24] Jim Wallace decided to open a hotel at Princeton that would be close to his saloon at Granite Creek and was looking for contractors to build it. "The structure was to be 30 × 60 feet of modern build and first-class finish." Wallace had the liquor licence approved before shovels went into the ground.[25] Born in Wesley, Ontario, on August 10, 1850, Wallace eventually came west, settling for a time in San Francisco before moving to Victoria, BC. He had the means to follow his dreams and spent much of his time prospecting for gold, which took him on adventures to the Yale district, the Cariboo, and Nicola before settling at Granite Creek in time for their gold rush.[26]

The Princeton Hotel cost $10,000 to build and was the first hotel in the growing town during the summer of 1896.[27] Wallace was an affable proprietor who enjoyed hosting Saturday night dances at his new hotel. Everyone was welcome to drop in and dance to live music, gorge down delicious and plentiful dinners, and consume the wide variety of spirits and other beverages on offer at very reasonable prices. Brave souls usually well into their cups were invited to partake in consuming a concoction named "Wallace's Best," which came with a warning to not overindulge. Imbibing the smallest amount of Wallace's elixir miraculously gave those who would normally never dance the ability to dance like a damn fool and did wonders for their confidence. Drinkers of this intoxicating beverage woke the following day with a big head but mercifully had no recollection of the tomfoolery they displayed in front of family and friends the night before. Saturday night dances became very popular as folks could blow off a little steam and enjoy a good time.[28] Wallace advertised his hotel in the weekly local newspaper, the *Similkameen Star*, mentioning his "First Class Dining Room and Bar," and adding, "No trouble to talk to guests. The Boer War and Fighting Joe's campaign discussed every night." He would make each ad unique by including a different parting line—for example, "Come and hear the phonograph," or, regarding the latest international news, "Mongolian sympathisers excluded."[29]

It was a shock to the citizens of Princeton when they woke on that fateful day in March 1911 to learn that the Princeton Hotel had been destroyed by an early-morning fire. There hadn't been a fire this big and destructive in town since the Tulameen Hotel and adjoining buildings were destroyed in March 1904. The Princeton Hotel fire began very early on a Sunday morning and wasn't discovered until much later, when thick black smoke came billowing out of the structure. "It was with difficulty that guests of the house were aroused, some escaping with only a suit of clothes." Others did not have that luxury as they ran for their lives in their night clothes. Some guests found themselves unable to use the staircase as the flames beat them to it, so they resorted to any means of escape; witnesses saw a few guests climbing down the posts of the verandah. One person, Yoza ("Joe") Djekovic, visiting from Horvatsko, Austria, died in the fire.[30] It was later determined that the fire most likely started when some candles may not have been extinguished properly and ignited the wooden cupboard in which they were kept, causing a fire that spread throughout the hotel. The fire initially burned the top floor of the structure, which gave citizens, staff, and some guests time to remove as much furniture from the burning building as possible before the whole hotel was consumed. The spreading flames damaged other businesses, including the Great Northern Hotel.

Wallace only had partial insurance, and in spite of saving most of his first-floor furnishings, he decided not to rebuild but to join in a partnership with the proprietors of the Similkameen Hotel. The site where fire had destroyed the Princeton Hotel was soon put to good use when a much needed short-order café opened in October.[31] Princeton had two main hotels left, the Similkameen and the Tulameen, the latter rebuilt in the summer of 1906 by the McCoskery Brothers.[32]

It wasn't long before plans were made to replace the Princeton Hotel. The damaged Great Northern Hotel (named for the Great Northern Railway) on Bridge Street was dismantled and the site cleared to rebuild that hotel, but this time it would be constructed in brick, would take up the whole block, and include other businesses that would lease space on the ground floor. By June 1912, the foundations of the new hotel were close to completion. The bricks were supplied by the Idaho Brick & Lime Company in Spokane, and the lumber sourced locally by the Similkameen Lumber Company, whose manager was W.C. McDougall. The two-storey structure measured 100 feet by 100 feet, and the walls were constructed to withstand the pressure of a four-storey building if, in the future, additional storeys were to be added. Plate glass fronted Bridge Street and Harold Avenue, and a marble vestibule and tile floor gave the new hotel a striking appearance. The costs of building and furnishings were estimated at $55,000, and opening day was planned for October 1.[33]

When it came to new construction especially, 1912 was a boom year for Princeton. The two other major hotels in town were experiencing additions and improvements while the Great Northern Hotel was being built. The Wilson Brothers added an annex building to the Similkameen Hotel, while at the Tulameen, proprietors Kirkpatrick and Malone had completed the foundation work for a large addition to their hotel that would double its capacity. Meanwhile, contractor Charles Stanley was nearly finished erecting the fine brick walls of the new Great Northern Hotel for proprietors Peter Swanson and Alex D. Broomfield (incorrectly written as Bloomfield on occasion).[34]

You may be asking whatever happened to the rebuilding of the Princeton Hotel. Sometime between late June and early October 1912, the name of the as yet unfinished and promising Great Northern Hotel was changed to the Princeton Hotel. By early November, the local newspaper announced that "a small army of employees are getting things in shape for the grand opening," which was promised to be in a week to ten days.[35]

Finally the day came and the wait was over. The brand-new, handsome Princeton Hotel opened on December 6, 1912, with a dinner party given by the contractor, Charles Stanley. The new hotel was a marvellous two-storey brick structure and the first brick building to open in Princeton. It was designed by architects Emanuel J. Bresemann and Morien E. Durfee, who had offices in

Princeton Hotel on Bridge Street, 1915. COURTESY OF PRINCETON MUSEUM

Victoria and Vancouver. The partners had designed other substantial hotels, including the St. James Hotel on Johnson Street in Victoria and the Commercial Hotel, for co-proprietor of the Princeton Hotel Peter Swanson, in Nanaimo.[36] Businesses in town would vie for a spot in the new Princeton Hotel block, and the first to open there was the Bank of Montreal. The corner of Bridge (later Main) Street and Harold Avenue became a vital addition to the continued growth of Princeton from a pioneer town into the major urban centre for the Similkameen.

Proprietors Peter Swanson and Alex D. Broomfield took charge of the most modern and elegant hotel in Princeton. The red brick gave the hostelry a look of permanence and grandeur. Within two years, Swanson had stepped away from the Princeton Hotel, leaving Broomfield as sole proprietor. By August 1914, Swanson had died in Seattle although no details of the nature of his passing were forthcoming.[37]

The new Princeton Hotel didn't have any trouble attracting clientele, including one famous guest, billionaire John D. Rockefeller, who had business in the region.[38] Mr. Broomfield was well connected to the local businessmen of Princeton who operated the large coal mines located on the shelf above the town. The Princeton Coal & Land Company employed several hundred residents. Another major employer was the Canada Copper Corporation, whose mine at Copper Mountain, about twelve miles (twenty kilometres) south of Princeton along the wagon road, was a major producer. Mr. Broomfield would often host out-of-town guests connected with the large coal and copper companies.[39]

In November 1922, a significant luncheon took place in the dining room of the Princeton Hotel. The Princeton Board of Trade invited the Honorable W.H. Sutherland, the minister responsible for BC highways, to speak about an exciting new project, the Hope-Princeton Highway, which would connect the southern Interior of BC to Vancouver and the coast. It was still the age of the railways, but times were changing and commercial and recreational vehicles were becoming the wave of the future. Highway construction was an essential key for moving goods and linking communities. Minister Sutherland confirmed that the government was committed to the project and work was underway to determine the best route to use before shovels went into the ground.[40]

Alex Broomfield of the Princeton Hotel and his wife proved to be popular hosts and were involved in a variety of clubs and charities in town. In May 1925, their thirteen-year-old daughter, Truda, was chosen as Princeton's first "May Queen."[41] The Broomfields enjoyed their job serving guests at their fancy hotel and would continue to do so for another twenty years, making their tenure the longest of any owner—thirty-three years in total—when they sold it in 1945.

In March 1928, news was received that Jim Wallace, who built and operated the first Princeton Hotel, had passed away in the Princeton Hospital. He was seventy-eight years old.[42] In December the same year, Princeton finally received twenty-four-hour phone service when the BC Telephone Company completed the line. To celebrate, the general manager of the BC Telephone Company spoke with several citizens of Princeton, including E.E. Bur, president of the Princeton Board of Trade, H.C. Smith, general manager of the Granby Company, and A.D. Broomfield, proprietor of the Princeton Hotel. The line to the Princeton Hotel lobby worked splendidly and hearty congratulations were exchanged.[43]

On the eve of the crash on Wall Street in New York and the onset of the Great Depression, the three main hotels in Princeton received some good news. By a vote of 293 to 48 in a local referendum, Princeton voters approved of the sale of beer by the glass. The Similkameen, Tulameen, and Princeton hotels applied for beer-parlour licences immediately after the results of the vote were released. The cost of adding a beer parlour or modifying existing space in their hotels to accommodate one was well worth it—it had been shown that hotels that were licensed in Vancouver and Victoria as early as March 1925 did extremely well financially from their beverage rooms. All three Princeton hotels were granted beer-parlour licences. The Princeton Hotel Company invited tenders to contractors to renovate the Princeton Hotel to include an addition of another floor that would add an additional thirty-four rooms; each of the new rooms would have their own baths.[44]

Just as things were looking up and the future looked promising, with the new beer parlour making money and plans in progress for an addition to the hotel, every hotelier's worst fear occurred: a fire broke out in the Princeton Hotel. In the early morning hours of a day in early May 1930, a small but growing blaze was discovered by a guest, Nichol Thompson. Largely due to his alacrity and presence of mind, the hotel was not totally destroyed. The fire was caught in time but still did considerable damage to one corner of the structure, and when taking into account the water damage to a portion of the rooms, the dining room, the café, and the beer parlour, the estimated cost was put at $100,000. But the forty-room Princeton Hotel was saved. The cause of the fire was believed to have been a spark from a short circuit.[45]

Plans for a Hope–Princeton Highway connecting the BC southern Interior to Vancouver and international markets had been promised since the 1860s. By 1932, it looked as though the new highway would finally be built. Some construction was taking place as trucks and bulldozers began clearing a rough road into the Interior for the beginning of the highway.[46] It would take another seventeen years before the highway was finished and the final twelve-mile gap (nineteen kilometres) was paved. The Hope–Princeton Highway opened with much fanfare on November 2, 1949. Premier Ingemar ("Boss") Johnson, with a turn of a key, opened the padlock that launched the $12 million, 1,147-kilometre

(713-mile) highway.[47] The Depression and the Second World War had slowed down progress, but a post-war push saw the long-promised highway completed at last. Initially the opening of the highway had a positive financial impact on businesses in Princeton, including the Princeton Hotel, but over the next few years, passenger rail service declined rapidly as most people preferred to drive over taking the train. The hotels were affected by this change and had to adapt by remodelling their rooms into suites for long-term residents.

Another chapter in the hotel's history ended when the original co-owners, Mr. and Mrs. Broomfield, sold the Princeton Hotel to Mr. and Mrs. Robert G. Hunter of Vancouver in March 1945. Customers were sad to see the Broomfields depart, as it was like the end of a long friendship. People were just used to the Broomfields running the Princeton and had known no other proprietors. The Broomfields retired from the hotel but remained in town. At least one familiar face at the hotel remained: Mr. Roy Curran, the manager of the Princeton Hotel for the past sixteen years under the Broomfields, would be staying and assisting the new owners.[48] Within nine months, the Hunters sold the Princeton Hotel to business partners Mickey King and Charles Reda, also from Vancouver. Mr. Reda gained his hotel experience when he owned and operated the Wakefield Inn at Sechelt on the Sunshine Coast.[49] The partners had an addition put onto the west side of the hotel, increasing the number of rooms.

In June 1956, Mrs. Broomfield suffered serious injuries when she took a tumble down the basement stairs of the couple's house. People were shocked when they found out that her fall was fatal; she died in the Princeton Hospital the following day.[50] Four years later, in June 1960, Alex Broomfield was reunited with his beloved wife when he passed away at the age of eighty-one.[51] The Broomfields played a crucial role in the early development of Princeton, and the hotel that they helped build became a landmark building in the community.

On a personal note, my wife and I had the pleasure of dropping into the Princeton Hotel one fine sunny afternoon while we were on holiday. We had arrived in town from Vancouver, along the

Hope–Princeton Highway, on our way to Penticton in the summer of 2000. After driving around Princeton, taking in the town, we decided to stop in at the Princeton Hotel for lunch and a few beverages. I will never forget what I saw when I opened the door into the hotel's pub: a real, live adult horse standing on the dance floor. Our server explained that a film crew from Australia was filming a new reality program (it may have been *The Mole*, but my memory is a bit cloudy). She added that under normal circumstances, horses are not allowed in the Princeton pub. It sure gave us something to talk about.

We were sad when we heard the news that the Princeton Hotel was destroyed by fire in April 2006. The fast-moving fire started in the basement and quickly engulfed the rest of the hotel. No one was injured, but the fire left seven people homeless.[52] It also destroyed one of the most important landmark hotels in Princeton and indeed in the whole of British Columbia.

COALMONT HOTEL

(1911–Present)
Coalmont, BC

THE COALMONT HOTEL refuses to quietly fade away. For the last twenty years, it has hovered between being temporarily open to temporarily closed as subsequent proprietors arrive with their ideas and dreams for the historic hotel and then eventually move on. At the time of this writing, the Coalmont Hotel was sitting empty, perhaps hoping for a new owner to breathe life back into the old historic hotel.

It's hard to imagine that the tiny hamlet of Coalmont, northwest of Princeton on the Tulameen River, once promoted itself as "the city of destiny," and predicted it would grow to have a population of ten thousand one day. That day never came, and at its highest, the town's population never exceeded two hundred souls.[53] Coalmont got its name from the belief that there was a mountain of coal to be found beneath its surface: one had only to dig for it. Speculation built the town, with the Columbia Coal and Coke Company legitimizing the speculation by moving its operations to the new townsite from Granite Creek in 1911. The boom was on as hammers fell and buildings rose where before there had been bush and forest. Restaurants, a blacksmith, barbers, a clothing store, a pool room, an insurance company, a Chinese laundry, and a new hotel were built between 1911 and 1912.[54]

The history of the Coalmont Hotel goes back to the summer of 1911, when Louis Napoleon Marcotte partnered with J.T. Ryan with plans to build a major hotel in Coalmont. Marcotte was an experienced hotelier, having owned and operated the nearby Granite Creek Hotel since 1909. In May 1911, he sold his hotel to Herbert Goodison of Merritt.[55] The owners of the future Coalmont hired A.V. Anderson and P. McRae to build their hotel at a cost of $26,000. Construction began in June 1911 and continued into the winter as the large and impressive fifty-five-by-seventy-six-foot, three-storey building took shape. There were some delays along the way such as the little matter of Marcotte getting married to his sweetheart, Myrtle Schisler, in September. By the following spring, the finishing touches were added, such as painting the exterior "CPR red" with white trim.[56]

On April 26, 1912, the Coalmont Hotel held its gala opening, organized by manager Marcotte. "The Princeton Orchestra was engaged to entertain the two hundred guests 'of both sexes,' at the grand ball held in the hotel's large dining room as a 'discourse of sweet strains for the benefit of the terpsichoreans till an early hour.'"[57]

Sadly, within four months of the Coalmont Hotel's opening, nineteen-year-old Myrtle Marcotte died during childbirth in the Princeton Hospital. Her healthy baby girl was named Myrtle. Mrs. Marcotte was laid to rest in the Princeton cemetery and little Myrtle Marcotte was raised by Mr. and Mrs. Schisler. As the little girl grew, she made frequent trips to visit her father in Coalmont.[58]

One of Louis Marcotte's passions was duck hunting, and he would go in all kinds of weather. A multitude of stories circulated throughout Coalmont, told in the bar and on porches on summer evenings, of the adventures of Louis Marcotte. One such story had Louis and his good friend Fred Pope hunting ducks on one particularly foul day. Someone had the bright idea to shoot at the ducks while floating on a raft in the middle of Hastings Lake. When the unsteady craft began to sink, Fred Pope grabbed his rifle, hoisted it over his head, and swam for the nearest shore. Marcotte was urged to follow, but in a panic the hotelier confessed that he couldn't swim. Fred exclaimed, "You gotta!" Fortunately for Marcotte, when Fred Pope, who was a big man, left the raft, it became buoyant again, much to the relief of Marcotte, who quickly paddled to shore.[59] Score one for the ducks.

The Coalmont Hotel, 1912. COURTESY OF PRINCETON MUSEUM

Except for Coalmont, where coal was king, the biggest bountry in the surrounding creeks and the Tulameen River was gold. Granite Creek, which later became Granite City, was built on gold, and while that attracted prospectors and new businesses, it also brought the undesirables, such as thieves and murderers. A couple of robbers visited the Coalmont Hotel in the days just prior to Christmas 1912, with the intent of stealing the cash box from the hotel's bar. Quick action by an employee thwarted the would-be robbers, who landed themselves inside the Kamloops jail awaiting their trial for attempted robbery.[60] After that close call, it was decided that gold nuggets would no longer be put on display at the Coalmont Hotel. The large gold nugget found by Coalmont Hotel co-owner J.T. Ryan was moved out of town to Princeton.

The Coalmont Hotel was doing well and making money during those pre-Prohibition years. In the spirit of giving back to their community, Marcotte and Ryan financed the construction of a hockey rink for the fledgling Coalmont hockey team.[61] The excited Coalmont boys, in a fit of bravado, swore to "wipe the earth" with their biggest rivals, the Princeton hockey team, who had their own hockey rink, dubbed "the Owl."[62] The other team was the Tulameen–Granite team, which found little time to practise. These early hockey teams were not exclusive to the male domain. Princeton's All Ladies Team was a force to be reckoned with, as they proved in a victory over a boys' team, to the surprise and dismay of the coach and opposing players and the delight of onlookers at the Owl rink.[63] Louis Marcotte, an avid sports fan, supported and sponsored various local teams through the years.

In June 1916, business partner J.T. Ryan sold his share in the Coalmont Hotel to the locally well-known and even-tempered Louis Henry ("Harry") Brooks. Within a month, Brooks died from heart failure and Louis Marcotte became the sole proprietor of the hotel.[64] On October 1, 1917, Prohibition came to British Columbia, causing business to slow in the Coalmont Hotel bar. A substandard low-alcohol beverage known as "near-beer" was permissible to sell, but was certainly not popular with the patrons. The population of Coalmont sank to eighty-five year-round residents.[65]

By 1922, liquor was again legal but only for sale in liquor outlets operated by the government. The return of the saloon was forbidden. Instead, the BC government was preparing licences for government-controlled rooms known as beer parlours, but that was still at least three years away. In August, a number of hotels were raided by the "wet police" searching for the illegal sale of booze. The Coalmont Hotel was one of the places where illegal liquor was being sold in the bar.[66]

Meanwhile, Louis Marcotte married Mary Faulds in a quiet ceremony in Vancouver. The happy couple returned to Coalmont and the Coalmont Hotel.[67] By 1922, Mr. Marcotte had owned the hotel for eleven years, and after discussing matters with his wife, they decided to sell. James McKiernan and Frank M. McMahon purchased the Coalmont (the McMahon Stadium in Calgary is named after Frank and his family). In turn, they sold the hotel to the Miller Brothers in 1928, who owned it for less than two years before selling it to David ("Jerry") Paterson Brown and his wife, Elizabeth. The Coalmont Hotel was partially a wedding gift to Elizabeth from Jerry; the couple had married in Blakeburn just weeks earlier, spent their honeymoon driving to Mexico, and then settled in Coalmont.[68] The Browns ran the Coalmont Hotel for the next thirty years.

Jerry Brown was born in Edinburgh, Scotland, on December 20, 1882, and throughout his life was involved in sports and entertainment. Brown was a Sapper in the 2nd Canadian Tunnel Company, 1st Battalion Canadian Expeditionary Force, serving in Belgium and France during the First World War. When the war ended, Brown moved to Blakeburn and took up mining in the Coalmont Colliery's Number 3 mine. Brown also operated the local taxi and garage.[69] Brown was a natural storyteller and became very popular with the customers when the Coalmont Hotel beer parlour was finally granted a licence. A bottle of beer cost twenty-five cents in 1931, and Jerry Brown insisted that no one leave a tip, as beer was expensive enough. Brown proved to be a kind and generous man. Every Christmas Eve, he would stand at the door of the hotel and shake guests' hands as they departed while giving each a free bottle of beer.[70] Such was the nature of the man—a people person in a job that caters to people.

Between the years 1936 and 1940, the Coalmont Colliery saw a steady decline in coal production. "In three years production dropped by 20 percent and the workforce decreased by greater than one-quarter." By 1940, mines Number 1 through Number 5, which had extracted two million tons of coal, shut down one by one, forcing the company to cease operations and sell off or move their equipment.[71] When the mines closed, the powerhouse that produced electricity for the mines and the community of Coalmont shut down as well, leaving folks literally in the dark. Electricity would not return to Coalmont until 1965—twenty-five years later.[72] Those persons who did not leave the town when mining operations shut down learned to cope with the loss of electricity as best they could. Dances and high school concerts continued in the dining room of the Coalmont Hotel as alternative methods of power were used, taking the town back to pre-electricity years.

If the loss of electricity wasn't enough of a shock to the good folks of Coalmont, sad news of the death of pioneer Louis Marcotte came in July 1948. A healthy and active sixty-three-year-old,

Marcotte met his end while prospecting in a mine at Tulameen that caved in, killing him instantly. He was survived by his wife and his daughter, Myrtle Parks, of Port Alberni.[73] People left Coalmont over the next ten years, but the town was still active. The Coalmont train station went up in flames in May 1957, and less than seven years later, passenger service ceased.

The remaining townsfolk were saddened to hear that the Browns, who had successfully run the Coalmont Hotel for thirty years, had announced their retirement. On July 30, 1960, a celebration was held in the hotel to honour Jerry and Lizzy Brown and to thank them for the wonderful job they had done serving travellers and locals over such a long period of time. A week after the retirement celebration, seventy-nine-year-old Jerry Brown passed away. Elizabeth Brown lived a good life until 1985, and their only son, David, became mayor of Princeton.[74]

The Coalmont Hotel was purchased for $17,500 by the new owners, Mr. and Mrs. F. Norheim. Although empty at the time of this writing, the Coalmont Hotel building is still there. If you're considering becoming a hotel owner, the Coalmont is waiting.

DRIARD HOTEL

(1890–1910); Nicola Hotel (1910–23)
Nicola Lake, Yale District

OUR JOURNEY TO the next historic hotel takes us eleven kilometres east from Merritt to the small community on the western shore of Nicola Lake. The name Nicola derives from the English name for the famous Syilx Chief, Hwistesmetxē'qen or Nwistes-meekin (meaning "walking grizzly bear"), who, it is claimed, had seventeen wives. Early white traders, unable to pronounce his name, simply came up with their own, calling him Nicolas, which eventually became Nicola or N'Kwala.[75] The territory of his community was likewise called the Nicola Country.

The pioneer history of Nicola and the Driard Hotel began with one extraordinary man: Albert Elgin Howse. Howse's background is just as interesting as his achievements later in life. The youngest of two children, Albert Howse was born in Lincoln County, Ontario, in 1855 to Frederick and Sarah Howse (neé Beamer). He grew up in a sixteen-room brick house that had served as a hiding place for William Lyon Mackenzie, a prominent political leader and the first mayor of Toronto, during the political upheaval taking place at that time.[76] At the age of twenty-one, Howse landed a job with a publisher in California. After a year in California, he heard about a settlement at Douglas Lake, British Columbia, and decided to go there. He left San Francisco by steamer for Esquimalt, where he then took a boat to New Westminster and hired pack animals and helpers to get him to Hope. He then travelled along

The Driard Hotel, Nicola Lake, 1899. COURTESY OF THE NICOLA VALLEY MUSEUM AND ARCHIVES/NVMA

the Coquihalla trail to the Nicola Valley, arriving on July 4, 1877.[77] Howse got a job with a road crew that was building a wagon road to Kamloops. With his pay, he purchased 320 acres of ranchland located between Douglas Lake and Quilchena and stocked it with cattle.[78]

In 1880, Howse visited his hometown of Grimsby, Ontario, where he married his sweetheart, Agnes Armstrong, in a pleasant summer wedding on June 2, 1880.[79] The couple travelled to Ottawa, where Howse applied for a position as an Indian Agent for the Nicola District. It didn't hurt that Prime Minister Sir John A. MacDonald was a good friend of the Howse family, and in 1881 Howse was appointed to the position, which he held until 1884. In 1882, he partnered with George Petit and opened his first general store in Nicola. He went on to open four more stores—in Granite Creek, Princeton, Hedley, and finally, Merritt. Howse was a forward-thinking man. In 1887, he could see the growing demand for local lumber, so he went to Toronto, bought a portable steam sawmill, and brought it home with him. It was the first of its kind in the Nicola Valley. Howse's other interests included a flour mill, the first in the valley, and of course, the Driard Hotel, which he built with lumber from his own sawmill.[80]

The Driard Hotel, like most things in town, was owned by Albert Howse but was well managed by Clair Smith.[81] The name of the hotel is believed to be from the first-class Driard Hotel in Victoria and its popular owner, Sosthenes Maximilian Driard.

Around four in the morning on April 19, 1895, the modest but popular Driard Hotel was quickly consumed by fire, with the tragic loss Alex Ferguson, a miller, and a brother of the city clerk of Brandon, Manitoba, who were boarders, and Joe Moore, a visitor. Other guests escaped unharmed and the estimated cost of the loss was set at $3,000.[82] The Driard was replaced with a commodious two-storey building that was completed and opened that summer. A petition circulated against allowing the rebuilt Driard Hotel to have a liquor licence due to the many fires the previous hotel had suffered, but due to Howse's influence and the fact that the new hotel had fire-preventive features that the previous hotel lacked, a licence was granted.

A "grand ball" was held at the Driard Hotel in February 1896, hosted by Albert Howse with the aid of manager George Buse. Over one hundred people were invited from the district covering the Nicola Valley, Douglas Lake, and as far away as Kamloops. The exterior of the new hotel looked magnificent, illuminated from cellar to garret in the gloaming, and inside, the spacious dining hall was beautifully decorated and fitted for the occasion. Live music with violin and banjo entertained the guests, and at midnight, a call to the table welcomed guests to a scrumptious repast of turkey, chicken, and other meats, with coffee, pies, and cakes for dessert. When supper ended, the music and dancing began again and continued until dawn, which saw most of the happy participants make for home while a handful decided to stay and recover in one of the hotel's rooms.[83]

Busy with his other ventures, Albert Howse hired John Clark as proprietor of his hotel; in turn, Clark hired experienced hotelier Joe Richards to manage it from 1899 to 1902. Mr. Richards is profiled later in this chapter—he and his wife operated the Montebello Hotel in Salmon Arm. Another significant dance was put on at the Driard in February 1901, even more elaborate than any other, thanks to the fine efforts of Mr. and Mrs. Richards. The interior of the hotel had recently been painted and the decorations in the dining room were spectacular.[84]

The population of the village of Nicola was 150 but slowly growing. A stagecoach brought the mail twice per week, and the nearest railroad station was at Spences Bridge. Soon that would change as plans were in the works to extend the Nicola Valley Railway Company line from Spences Bridge to Nicola. In addition, the Dominion Government was considering subsidizing a wider new road to the headwaters of the Nicola River. Directors for the company were elected at a meeting held in the Driard Hotel.[85] The infrastructure of these new transportation routes was improving; they were vital if the community was to grow and develop. Albert Howse played a significant part in making it all come to fruition.

It was around this time that management changed at the hotel. G.W. Simpson from Victoria replaced John Clark, and J.H. Jackson became the new manager. A large addition was built onto the Driard in the summer of 1905. In July the same year, thieves managed to break into the basement of the hotel, where they helped themselves to a large cache of whisky.[86]

Howse was working a rare shift in the Driard bar when one customer who had too many became belligerent and caused damage to hotel property by smashing a mirror, bottles, and glasses. Howse was threatened by the distraught man and managed to duck when a large glass pitcher was flung at him. The man was up on charges the following day.[87] After this, Howse left the bartending to his staff.

The biggest change for the Driard Hotel took place in the spring of 1908 when Howse sold his hotel to Stanley Kirby.[88] Howse had been involved in a multitude of investments and owned a variety of businesses that he had worked hard to build up over the previous thirty years. He simply felt it was time to (semi-) retire and enjoy life. After selling the Driard Hotel, Mr. and Mrs. Howse took an extended and well-deserved vacation to Great Britain and Europe.[89]

Kirby continued with the popular dinner-dances at the hotel and made only one notable change in December 1910, when

A team of horses and people in a wagon at the Driard Hotel at Nicola.
COURTESY OF THE NICOLA VALLEY MUSEUM AND ARCHIVES/NVMA

the Driard Hotel became the Nicola Hotel.⁹⁰ Kirby operated the Nicola Hotel successfully for the next eleven years until something quite unprecedented took place in the spring of 1921. Major Charles Sydney Goldman, former member of the British parliament and well-known South African capitalist, had his eye on the village of Nicola and had been making enquiries with the intent to buy property there. Temporarily living in the Nicola courthouse, Goldman not only purchased 20,000 acres but also the entire A.E. Howse holdings in the area. Goldman then snapped up the rest of the buildings, in effect buying the whole village of Nicola. Here was a man with a plan. Goldman intended to change the village of Nicola "into a model English town."⁹¹ A perfect village green was on the drawing board for the current business section of Nicola. His ambitious plans also included building a large summer resort on the shores of Nicola Lake and to eventually buy up thousands of acres that would be put under cultivation using an elaborate irrigation system. The "Major" had a stellar reputation in the British Army and had written a number of books on the subject of mining.

He planned to stay in Nicola for a few months in order to begin his grandiose scheme for his new town.[92] This extraordinary change of events meant that Kirby no longer operated the Nicola Hotel; the new owner was Major Goldman. Mr. Kirby returned to running his ranch while the Nicola Hotel was owned by Major Goldman until 1923.

A footnote regarding Albert Howse and family. Shortly after Major Goldman dropped his bombshell and proceeded to buy up the town, Fred Howse, Albert's son, who lived and worked in Princeton, went missing. He had not been seen in four days, ever since he took his car out for a drive. Fearing the worst, search parties were organized and fanned out over the countryside. His wife and friends were relieved when a dishevelled but very much alive Fred Howse eventually showed up at home. His absence was caused by a terrific accident in which his car plunged over an embankment and came to an abrupt crash at the bottom of a ravine. The young Howse was knocked unconscious, and when he finally came to, he was in a state of "temporary asphasia [sic] which caused him to wonder [wander] aimlessly into the hills." At home and in the care of his loving wife, Fred Howse fully recovered from the ordeal.[93]

Mr. and Mrs. Howse retired to Princeton, where Mr. Howse remained somewhat active in his various business interests. In his senior years, the highly esteemed Albert Howse could be regarded as walking history, not only because he was a pioneer of the Nicola Valley who had arrived in 1877, but because the teak walking cane he used on occasion was fashioned from a salvaged piece of the famous Hudson's Bay Company ship SS *Beaver* that ran aground at Prospect Point in 1888.[94] Howse was active right up until his final illness. On December 14, 1938, the old pioneer Albert Elgin Howse passed away in the Princeton Hospital at the age of 83.[95]

SPENCES BRIDGE HOTEL

(1881–1939)
Spences Bridge

According to its current owners, the Spences Bridge Hotel is still in business today, operating under the name "The Inn at Spences Bridge." The original hotel was reputed to have opened in 1862, with modifications and additions taking place over the years until a disastrous fire in June 1939 burned it down. The hotel was rebuilt and continues to this day. Located between Lytton, fifty kilometres to the south, and Ashcroft, forty-four kilometres to the north along the Thompson Plateau, the community of Spences Bridge was originally called Cook's Ferry, after Mortimer Cook, who operated a rope-pull ferry on the Thompson River from 1862 to 1865. Cook's Ferry provided a vital service as part of the wagon road that led to the Cariboo goldfields.[96] Our profile of the Spences Bridge Hotel covers the period from 1886 to 1939, when the original hotel burned down, with an emphasis on the Clemes family.

Our story begins during the tenure of Archibald (Arthur) and Esther Clemes, who owned and operated the hotel from the summer of 1886 until Arthur's death in 1922. Archibald Clemes was born in Cornwall, England, on November 13, 1851. He was known as Arthur, then simply Art in his senior years. There was a discrepancy as to the spelling of his surname, which is sometimes written as "Clemis" in early records, but Clemes appears to be the proper spelling. Arthur's parents, William and Jane Clemes, immigrated to Canada in 1854. At the age of three, Arthur Clemes found himself in a new country and a new home in Lindsay, Ontario. Mrs. Clemes next gave birth to James and later to two daughters. The youngest, Dorothy Anne ("Dolly") Clemes was born on November 5, 1878, in Victoria, Ontario.[97]

The 1881 British Columbia Census lists Arthur Clemes and his wife, Esther, as "hostelers" at Nicomen Falls, BC (variations on the spelling include "Necomin"), at the BC Express House and Stables, which was situated on the busy wagon road between Spences Bridge and Lytton. The BC directories from 1881 to 1883 also list them working there. The couple were described as "a colourful pair, with Esther known as a formidable woman." On one occasion, she had to subdue a quarrelsome customer, which she achieved by hitting him over the head with a chamber pot, an act that sent the unfortunate man to hospital in Lytton, where he was treated for a concussion.[98] They were well suited for the job as they were both no-nonsense people and hard-working. Their house was a popular stop along the Cariboo wagon road.

While Arthur and Esther Clemes were running the BC Express House at Nicomen Falls, Charles Morton opened his Morton House at Spences Bridge on July 1, 1881, in a building leased from pioneering orchardist John Murray. Morton moved to Victoria in March 1883 and, by 1886, he had opened a new Morton House at Shawnigan Lake in anticipation of the Esquimalt and Nanaimo Railway running through that community.[99] Meanwhile, the Morton House at Spences Bridge retained the name under a new lease agreement with former blacksmiths E.E. Bligh and Tait. Within a year, Mr. Tait had sold his portion of the Morton House to Arthur Clemes. It is very likely that Esther Clemes managed the BC Express House while Arthur co-managed the Morton House. These were very busy times, and the money kept rolling in. By the summer of 1886, more changes took place as Reid and Neff took over the lease of the Morton House from Bligh and Clemes.[100] In June 1886, Arthur and Esther Clemes went to work in what became the Spences Bridge Hotel. Besides co-managing the hotel with his wife, Arthur was also ran the general store, was postmaster, and was listed in the directory as a farmer. I believe we have a word today for what he was: a "workaholic."

Arthur and Esther Clemes had worked in the hospitality industry for ten years by 1900. By that time, they had socked away their hard-earned profits. In the spring of 1900, the Clemeses decided to take a well-deserved holiday to Europe. Paris was one of the cities they visited, just when the Exposition Universelle of 1900 (better known in English as the 1900 Paris Exposition) was taking place between April 14 and November 12. The Exposition in the City of Light celebrated the human achievements of the past century.

It was at the Paris Exposition that Arthur saw an astonishing exhibit put on by the Wolseley Motor & Tool Company of England. The first 1901 Wolseley Motor cars were on display, featuring a one-cylinder and two-cylinder model. Arthur was fascinated by what he saw to the point where he considered buying one of these brand-new automobiles. The automobile industry was in its infancy, but I can just imagine what was going through Arthur's head at the thrill of driving the first automobile in the BC Interior. He could see himself driving down the only decent eight miles of road available around Spences Bridge with Esther by his side and with the townsfolk gaping in amazement as he zoomed by at three miles per hour. As their whirlwind trip to Europe ended and on the return trip home to Spences Bridge, Arthur couldn't get the English motor car out of his mind.

In 1904, Arthur Clemes ordered a Wolseley. It was shipped via Cape Horn; if it had come on the more convenient route across the Atlantic, it would have had to be stripped down and crated, and nobody in Spences Bridge or Kamloops at that time knew how to assemble an automobile, simply because none had existed until then. I would have loved to have been there when the automobile came off the ship at the dock in Vancouver, was ferried by rail to Spences Bridge, and then taken off the flat car and started up for the first time. It caused tremendous excitement as the whole town came out to see the future of transportation. Painted flaming

The Spences Bridge Hotel, 1894. CLEMES HOTEL, COURTESY OF THE CITY OF VANCOUVER ARCHIVES, HOT P60

scarlet, its driver and single passenger attired in heavy veil and dustcoat, the car made a short run on the only good road in town but had to be towed back to the hotel by a team of horses.[101] It did come with an instruction book, but parts could only be had from the company, weeks away in England.[102] Still, Arthur and Esther owned the first gasoline-driven automobile in the Interior of British Columbia.

When Arthur and Esther weren't driving around town, they were kept very busy with their various jobs. The 1901 BC Directory described Clemes as a hotel keeper and rancher. Clemes proved to be an excellent businessman, which eventually led to him making a substantial amount of money from his shrewd real estate investments at Spences Bridge and especially in Vancouver. By 1901, he was the leading business figure in Spences Bridge, owning the general store as well the hotel, in conjunction with his duties as postmaster and later as justice of the peace.

In 1906, Clemes leased his ranch to Chinese growers. The *Nicola Herald* reported that "the enterprising Celestials intend supplying the various railroad camps with fresh vegetables. Rumour has it that $1,000 rental was paid in advance."[103] In February 1910, an ad ran in the *Nicola Valley News* for the Spences Bridge Hotel, with A. Clemes, proprietor, stating that a "Porter meets all trains."[104] I wonder if the porter drove the Wolseley automobile to pick up hotel guests—I'm sure they would have been impressed.

By 1911, Arthur and Esther were still listed in the census as living in Spences Bridge, with many employees and lodgers living in the same accommodation (their hotel). They seem to have travelled more, as they had visited South America, Mexico, and the US by 1915. You would think that the Clemeses had little time for anything else, but the resourceful and energetic Arthur Clemes started the Spences Bridge Light and Power Company, establishing it in 1912.[105]

While performing his numerous duties at Spences Bridge, Arthur Clemes was also active in developing his investment properties in downtown Vancouver. In fact, Clemes had invested a substantial amount of money in Vancouver real estate, having purchased several lots in that city. Clemes built six brick dwellings on Hamilton and Georgia Streets from 1903 to 1904: "Two lots on the south side of Hastings street just west of Columbia avenue (52–64 East Hastings) which a year ago sold for $7,000, today brought $18,000. The purchaser is Art Clemes, hotelkeeper of Spences Bridge..."[106]

Between 1906 and 1907, Clemes built the Pantages Theatre on East Hastings after securing a long-term lease with Alexander Pantages. Designed by local architect E.E. Blackmore and costing $100,000, it was bankrolled by Art Clemes, who would go on to build the Regent Hotel next door to the theatre a few years later. The Pantages Theatre opened in January 1908. Alexander Pantages supplied the acts and developed a circuit that saw his shows tour throughout North America.[107] The Pantages Theatre, which was both a vaudeville and film theatre, booked the "Three Marx Brothers," appearing for the first time in Vancouver in 1909 and then again in 1911 in the sketch "Fun in Hi Skule." Groucho Marx played a Dutch- (or German-) accented schoolmaster, alongside his brothers and his Aunt Hannah, portraying one of the pupils. The Marx Brothers returned again to play a week's residency in 1913 as "The Four Marx Brothers."[108]

In its heyday, the Pantages's stage was graced by vaudeville stars like Charlie Chaplin, Harry Houdini, and Fatty Arbuckle before it became a movie theatre. The Pantages was converted in the 1920s to a movie house and operated under several names during its lifetime, among them the Royal, State, the Queen, the Avon, and the City Nights. It was later a Chinese-language theatre named Sun Sing until it closed in 1994. It stood vacant until its demolition in 2011.[109]

Arguably, Clemes's greatest investment was developing his property on East Hastings. On January 2, 1913, the *Daily Building Record* announced that a building permit was issued to build the new Regent Hotel on Clemes's property on East Hastings, east of the Pantages Theatre, at the cost of $150,000.[110] Two days later, it was announced that J.J. Frantz Construction would begin work on the eight-storey hotel on February 1, 1913. When completed, the hotel had "one hundred and sixty rooms, all light and airy, seventy-five with private bath ... rooms without a bath $1.00 per day for one and $1.50 per day for two. Rooms with bath $1.50 to $2.00 for one, and $2.00 to $2.50 per day for two persons ... a free bus meets all trains and boats. H.M. Cottingham, Proprietor."[111]

I imagine Clemes would be turning in his grave at how his once magnificent hotel met its eventual end with a slum landlord and hard times. But when it was completed in 1913, the Regent was a first-class hotel with a promising future. This part of Vancouver was considered the centre of town at the time, and the Regent fit right into the growing needs of the city.

On the morning of May 24, 1918, Esther Clemes died at Spences Bridge. Arthur Clemes lost his beloved wife and hotel-business partner, while the sons and daughters lost their mother. Esther was laid to rest at Spences Bridge two days later, with Reverend Father Sandilands of Ashcroft officiating. Attendees spilled out of the church, as the late Mrs. Clemes had many friends throughout the Nicola region and further afield who came to show their respect.[112] Less than four years later, on February 16, 1922, Arthur Clemes died at the age of seventy at Spences Bridge.[113] He was buried beside his wife. Some accounts mention that his favourite horse was also buried nearby.

Arthur and Esther Clemes had lived and worked in Spences Bridge for forty years and in that time managed to accumulate an astonishing record of accomplishments, not only successfully operating a number of hotels over the years, but also their significant contribution to the community of Spences Bridge and to the growth of Vancouver. They earned a place in the pioneer history of British Columbia.

Immediately following the death of Arthur Clemes, a trustee looked after the Clemes estate while the family ran the Spences Bridge Hotel and William Clemes operated the general store. The hotel stayed in the family until it was leased in August 1935 to H.H. Vickers. The transaction included the hotel, annex, dining room, beer parlour, and community hall.[114] Vickers's lease expired in 1938 and the hotel fell to Mr. H. McArthur, a trustee.

In September 1938, Robert and Mary Ellis leased the hotel from the Clemes estate. On a tragic day in June 1939, Mrs. Ellis was cleaning one of the rooms when a nearby coal-oil lamp exploded, setting fire to the room and Mrs. Ellis's clothing. She was badly burned before the flames engulfing her were extinguished. Meanwhile, the fire had spread to other rooms and quickly got out of control. The hotel was destroyed, with estimated damages of $12,000. Mrs. Ellis was rushed to the hospital in Lytton, forty miles away, where, after eight hours following the accident, she succumbed to her burns. Police from Ashcroft investigated the fire and concluded that a gas line had accidentally been punctured, causing the explosion.[115] A grieving Robert Ellis stayed on temporarily as proprietor with business partner A.J. Tyson, helping the Clemes family rebuild the hotel.

The history of the Spences Bridge Hotel continues to this day as the Inn at Spences Bridge and, by all appearances, will continue for many more years.

ASHCROFT HOTEL

(1885–1916, 1917–74)
Railroad Avenue and 4th Street, Ashcroft

THE TOWN OF Ashcroft was originally known by its Indigenous inhabitants as Tuk-tuk-chin (pronounced dee-duck-cheen; it means "speaking the truth" in the Nlaka'pamux language). It was nestled on a river and surrounded by hills where fish, game, roots, berries, and vegetables were plentiful. The Nlaka'pamux and Secwépemc Peoples established winter homes there.[116] Europeans arrived in the area around 1860, when lawyer Clement Francis Cornwall and his brother, Henry Cornwall, established a ranch that they named Ashcroft (later Ashcroft Manor) after their family home in England. It eventually became a stopping place for the stagecoach and other travellers on the wagon road between Spences Bridge and Kamloops.[117] The name Ashcroft was later adopted for the growing community.

In 1883, landowners John Christopher Barnes and American Oliver Evans were quick to realize the value of their land for the anticipated arrival of the Canadian Pacific Railway (CPR) and struck a partnership. Together with Evans's pregnant wife, Ellen, the two men began surveying a townsite and taking stock of the landscape. They decided it would be an excellent idea to have a hotel nearby if the CPR were to establish a station and depot there.[118] The Thompson River Hotel opened in 1883 close to the river it was named for, but on a different part of the shore than the proposed community. Barnes and Evans strung a heavy cable across the Thompson River for their new cable ferry and waited for the CPR to bring customers to their door.[119]

The Ashcroft Hotel, 1891. COURTESY OF THE CITY OF VANCOUVER ARCHIVES, HOT P61

The following year saw the San Francisco Bridge Company build a bridge, at the cost of $17,000, across the Thompson River that connected to the Cariboo Road.[120] The much-anticipated CPR tracks finally reached Ashcroft but, to the dismay of Barnes and Evans, they were nowhere near their hotel. The partners scrambled to find a suitable piece of land close to where they now knew the CPR would construct its railway station. Once land was secured, they set to work dismantling the Thompson River Hotel and rebuilding it near the CPR railway station on the appropriately named road, Railway Avenue.[121] It was worth the effort and expense to move their hotel because the benefits of being within walking distance of the railway station far outweighed the cost of the move. Ashcroft was the northern terminus of the CPR line, as the tracks then headed east to Kamloops. Anyone wishing to go farther north would have to get off the train in Ashcroft and wait for transportation north along the Cariboo Road at all hours of the day and night. Many would overnight at the Thompson River Hotel.

Sometime between 1885 and 1887, the name of the Thompson River Hotel was changed to the Ashcroft Hotel, and John Barnes left to work on his nearby farm and ranch. Oliver Evans's new business partner was E.E. Bligh. The gamble to move the hotel in 1885 had paid off handsomely: "The Ashcroft, boasting 54 rooms, was considered the best of Ashcroft's hotels, with linen tablecloths, fine china, silver, a reading room, and excellent food that attracted locals as well as travellers. A room in the hotel cost $1 per day, and a meal was 50 cents; and because some travellers passing through town only needed a room for a few hours to rest and freshen up before continuing their journey, the hotel was able to rent out a single room as many as three times in one day."[122]

Oliver Evans, co-owner and co-founder of the first-class Ashcroft Hotel, retired from the business around 1891 and was replaced by William Lyne. Messrs. Bligh and Lyne now operated the best hotel in town. A story published in the *Vancouver Daily World* described the first-rate hospitality at the time: "Our train arrived about 2 AM and some three or four passengers got off, all of whom put up at the Ashcroft Hotel, where they were cared for by the courteous proprietors, Messrs. Bleigh [sic] and Lyne."[123] Both Bligh and Lyne lived a good part of their youth in the United States—Bligh in Pennsylvania[124] and Lyne in Little Rock, Arkansas,[125] and Illinois. They both came to British Columbia during the early gold rush period in the late 1850s and stayed on.

The Ashcroft Hotel was a busy place and business was very good, but nothing would prepare the owners for the mad rush of customers making their way north at the time of the Klondike Gold Rush, from 1896 to 1899. By this time, William Lyne was the sole proprietor of the Ashcroft Hotel, and when he got the news about the gold rush, he knew his hotel rooms would be in great demand. Fortunately, Lyne had an experienced staff and employed Mr. John Glassey as manager. "Ashcroft appears to be busier than the coastal towns over the 'Klondike excitement.' Hundreds of men making there [sic] way to the coast from the east who never intended to go to the Klondike but took advantage of the cheap fares to realize their dreams... Carlyle [Cargile] House and the Ashcroft Hotel are taxed to the limit to find space for the demand."[126] By the spring of 1899, the rush had subsided and Lyne was exhausted. He put the hotel up for sale, but there were no takers.

Months later, long-time manager John Glassey had a dreadful accident when he fell off a wagon while journeying from Ashcroft to John Wilson's ranch at 8-Mile Creek. He was found lying unconscious on the road just outside Ashcroft and was immediately brought to the Ashcroft Hotel and put under the care of Dr. Williams. He died that afternoon in the hotel he had managed for years under various owners. Glassey was well known and liked in Ashcroft and many were surprised that his injuries were so severe as to cause death.[127] Mr. Wyness later became manager. The bad-luck streak continued when Tom Hamilton, the night clerk living at the Ashcroft Hotel, didn't show up for his shift. His door was locked and entry had to be made through a window off the verandah. He was found dead in his bed from an apparent suicide; an empty bottle of morphine was on the night table and he had left a suicide note. Hamilton had been known as a heavy drinker. He was survived by a brother, Gavin, at Lac la Hache, and a daughter at 150 Mile House.[128] They say bad news comes in threes, and in this case, they were right. In April 1903, seventy-five-year-old William Lyne, prospector, hotelier, and father of four, died after a brief illness.[129]

One important historic figure visited Ashcroft in September 1904 and rented a room for the night at the Ashcroft Hotel. A Mr. George Edwards is on the registry of the Ashcroft Hotel for September 6, 1904. The soft-spoken Mr. Edwards was an older gentleman who enjoyed a dinner at the hotel then joined in a game of poker for a few hours before retiring for the evening to his room. The following day, he signed out and went to work. His job, it turned out, was robbing trains, for George Edwards was none other than the infamous American bandit Ezra Allen ("Bill") Miner. Miner, "the gentleman bandit," and two accomplices stopped and then boarded the southbound CPR train at Mission, relieving it of its gold shipment. "The gold was valued at a mere $6,000. Authorities later reported that, if Miner had waited for the next stage shipment from Barkerville, he would have netted $60,000."[130] On May 14, 1906, the law finally caught up with the desperados near Douglas Lake, and, after a very brief confrontation the trio were captured by the North West Mounted Police and the BC Provincial Police and taken to jail at

Kamloops.[131] The prisoners were tried in Kamloops, where an American prison official identified the gang leader as Bill Miner. All three were convicted, with robber Louis Colquhoun sentenced to twenty-years and Tom ("Shorty") Dunn and Miner given life sentences.[132]

A parade of proprietors followed over the next twelve years: Johnson and Perkins (1904–1905); Al Johnson as solo proprietor for a year in 1905; Fletcher and Dickson (1906–1907); George Ward and James Veasey (1907–13), who also leased out the hotel at various times during their ownership; Hobson and Hobson (1913–16); and finally, Hobson and Charles Crotts, who ran the hotel right up until disaster struck in July 1916.

Co-proprietor Harry Hobson sold his share of the Ashcroft Hotel to Charles Crotts of Vancouver on March 16, 1916, but just over three months later, the thirty-year-old Ashcroft Hotel burned to the ground. According to an article in the *Calgary Herald* on July 6, 1916, the "fire broke out on the second story [sic] of the Ashcroft hotel last night around 7 p.m." By the time the volunteer firefighters arrived the structure "was a mass of flames." A brisk west wind carried the flames onto adjoining buildings, which included the Central Hotel. "The fire leaped from block to block faster than the fire hose could be adjusted to the hydrants." Five blocks were consumed by the fast-moving fire before it was put under control. It would have continued but there was nothing left to burn. Losses were first estimated at half a million dollars, with few businesses carrying full insurance. The entire Chinatown district was destroyed, as was the business section of town.[133]

BEFORE LONG, a second Ashcroft Hotel had been built, standing from 1917 to 1974. Ashcroftonians owe a debt to their Chinese citizens, who got to work rebuilding Chinatown and parts of downtown Ashcroft once the embers cooled: "Almost immediately after the Great Fire, Chinese carpenters were hard at work rebuilding Chinatown on both sides of north Railway. Wing Chong Tai, Wing Wo Lung, and some eighteen other Chinese-owned businesses were soon back in operation.[134] While many of the white businesses also rebuilt quickly, some did not, and a year after the fire, none of Ashcroft's three hotels had been rebuilt."[135]

Since the great fire in July 1916, Ashcroft was without a hotel. People bypassed the recovering town who would normally have stayed in the local hotels, so the revenue that would have been generated at the hotels also passed by the town. After housing those citizens displaced in the fire, the main priority was to rebuild the hotels. In 1917, a group of Chinese merchants banded together and rebuilt the Ashcroft Hotel and, later on, the Central Hotel; both were bigger and better than before. A third hotel, the Chinese Hotel and Tea Room, made a fine and unique addition to the town.[136]

The new Ashcroft Hotel opened in 1917, less than a year after the devastating fire. It is no surprise that a Chinese proprietor, Joy Shung, managed the new hotel and would continue to do so until she stepped down in 1928.[137] The two-storey wood structure was modest at first, but with a sixteen-room addition in May 1918 and continual improvements in July 1919 adding a further fifteen rooms with a new wing for the hotel, the Ashcroft came into prominence once more.[138] The new Ashcroft Hotel faced its first hurdle when its application for a liquor licence was turned down.[139] This was not unusual in the months leading up to Prohibition, which affected all of British Columbia by October 1, 1917. A portion of the good citizens of Ashcroft wanted their community dry from the evils of alcohol and got their way for the time being. Those who grew thirsty could be satisfied at any of the surrounding towns.

Joy Shung had done a fine job operating the Ashcroft Hotel and when she stepped down, Charles H. Croke, David B. Derbyshire, and A.M. Sparling tried their hands at operating the popular hostelry. Over the years, a steady stream of new proprietors came and went, adding their touches and ideas and further modernizing the historic twenty-seven-room hotel.

In November 1974, the fifty-seven-year-old landmark hotel burned down. Two men and a woman died in the fire; thus ended the legacy of the landmark Ashcroft Hotel, which had served the community since the founding of the town itself.[140]

WALHACHIN HOTEL

(1910–21)
Walhachin

THE HAMLET OF Walhachin was a fruit-growing settlement located on the south shore of the Thompson River between Ashcroft to the west and Kamloops to the east. The community only lasted for fifteen years, from 1907 to 1922, and thrived for less than eight before it was abandoned. The dream of becoming a prosperous and growing town based on a productive apple orchard was never realized for various reasons, some which will be discussed here. Its very English Walhachin Hotel, overlooking the few houses and businesses locally known as "Little England" was, like the town, doomed from the beginning.[141]

Sir Talbot Chetwynd, manager of the 111 Mile House Ranch, suggested the name Sunnymede for the new settlement, but the name was rejected in favour of the Nlaka'pamux name, Walhachin (pronounced Walla-sheen).[142] Originally spelled *Walhassen*, it was promoted in the London-based brochure for the settlement to mean "bountiful valley," but its actual meaning was "land of round rocks."[143] Not a particularly inviting slogan if one is trying to entice settlers to the area.

In 1907, American Charles E. Barnes was surveying nine kilometres east of Ashcroft when he came upon a lush two-acre apple orchard cultivated by Charles Pennie on his ranch. Although inexperienced in the intricacies of fruit growing, Barnes came up with an idea to cultivate the entire area with fruit trees, and he began to seriously look into this exciting plan.[144] Barnes approached the British Columbia Development Association (BCDA), which, oddly enough, was based in London, England. The association sent one of their leading directors, Sir William Bass, accompanied by two associates, Palmer and Ashcroft, to determine if the plan was worth backing financially. After a review of the landscape, "Bass was convinced of the area's speculative value and advised the BCDA to invest in a land colonization scheme to be built around the Pennie ranch with Barnes as manager."[145] In January 1908, the Pennie Ranch plus an additional 930 acres on the south bank of the Thompson River and 3,265 acres on the north bank were purchased by the BCDA for development.[146] The BCDA created the Dry Belt Settlement Utilities Limited to oversee the development of a townsite that would include the Walhachin Hotel.[147]

The building of the town of Walhachin and development of the surrounding orchards would not be possible without the CPR and the Canadian National Railway (CNR), which provided essential links to outside markets and would bring in potential settlers. The construction of an elaborate irrigation system to water the thousands of fruit trees planned was the second vital component for success for Walhachin. Work got underway to build up the townsite, and in April 1910, the two-storey Walhachin Hotel was opened by none other than Prime Minister Sir Wilfrid Laurier, who was visiting Western Canada at the time.[148]

A reporter for the *Ashcroft Journal* wrote: "The Walhachin Hotel is delightfully laid out and furnished. The large dining room overlooks the orchards and from the balcony on the north side is a good view of the orchards and the Thompson River. Spacious billiard, card and ladies' and gentlemen's sitting rooms occupy the east wing. Hot and cold water, gas and all comforts have careful attention."[149]

The luxurious Walhachin Hotel was initially closed to the general public as it served as temporary lodging for the select English settlers waiting for their homes to be completed. By July 1910, fifty-six settlers had arrived and within five years, there were 150 permanent English settlers, 50 Chinese ones, and about 200 seasonal workers.[150] The hotel provided two bars, one for the refined English upper class that adhered to a strict dress code and one

The Walhachin Hotel. IMAGE D-03192 COURTESY OF THE ROYAL BC MUSEUM

for "others."[151] As the Canadian settlers living in the surrounding communities of Ashcroft, Savona, Kamloops, and neighbouring ranches passed through Walhachin, those that stopped for a drink were restricted to the "other" bar and were never invited to formal functions.[152] It was common to find separate bars divided by gender, especially during the beer parlour era, but it was rare to find bars separated by class, and this was one of the problems that contributed to Walhachin's downfall. The new English upper crust that made up most of the population of Walhachin ignored or dismissed advice from locals who knew how to manage the land.

Proper attire was expected in the dining room, where Miss Eleanor Flowerdew was manager and housekeeper. Miss Flowerdew lived up to her name, providing fresh flowers or sprigs of fern at every table setting throughout the summer and potted plants in the winter months. She also continued the English tradition of afternoon tea for the ladies of the village. When the hotel's first general manager, Mr. R. Colson, became ill, Miss Flowerdew took over his duties as well. "The dining room had established a reputation for serving excellent meals and on Christmas Day, 1910, fifty guests sat down for Christmas dinner."[153] In the winter of 1911, Miss Flowerdew was the first bride in Walhachin when she married poultry farmer Mr. Higgs.[154] A shame to give up such a wonderful surname as Flowerdew.

Several musical evenings were held and monthly formal balls took place in the hotel common room as one way of relieving the tedium of living and working on the Dry Belt. Mrs. Al Faucault and Mrs. Charles Barnes would take turns providing the music, with musically inclined others waiting in the wings. If for any reason live music was impossible, a gramophone served the purpose, as it was sure to attract record crowds. Bachelors' and Spinsters' Balls were highlights as a string of carriages was on hand for tours among the apple trees.[155] The singing of "Auld Lang Syne" followed by "God Save the King" signalled the close of the balls.[156]

Ralph ("Rafe") Chetwynd purchased a grand piano from the famous virtuoso, Ignacy Jan Paderewski, to be used in the Walhachin Hotel. Unfortunately, it turned out that the piano didn't fit through the doors, so it was moved to the new community hall that was completed in 1912. (The piano survives to this day and can be found at the University of British Columbia.) The fancy balls and concerts moved to the new hall that claimed to have the only spring dance floor outside of Vancouver.[157]

Also in 1912, a big change took place in the small community when twenty-eight-year-old Charles Henry Alexander Paget, the Sixth Marquess of Anglesey, came to Walhachin and bought up everything in town including the Walhachin Hotel. The first change he made at the hotel was to put an end to the two-bar system, allowing all guests access to the bars in the hotel regardless of class.[158] A good start. The hotel was advertised as "the most comfortable hotel in the interior, on the CPR transcontinental main line. All meals served by Old Country cook; best river fishing in British Columbia, climate superb—American plan, $3 per day…" The description was perhaps a bit exaggerated, but the hotel was becoming popular and open to the public. Monthly rates for full room and board were $35, or one could get just a room for $10 per month.[159]

The Marquess of Anglesey found a location approximately six kilometres west of the town where he began construction of his estate. He added a swimming pool for family and invited guests only. The estate was completed in 1914, a watershed year for the young village. The population of Walhachin had reached three hundred, but by the end of July those numbers would begin to fall due to the UK and the British Empire declaring war on Germany and the Axis powers.

The need for men to do their duty for King and Country was met with a rousing wave of patriotism, and the enlistment rolls saw tens of thousands join up. Volunteers soon included 97 out of the 107 men from Walhachin, who joined the army to fight in Belgium and France. This left the women and a small number of men to work the orchards and attempt to repair the faulty, poorly constructed wood flumes that carried water to the trees and seemed to constantly require attention.[160] While the drain of young men eager to enlist caused a shortage of labour at home, the war was not the sole reason why most men left. "The war provided an honourable excuse to escape the ever increasingly unacceptable social situation. Single men had grown weary of the social and sporting life and of dancing only with other men's wives. Many wished to date, marry, and raise families of their own, but there was an extremely limited number of girls of their class available. Forty of the forty-one bachelors in town signed up right away."[161]

By 1916 and 1917, it became more and more obvious that the wood flumes that carried water from Snohoosh Lake, forty kilometres from Walhachin, were totally unsuitable for the job. They kept breaking down and were only supposed to be temporary until much stronger and better-built flumes would take their place. High wood trestles that were constructed over ravines also required constant upkeep and regular repairs. The marquess helped all he could with finances and hands-on work, but he was certainly not an engineer nor would he take the advice of the Canadians who had knowledge about such things.

Meanwhile, life continued, albeit with fewer folks around to lend a hand or to participate in social activities. The Walhachin Hotel was still operating, advertising itself as one of the most comfortable hotels in the province, with electric lighting, steam heat, and hot water in every room. The new proprietor, A.E. Axten, mentioned the good hunting and trout fishing to be had on the Dry Belt. Rates dropped for weekly and monthly rentals.[162]

Troubles for the village intensified by 1918. A great storm slammed Walhachin for two days, resulting in more serious damage to the irrigation infrastructure and ripping out a mile of valuable flumes. Estimates in excess of $240,000 to get the flumes replaced and working again were beyond the capacity of the Marquess of Anglesey to pay, and the provincial government was unwilling to put up that kind of money for the restoration.[163] In November, the hotel needed a manager and advertised extensively: "Married man preferred."[164] The Marquess of Anglesey ended up operating it on his own and by the following summer announced the hotel would close temporarily in August until further notice, with special arrangements made for a bed and breakfast only to accommodate the travelling public.[165] The state of things at Walhachin went from bad to worse as the marquess made a major blunder when he replaced the energetic Charles Barnes, the man with a dream, with Ralph Chetwynd, the man without a clue, at the critical moment when strong leadership was essential. Chetwynd proved to be too inexperienced to do the job.[166] On top of that, some of the sons of Walhachin returned with their new brides to a disorganized, failing community and decided to move on to Vancouver or Victoria to raise their families.[167]

One bright light in these dark days was that a new proprietor was found for the Walhachin Hotel. Captain Askew breathed new life into the fading hotel and ran ads in the Vancouver newspapers attempting to attract business to the hotel and the town. The captain reopened the hotel, emphasising the comfort and quiet to be found in Walhachin and the many activities on offer that included outdoor tennis, badminton, and swimming in the summer, and skating on the Thompson River and billiards in the winter.[168] The last ad was dated March 5, 1920, and then all was quiet from the Walhachin Hotel.

In 1920, the exodus was intensifying as it became clear that there was no future in the village, and within two years, the last of the English immigrants to Walhachin had left the community and it became a ghost town. The experiment at Walhachin failed for many reasons. The soil was not suitable for large-scale cultivation for orchards, and the fact that the English settlers did not seek help from their experienced neighbours but stayed in isolation with their flawed schemes was a factor in the community failing. "The elegant Walhachin Hotel resides only in memory and Eden is inherited by dust devils."[169] A few years after the English had left, a few people moved into the deserted village and lived there year-round. The old community hall survived the years, spring floor and all, and today contains the Walhachin Museum. A modest stone house and a handful of other buildings have been carefully restored and are in use today.[170]

MONTREAL HOTEL

(1898-1903, 1905-1906); Leland Hotel (1906-79)
301 Victoria Street at Third Avenue, Kamloops

THE FOLLOWING PROFILE of the Montreal and Leland Hotels covers the years 1891 to 1946.

Kamloops received its name from the Secwépemc words meaning "meeting place" or "where the rivers meet." The Hudson's Bay Company built a fort in the area in the 1830s, naming the settlement Fort Thompson. In 1870, when the post office was established, the name was changed to Kamloops. The city of Kamloops was incorporated in 1893.[171]

In 1891, Napoleon Latremouille arrived in Revelstoke from Ottawa and opened a bakery, advertising that he "is prepared to supply the finest in bread, buns, cakes and pastries. All kinds of baking to order."[172] Sometime between 1892 and 1897, Latremouille went from baking hot cross buns in Revelstoke to managing the Queens Hotel in Kamloops. By the following year, he had leased the Montreal Hotel in Kamloops.[173] Latremouille leased the Montreal from owner J. Peterson from 1898 until 1903. He refurbished the popular hotel in 1901 and must have been doing well because, in 1902, he became one of the very first in Kamloops to purchase an automobile.[174] The automobile was all the rage at the time, especially in New York, where sales were soaring.

On November 9, 1903, the attractive two-storey (see photograph) Montreal Hotel in Kamloops burned to the ground. The origin of the blaze was never determined, and the unhappy owner was uninsured and lost a total of $6,000 to the fire—$4,000 for

The Montreal Hotel in Kamloops, ca. 1900. KMA 9714. COURTESY OF THE KAMLOOPS MUSEUM & ARCHIVES

the building and $2,000 for the new furniture.[175] There was some question if the Montreal Hotel would be rebuilt. In September 1904, ten months after fire destroyed the original Montreal Hotel, Mr. R. McKay was given the contract to build the replacement at the corner of Victoria Street and Third Avenue.[176] Napoleon Latremouille was taking no chances on this new structure burning down, so he paid $7,000 to protect the exterior of the new Montreal by investing in a brick finish.[177] Wooden structures were being replaced with brick throughout town to provide at least some protection against fire, but brick was also modern and had an aesthetically pleasing appearance.

The three-storey brick Montreal Hotel, designed by Vancouver architect William Tuff Whiteway, opened in 1905 with C.F. Armstrong as hotel proprietor and Latremouille as manager of the bar. When completed, the new Montreal Hotel was, in the words of a local news writer, "one of the best, if not the best hotel in the city."[178] Views of the interior and exterior of the building in those early years show off a first-class hotel ready to wow the travelling public. The partnership of Armstrong and Latremouille lasted about a year before a new buyer came along in February 1906, purchasing the Montreal Hotel for $18,000.[179]

Mr. Robert ("Bob") Dowswell (1857–1944) was experienced at running a hotel in Vancouver before arriving in Kamloops and would continue to buy and operate hotels in British Columbia long after his four years, from 1906 to 1910, at the Montreal Hotel. His father, Ambrose Dowswell, was the proprietor of the Claremont Hotel in Pickering, Ontario, where Bob literally grew up in the business. Dowswell came from Ontario but found himself working in Vancouver, where he operated the old Leland Hotel on West Granville Street from 1901 until he left in 1904 to co-manage the Merchants Hotel on Seymour Street, also in Vancouver. At the Leland Hotel, he gained a reputation as a no-nonsense manager who would not tolerate rowdiness or rude behaviour, but he and his lovely wife Bertha (née Moen) were well liked by the guests and long-term residents of every hotel they operated. At the Leland, Bob, would cheerfully offer to take guests who were new to the city on a tour through Stanley Park or help out in other little ways beyond the measure expected of a hotel manager. On more than one occasion, long-time guests staying at his hotel would present token gifts as thanks for his honest and even-handed management and in appreciation of his hard work with their comfort in mind. On one occasion, the Dowswells were presented with two beautiful gifts: for Bob, an attractive cigar case, and for Bertha, a beautiful silver tea service.[180] Bob was a genial soul and made friends wherever he went.[181] This was the nature of the man who took control of the Montreal Hotel in Kamloops in February 1906.

The first thing the Dowswells did was to meet and talk to the long-term guests and staff at the hotel, and the second was to announce that the hotel name would change from the Montreal to the Leland Hotel. The Vancouver Leland, where the Dowswells had lived and worked for four years, had obviously made an impression on the couple.[182]

Bob Dowswell enjoyed travelling and made frequent trips to Vancouver and Victoria during his time at the Leland Hotel in Kamloops. He also had a passion for lawn bowling, something that would remain with him the rest of his life. The Dowswells managed the Leland Hotel in Kamloops for four years and then sold it to a consortium under the name of the Leland Hotel Co. Ltd. The provincial directors were G.N. Barclay, F.T. Cornwall, M.F. Gesner, J.M. Scott, and B.S. Burchell, with E. Gesner in charge as manager.[183] Meanwhile, the Dowswells moved to Victoria and would reside in a fine, comfortable home on Wark Street for the rest of their lives. But they certainly did not fade into retirement—far from it. Robert Dowswell continued to work, first opening an insurance company, and in 1915, becoming the proprietor of the very popular Brown Jug Hotel on Government Street, where he continued until Prohibition cut off the major revenue stream to the hotel in October 1917.[184] Robert Dowswell remained active in business, sports, and current affairs until his death in Victoria at the age of eighty-six on January 12, 1944.[185]

The owners of the Leland Hotel planned for some minor improvements in the hotel's interior, such as the installation of a modern switchboard built by the Marcus Electric Company, which would connect every room to the office.[186] They also planned for a large expansion of the hotel to be completed in two stages. The first stage would see a significant three-storey brick extension at the rear of the existing structure with a frontage of 50 feet on the north side of Seymour Street and 120 feet on Third Avenue. The ground floor would be fitted for retail stores, and a large basement would be built. This addition added 35 rooms to the Leland, giving the hotel a total capacity of 110 rooms. When completed, the Leland Hotel in Kamloops would be the largest hotel between Vancouver and Calgary.[187]

The new wing cost $20,000, but the owners weren't finished yet. A further expansion would see the cost double to $40,000 for the final phase of the massive project planned for some time in 1912.[188] Kamloops was growing, and the business community was very optimistic regarding the future of the city, as reflected in the expansion of the Leland Hotel and the building activity taking place throughout the city. Just as significant as the major expansion of the Leland, which helped open Third Avenue to retail businesses, a change in ownership of the Leland took place in 1911

The Leland Hotel, 1911. KMA #1987.018.001. COURTESY OF THE KAMLOOPS MUSEUM & ARCHIVES

when A.E. ("Arthur") Meighen purchased the hotel and formed the Leland Hotel Company, with A.E. Axton as manager.[189]

Meighen was a man with boundless energy that went hand in hand with his ceaseless political ambitions. He was born in Perth, Ontario, and when he was a young man, he moved to California, where he was engaged in the irrigation business on a large orange orchard estate. In 1906, Meighen moved to Kamloops, where he was hired to build and maintain a sophisticated irrigation system for the Fruitland Company. In 1911, he searched for a sound investment and found one in the expanding Leland Hotel. It didn't hurt that he just happened to be the first cousin to Arthur Meighen, leader of the federal Conservative Party from 1920 to 1926 and from 1941 to 1942 and the ninth prime minister of Canada, serving from July 1920 to December 1921, and from June to September 1926.[190] A.E. Meighen would end up owning the Leland Hotel for the next thirty-five years.[191]

On a cold day in November 1912, Captain Edwards, who owned a large ranch just outside of Kamloops, had his workers bring two heavily loaded horse-drawn wagons into the city. While pulled over to the side of Third Avenue, the untended horses of one of the carts became spooked from the noise of a threshing machine passing by and bolted down Third Avenue, running smack into a light standard in the intersection of Third and Victoria. The cart, its contents, and the horses were all knocked over. The horses were not injured, but as onlookers gathered, one of the horses kicked a man, Mr. Solburg, causing serious injury to his leg. He was taken into the Leland Hotel, where the wound was dressed before he was transported to hospital.[192]

Meighen became president of the Cariboo Central Unionist Association in Kamloops and decided to run in municipal politics for alderman. Meighen was elected alderman in January 1923, thus beginning his career in politics.[193] The following year, he was elected president of the Conservative-Liberal Association for the Kamloops riding, and in January 1925, he became the mayor of Kamloops.[194] Meighen led a charmed life. Not only did he win the mayor's chair three times, but in January 1928, he was elected with 386 votes to be the head of the police commission; his closest competitor, G.D. Brown, received 314 votes.[195] In addition to his duties as mayor and police commissioner, Meighen maintained his position as managing director of the Leland Hotel Company, and in 1930, he became the manager of the other significant hotel in Kamloops, the recently built, modern Plaza Hotel.[196]

In 1936, the *Vancouver Sun* reported: "The Plaza and the Leland, first-class hotels of Kamloops, are managed by A.E. Meighen. The 75 modern rooms at the Leland and its excellent dining-room have been managed by Meighen for the past twenty-five years (1911–1936), and the newer 57-room Plaza with its beautifully finished lounge room inside the striking stuccoed building has been managed by Meighen these past five years (1930–1936)." Meighen's son, H.A. Meighen, joined his father as assistant manager for both the Leland and Plaza Hotels; both enjoyed a booming business.[197] In October that year, hotel proprietors from many of the major hotels in the BC interior gathered at Kamloops to attend the first general meeting of the Interior of British Columbia Hotelmen's

Association. Naturally, A.E. Meighen of the Leland and Plaza Hotels was elected president of the association. The main topic on the agenda was whether the newly formed association should join with the corresponding body on the coast. Some of the major hotels represented in this meeting included the Kalamalka Hotel in Vernon, the Royal Anne Hotel in Kelowna, and the King Edward Hotel in Revelstoke.[198]

On July 24, 1946, Mrs. Ethel A. Meighen, former Revelstoke nurse and A.E. Meighen's wife, died.[199] The couple had been married since 1909. Meighen left the hotel business that year and retired to his home in Victoria, BC. He lived to the ripe old age of eighty-five, dying on April 28, 1956.[200]

The Leland Hotel continued to be a viable business right up until October 28, 1979, when it was destroyed by fire. Arson was suspected as the cause of the blaze as it was the fourth major fire to plague Kamloops that year. The fire had started on the top floor of the seventy-two-year-old hotel. Guests and staff all escaped without injury. Hotel employees had put out a small fire about ninety minutes earlier that was deemed suspicious before the fire that destroyed the hotel was detected.[201]

MONTEBELLO HOTEL

(1908–67)
Hudson Avenue at Alexander Street, Salmon Arm

BEAUTIFUL SHUSWAP LAKE is located in the Columbia–Shuswap region of British Columbia. The semi-nomadic Secwépemc People named the lake that their forefathers had fished for thousands of years. European explorers were the first white people in the region, followed by a handful of trappers, and then prospectors when a short-lived gold rush took place in 1865. Settlers trickled into the south arm of Shuswap Lake, where, it was claimed, pitchforks were used to extract the fish from the lake and streams as they were teeming. Farmers consumed some of the fish and used the excess to fertilize their fields.[202] But it wasn't until the CPR arrived in 1885, bringing with it an influx of settlers, that the community of Salmon Arm was born.

The two-storey Montebello Hotel (sometimes written as Monte Bello) was built in 1908. Designed by Vancouver architects Thomas Hooper and Charles E. Watkins, the Montebello was an attractive double-L-shaped structure that blended Swiss chalet and Mission styles, along with the addition of wide verandahs and balconies. The first phase contained twenty guest rooms and a bar that measured twenty by twenty-four feet, finished in oak and mahogany and featuring a large plate-glass mirror. A large McClary "Magnet" furnace supplied heat to every room, and electricity for lighting was generated on the spot by a five-horse-powered coal and oil generator. The Montebello Hotel had electricity four years before the rest of the town.[203] The new, first-class hotel eclipsed in style and comfort the Alexandra and Coronation Hotels in Salmon Arm at the time of opening.[204]

The proprietor of the Montebello Hotel was Joseph ("Joe") R.A. Richards. The Richards family had a long history in the service industry. Joe and his older brother, Frank G. Richards Jr., were born in New Westminster, where their father, Frank Sr., was one of the co-founders of the Hyack Fire Brigade.[205] The family moved to Victoria and Frank Sr. owned and operated Uncle Frank's Saloon on Langley Street downtown. He bankrolled his saloon from the proceeds of his modest but productive copper mine in Sooke.[206] His oldest son, Frank Jr., leased the brand-new, first-class Clarence Hotel, which opened in 1886 on the northeast corner of Yates and Douglas Streets. (A Bank of Nova Scotia occupies that spot today.) When his lease expired in 1888, Frank Jr. went into real estate and then in 1902 was elected sheriff.[207]

Joe Richards leased the Driard Hotel in Nicola (profiled in this chapter on pages 28) from 1900 to 1902. During that time he took a page out of his father's book and invested in a nearby copper mine on Mill Creek that he named the "Dandy Joe." Property along the creek was in great demand as Richards's claim "exposed some fine peacock copper."[208] Richards sold his copper mine and bought the Coutlee Hotel in the small community of Coutlee, just Northwest of Merritt on what is today Hghway 8. The Nicola Valley Coal and Coke Company owned the Middlesboro Colliery, the biggest employer in the region, and Richards had no problem filling his hotel and his bar with customers.[209] Joe Richards ran the Coutlee Hotel until May 1908, when he sold it to S.J. Solomon and took on the position of proprietor at the new Montebello Hotel in Salmon Arm. Mr. and Mrs. Joe Richards settled into their new business and home that summer. Joe set the daily hotel rate at $2.50 per room. The couple would operate the Montebello Hotel for the next eighteen years.[210]

Richards hired Bert Goodisson, a popular mixologist, as his head bartender and Barbra and Mary Macdonald as waitresses in the dining room. The lovely new and modern Montebello managed by the experienced and competent Mr. and Mrs. Richards

The Montebello Hotel, 1908. 2017.0020.0005. IMAGE COURTESY THE DENIS MARSHALL COLLECTION ARCHIVES AT R.J. HANEY HERITAGE VILLAGE & MUSEUM

gave the hotel a stellar reputation very quickly and attracted some well-known guests. The first of the rich and famous to arrive at the Montebello were Mr. and Mrs. Alvo von Alvensleben.[211] Gustav Konstantin von Alvensleben, commonly known as Alvo, was a German businessman who arrived in Vancouver in 1904. In less than ten years, this third son of a German count, Alvo Alvensleben, "became one of the biggest movers and shakers in the city. He brought millions of dollars of German investment into Vancouver and bought up large tracts of land and huge houses. Before going fabulously broke in 1913, he had a personal fortune of around $25 million."[212] From the famous to the common, the Montebello Hotel was the choice of thousands through the eighteen years that the Richardses were in charge.

In October 1926, Joe Richards died after a short illness.[213] Mrs. Richards became sole proprietor of the Montebello, but after a while she decided to put the hotel up for sale. Mr. James Bowes, proprietor of the Lake View Hotel in Kelowna (page 95) answered the advertisement and by September 1928 became the newest owner of the Montebello Hotel.[214]

James Bowes, like Joe Richards before him, had an impressive resumé, having managed hotels in Kelowna and before that in his hometown of Silverton. Also like Richards, Bowes had a very good reputation as a hard-working hotel manager who became very popular. Most of Kelowna came out for the farewell dinner for the Boweses. People were sad to see them go after twenty-six years at the Lake View Hotel, and without them the hotel would never be the same.

In the spring of 1936, the Bowes and the Montebello Hotel faced a serious challenge from an old familiar foe. A fire, believed to have been caused by a short circuit in the aging electric wiring, started in a corner of the attic. The fire spread to the roof and threatened to destroy the hotel. Early detection of the fire and quick actions by the fire department saved the hotel but not before considerable fire and water damage was done to the roof.[215]

A tragedy of a different sort played out in one of the rooms at the Montebello Hotel in January 1938. Mr. Kimoto, a guest from Japan, was staying at the hotel for a few days when he was accused of stealing. Details were not revealed in the newspaper report, but he was put under house arrest pending an investigation. When authorities went to his room, they found that Mr. Kimoto had committed suicide by hanging. He left a note behind that simply read, "Humiliated—please excuse."[216]

In spite of these grim events, life was generally quite pleasant at the Montebello for guests and staff. Although the hotel was thirty-three years old by 1941, tasteful renovations and meticulous upkeep over those years, in combination with consistent first-class service, gave the aging hostelry a reputation as the place to stay in Salmon Arm. In that time, the hotel had only known two owners, the Richardses followed by the Boweses, but that would soon change.

Mr. and Mrs. Bowes, having worked twenty-six years at the Lakeview Hotel in Kelowna followed by thirteen years at the Montebello, decided it was time to retire. The Montebello Hotel went up for sale. The popular and profitable hotel was not on the market long before it sold to a Vancouver man, George F. McEwan. The Boweses enjoyed their last days at the Montebello, receiving cards of thanks and well wishes from friends and customers. They retired to Vancouver, where Mr. Bowes lived to the ripe age of ninety-three.[217] Gone were the days of the long-term hotel owners—at least that was the case at the Montebello. The new owner, George McEwan, ran the hotel for less than a year before selling it to Mr. and Mrs. Glenn Huxtable, who sold it to C.L. ("Con") Whalen and sons Larry and Tom Whalen.[218] The Whalens stayed longer than the previous two owners and in their time spent money improving the Montebello and adding more rooms.

The Montebello Hotel was still the most popular hotel in Salmon Arm in 1954, the year when the BC government allowed a new licensed premises called the cocktail lounge. Up until then, the only outlets for drinkers other than in restaurants were the beer parlours, which could prove to be noisy and had too many restrictive rules and regulations to follow—besides, up until 1954, beer was the only choice of beverage in the beer parlours. The cocktail lounge broke their hold. Now couples had a choice and could enjoy a variety of drinks in a much quieter and calmer atmosphere in the cocktail lounge. Some were quite fancy, but all were popular, and this was the case with the new Mural Cocktail Lounge in the Montebello Hotel.[219]

By the Swinging Sixties, the Montebello Hotel seemed quaint and somewhat old-fashioned to some, but guests that stayed at the landmark hotel through the years and staff that worked there knew that the hotel kept up to date, and indeed it was its quaintness that gave it character and comfortable charm in a changing world. In 1963, the new Salmon Arm Motor Hotel was the new kid on the block and attracted out-of-town guests with its excellent location close to the highway. It may have eclipsed the older hotel, but it didn't hurt the bottom line as there were always enough customers who stayed loyal to the Montebello and looked forward to staying there and nowhere else when in town.[220] The question as to which hotel was the most popular became moot when, in the summer of Canada's centennial year, 1967, the fifty-nine-year-old Montebello Hotel was destroyed by a fire that started in the basement under the cocktail lounge after some lit cigarettes were tossed down the garbage chute.

The alarm was turned on around 12:20 AM by an employee, and by the time the fire was out, over a million dollars' of damage was done not just to the hotel but to a shoe store and other nearby businesses. Sadly, two people perished in the fire: H.G. Bert Slape, eighty-three, of Salmon Arm, and Mrs. Amy Topping of Oliver. Salmon Arm had lost its landmark hotel.[221]

CHAPTER TWO

The Okanagan

KING EDWARD HOTEL

(1905–47)
Maud Street at Mill Avenue, Enderby

THE ENDERBY HOTEL was the leading hotel in that North Okanagan community, and it served its purpose very well over the years, but the population of the region was growing, as was the demand for a second hotel. The recently completed Canadian Pacific Railway came with a promise of growth and prosperity, with a railway line coming right into downtown Enderby operated by the Shuswap and Okanagan Railway. Its scheduled arrival date was some time in 1905, giving further impetus for the construction of a second major hotel to temporarily house the influx of settlers and for passenger accommodation. Plans for a second hotel began in earnest by two rival parties.

The principal competitors to build the new hotel were Samuel Bell, a wealthy businessman from Armstrong, and Captain McAllister, retired after twenty years as a steamship captain on the local waters for the CPR. Bell appeared to get a jump over the captain when he purchased a 90-by-110-foot corner lot at the back of the CPR train station. Bell made clear his plans to erect a three-storey, first-class hotel, similar in detail to the popular Okanagan House operating at that time in Armstrong. Bell estimated it would cost between $7,000 and $10,000 to build.[1]

The timing for a new hotel could not have been better. Enderby was riding high from a boom that had begun in 1903 and showed no signs of slowing down. The economy was on the upswing, thanks to the sawmills in and around town operating at full

The King Edward Hotel, 1908. COURTESY OF ENDERBY & DISTRICT MUSEUM & ARCHIVES

capacity to provide material for the building boom that was taking place. In the summer of 1904, twenty-five residential houses were built, and the new King Edward Hotel was needed as temporary accommodations for people moving into the district and waiting for their houses to be constructed.[2] The other big employer in town was the busy Columbia Flour Mill.

The Bell proposal for a new hotel was finally accepted when Captain McAllister's elaborate plans for his hotel fell through. The reluctance and even opposition for some about McAllister's proposal was based on the idea of having another hotel with a bar in Enderby, but the owners addressed those fears: "it is my intention to give the town of Enderby a strictly first-class hotel, which I guarantee to operate as a quiet and orderly place, so that it may become a credit to the town."[3] Once the decision was made to allow the project to go ahead, anticipation of what the final appearance of the hotel would be was palpable. The Enderby and Armstrong newspapers, as well as the *Vancouver Province*, reported on every step of the building process, from the foundation to the gala opening in December 1905. "Keeping pace with the steady growth of the town, foundations are being laid for a three-storey brick veneered hotel on Mill Street. Mr. Thomas G. Bell of the Armstrong Horse Exchange states that when finished and furnished the hotel will represent an investment of approximately $18,000."[4]

People became very excited as opening day approached. For weeks they had watched the building rise from its foundation, and they looked forward to getting a peek inside Enderby's newest and finest hotel. The new hotel owners, Thomas G. Bell and Paddy Murphy, extended a cordial invitation to the people of Enderby and nearby Armstrong.[5] Admission was free, and judging by the gasps and wonderment on most of the faces that passed through the lobby doors, they were not disappointed. The three-storey King Edward was a majestic hotel built in stately brick manufactured from the nearby Enderby brickyard. It boasted a tall turret built onto the southeast corner, which gave the handsome hotel a regal appearance. All told, the King Edward Hotel cost $18,000, "not an inconsequential amount when you consider that wages in the sawmill were $2 per day."[6] A reporter for the local newspaper, *The Edenograph*, was given a guided tour three months prior to the opening and described what he saw:

> The new hotel was sixty-one feet long and forty-one feet deep where two doors opened in the front where one lead to the office and the other to the bar. The dining room was well lite [lit] with natural light and large enough to hold a substantial amount of diners, folding doors lead into the kitchen. A wide staircase leads from the office to the first floor where we find the Ladies parlour and writing room, Mr. Bell's room, and a number of guest rooms. There are twenty-two rooms in total.[7]

New hotel owner Paddy Murphy would become a giant in the community, but sadly, Thomas Bell died in 1906.[8] Paddy Murphy arrived in BC from the United States and eventually became proprietor of the Filbert Hotel in Sandon, BC, around 1902.[9] Murphy enjoyed horse racing, and his horse, Earl Junior, was raced on the grand circuit, winning twelve of the seventeen races he entered. Murphy brought his famous horse to Enderby, thrilling those who came out to see just what the fastest horse in the world looked like.

> When Paddy Murphy shook the snow of Sandon off his feet, he came here and now owns one of the finest brick hotels in the country. Although Paddy is an Irishman from Michigan, he calls his hotel the King Edward. In addition to the excellent meals, breakfast is served up to 10 o'clock, which is an added attraction to tourists.[10]

On the afternoon of July 26, 1911, a fire was discovered in the top floor of the King Edward Hotel. Quick action by the fire department contained the damage to the upper floor, which was estimated to cost between $3,000 and $5,000.[11] As the repairs were being done, a decision was made to replace the top of the original spire tower with a Gothic tower, and a fourth floor was added, capped with a mansard roof. These changes gave the King Edward a very different look from the original, and the tower now lent a castle feel to the finished renovation. Additional changes took place inside the hotel, as a large bar was completed (see photograph on page 74).

In 1912, Paddy Murphy's brother, James Francis ("Jim") Murphy, arrived from Ironwood, Michigan, where the Murphy family were early pioneers. Jim took over managerial duties at the hotel under proprietors Bell and Paddy Murphy. The renovations continued, doubling the size of the dining room and modernizing the kitchen. The owners of the King Edward purchased forty acres of land, where they grew their own fruit and vegetables in order to provide their guests with fresh food. Some of the plants were used as fodder for their stock of dairy cattle and hogs.[12] "From our garden to the table—these warm Sundays can be made a deal more enjoyable if you take dinner at the hotel. We have our own fruit orchards, vegetable garden, poultry yard and dairy, and our tables are supplied with the freshest & best. 'A1 quality' is our motto"— This was truth in advertising.[13]

King Edward Hotel after fire, 1947. COURTESY OF ENDERBY & DISTRICT MUSEUM & ARCHIVES

In December 1913, Paddy Murphy took time off from the hotel and went on an important trip back to his hometown of Ironwood to marry his sweetheart, Laura Brogan, also of Ironwood. The couple were wed at St. Ambrose Church, with Paddy's other brother, Cornelius Murphy, acting as best man. After the ceremony, both the bride's and the groom's families and friends enjoyed a dinner, and then the happy couple departed for St. Paul, Minnesota, to enjoy their brief honeymoon before going on to their home in Enderby. The local paper reported that Murphy is "an old Ironwood boy whom fortune has smiled and who has made good in the western country."[14]

The outbreak of the First World War in August 1914 and the arrival of Prohibition in October 1917 slowed business at the hotel and hurt the bottom line. The once-popular money-making King Edward Hotel bar was reduced to selling fruit juice, coffee, and tea as most patrons couldn't stomach the watered-down version of the legal beer dubbed "near beer." For regular bar patrons and

The King Edward Hotel bar, ca. 1913. Paddy and Jim Murphy at right.
COURTESY OF ENDERBY & DISTRICT MUSEUM & ARCHIVES

the discreet, illegal booze was available. Seventeen-year-old Clifford Hardwick was one of the bartenders at the King Eddy during the early days of Prohibition. No one questioned his age because most knew that Cliff was the nephew of bar manager Fred Abbott. Hardwick recalled that the law only permitted them to sell "near beer," but that didn't prevent them from selling "home brew" under the table. The illegal booze was produced by a prominent resident from up Marble Lake Way. The law caught up with young Hardwick when he was arrested while delivering two suitcases of assumed "goods" to the hotel. During the trial, the judge ordered the evidence to be examined and the two cases were brought into court. To the irritation of the judge and prosecution and to the astonishment of all, when the suitcases were opened, nothing was inside. It appears that the contents had "mysteriously disappeared." The case was thrown out of court, but not before the judge admonished the police for not confirming the contents in the cases before they charged Hardwick.[15]

In 1922, Patrick Murphy and his wife branched out on their own, first operating the King Edward Hotel in Revelstoke and then returning to the Okanagan to run the Kalamalka Hotel in Vernon from 1929 to 1936 (see page 82). Meanwhile, Jim Murphy continued to operate the King Edward in Enderby. Profits dropped off as the Depression came early to Enderby, causing the sawmill to close and prompting an exodus of a portion of the population, but the King Edward Hotel endured, thanks in part to travelling salesmen pitching their goods in the hotel's sample room at the rear of the building.[16]

The granting of a beer parlour licence for the King Edward Hotel was the first in a number of events that began to turn things around. Talk of a potential large-scale mica mine just north of Enderby was encouraging, as six tons of material was mined and shipped to Vancouver as a test shipment.[17] Unfortunately, it took the start of the Second World War to get the economy stimulated. In September 1939, war was declared on Germany, and industry all across Canada went into production to aid in the war effort. Logging and sawmilling went back into production in the Enderby area, and when off shift, many of the woodsmen tended to spend their time and money at the King Edward Hotel beer parlour. Bill Huffman was the elderly, experienced tap man at the King Eddy, having worked there since the beer parlour first opened. "The beer parlour became an institution in which the King Edward had a monopoly in town. When the bartender heard the roar of the logging truck across the wooden bridge into town, he would place the glasses on the bar and get ready to pour beer into them in anticipation of the loggers' arrival."[18]

After thirty-two years at the King Edward, first working with his brother Paddy, then on his own, Jim Murphy retired from the business in 1944, selling the hotel to David Parkin and his business partner Mr. Beckett.[19] Mrs. J. Litzenburger was the new manager of the dining room. It was the end of an era. There had been a Murphy at the helm since the King Edward opened in 1905, and now a new owner with new ideas had taken over. In the fall of 1946, Parkin, now sole owner of the Enderby landmark King Edward Hotel, had plans to totally remodel and modernize the inside of his new hotel, but an event in February 1947 put an end to his plans.

On Sunday evening, February 16, 1947, around 7:30 PM, a small fire began in the linen closet of the King Edward Hotel and rapidly spread. The Enderby fire crews were supported by the Armstrong and Vernon firefighters as the blaze lit up the night sky. Fifteen of the twenty rooms were occupied at the time, and fortunately, all the occupants escaped the inferno. Mr. Hedley V. Stevenson, a local insurance salesman, was rescued from the flames but not before he had suffered minor burns to his hands and face. It must have been an extremely horrifying few moments for him, not only due to the confusion of being in a burning building but because Stevenson was legally blind. The water pressure for the fire hoses was low, so the firemen had to break the ice in the Shuswap River to obtain more water.[20] In the end, the top two floors of the iconic hotel were totally destroyed and the cost was estimated at approximately $50,000. Fortunately for owner David Parkin, he had full insurance and vowed to rebuild.

But the old landmark was not rebuilt, and the remains languished for an additional two years before they were finally removed. There was strong speculation that the hotel fire was a case of arson, but that assertion was difficult to prove. Dave Parkin meanwhile managed a grill in town until he and his wife decided to move to Vernon in 1949. In March, friends of the Parkins put on a farewell party for the couple, who afterward drove to Vernon.[21] I wonder if, on their way out of town, Dave Parkin had one last look at the remaining main floor of the old King Edward Hotel.

James Frances Murphy outlived the destruction of the King Edward by ten years, passing away at the Memorial Hospital in Enderby at the age of seventy-one on March 4, 1957.[22] His legacy and that of the King Edward Hotel will live forever as an interesting part of Enderby's history.

Built in 1964, a one-storey, concrete-block workshop housing equipment for the telecommunications beacon on Hunters Range now occupies the spot where the historic hotel once stood.

ARMSTRONG HOTEL

(1892–2018)
3498 Okanagan Avenue, Armstrong

THE NORTH OKANAGAN city of Armstrong owes its existence and its name to the Canadian Pacific Railway (CPR). Originally named Aberdeen by the first European settlers, the CPR's subsidiary line, the Shuswap and Okanagan Railway (S&O), was built through the area in 1892 and its station was named Armstrong for William Charles Heaton-Armstrong (1851–1917), who was head of the London banking house that floated the bonds to build the railroad. Mr. Heaton-Armstrong visited the town that bore his name in 1892.[23] The CPR had the power to make or break a settlement in those pioneer days as the railway was a lifeline for the economy of every hamlet, village, town, or city. When residents of the village of Spallumcheen realized that the railway would miss their town, they packed up everything and moved to the new settlement of Armstrong to take full advantage of the railway.[24]

The first building erected in Armstrong was the Patchett home. Mrs. Patchett found herself cooking for a crew of approximately twenty men employed by T.W. Fletcher to build the first hotel, the Armstrong. The sounds of hammers and saws rang through the valley during the building frenzy of 1891 and 1892. Sunday service was held for the first time in the growing town of Armstrong in January 1892.[25]

Fletcher leased his handsome, two-storey Armstrong Hotel to Hughey Keyes for five years. Keyes was a well-known pioneer of the Okanagan district, with previous hotel experience as the former bartender at the Lake View Hotel and the Vernon House.[26] The

The Armstrong Hotel, ca. 1910. ARMSTRONG SPALLUMCHEEN MUSEUM AND ART GALLERY, ASMAS00372

perimeter of Fletcher's Armstrong Hotel was fourteen by fifty-eight feet and contained two storeys, with the upper storey having fifteen guest rooms. The main floor, with its ornate wraparound verandah along the entire north face of the hotel, had a lobby, two sitting rooms, a large dining room, and a barroom. Attached to the hotel was a large stable.[27] The hotel opened in March 1892, with an appreciative crowd from around the district in attendance.

On Sunday, October 28, fate played a cruel trick when the Armstrong Hotel burned to the ground. The fire started in the kitchen around 2:30 AM and, like many of these wood-building, fires spread rapidly throughout the structure. Guests ran for their lives, and thankfully there were no injuries or deaths. Proprietor Hughey Keyes lost everything, including his treasured gold watch. The estimated loss for the damage to the hotel was $6,000, but Fletcher had insurance for only a fraction of that amount.[28] Undaunted, he decided to rebuild, and Keyes continued leasing the rebuilt Armstrong Hotel.

Over the next six years, all was well at the Armstrong Hotel. Keyes took the option of extending his lease on the hotel and it proved a great money maker. In February 1899, Keyes was involved in an accident when visiting Vernon, where he suffered "severe bruising" after his handcart collided with a carload of flour. He was sidelined for less than a week but was back on the job after a full recovery.[29] On a happier note, Hughey Keyes and his wife, Ida (née Cornell, formerly of Brantford, Ontario), had their first child, a healthy baby boy, on July 30, 1901.[30] Shortly after the birth of his first son, Keyes left the Armstrong Hotel to manage the two-storey Benvoulin Hotel (opened in 1895) at Okanagan Mission. Mr. and Mrs. A. Gourlay took over Keyes's old job managing the Armstrong Hotel.

A footnote concerning Hughey Keyes. In November 1905, Keyes died quite suddenly in the Benvoulin Hotel. The report of his death mentioned there were "some suspicious circumstances surrounding his death." The post-mortem examination found a perforation of the bowels was the cause.[31]

The Gourlays had managed the Armstrong Hotel for five years when, in April 1906, Mrs. Margret Gourlay (née Jamieson, formerly of Blyth, Ontario) died of dropsy (known today as edema).[32] In the same year, an epidemic of glanders disease, a fatal horse affliction, break out in Armstrong and district. A large number of horses contracted the disease and had to be put down and then cremated in an effort to stop the spread. Consequently, there was a shortage of working horses for some time.[33]

Mr. Gourlay continued managing the Armstrong Hotel after the death of his wife. In January 1907, he took on a business partner, Mr. Skyrme. In February 1909, a great scare occurred when an errant lit match was carelessly tossed aside in the lobby office of the hotel. It landed on a pile of loose papers and immediately burst into a ball of flame. It was quickly (and frantically) extinguished.[34] The threat of fire, as we shall see throughout this book, was always present as most of the historic hotels were built out of timbers that become drier with each passing summer.

After Gourlay's and Skyrme's lease expired, two short-term proprietors came and went. In the fall of 1912, Mr. George C. Lembke of Vancouver bought the Armstrong Hotel for $30,000.[35]

Lembke was born in Petrolia, Ontario, near Sarnia, and came to Vancouver in 1897. He and his brother, William H. Lembke, had formed a contracting business, working out of Revelstoke, called the Lembke Brothers. As a side investment, they had owned part of a mineral claim at Trout Lake near Lardeau in the West Kootenay. Around 1904, George Lembke got a job as the head electrician for the city of Revelstoke. He stayed there until resigning in May 1908.[36] He then partnered with Mac House, a former barber in Revelstoke, and the two became co-proprietors of Vancouver's Imperial Hotel on July 14, 1910. (Eventually the Imperial became the infamous Marr Pub.)[37] Lembke left the Imperial Hotel and Vancouver to operate the Armstrong Hotel in 1912.

By the summer of 1916, there were rumours that Prohibition might come to British Columbia. Most owners and proprietors who ran hotels with a bar were against Prohibition, in part because it would cut off a lucrative stream of income for their business. George Lembke spoke to this issue:

> There is opposition to the Prohibition referendum bill as it is presented to the electorate. There is a chain of excellent hotels in operation throughout the Okanagan that contribute to the prosperity of the region and any legislation which would put them out of business is not viewed favorably.[38]

A week after George Lembke's speech on Prohibition, Mrs. Lembke and her two sons were in a serious automobile accident. A Mr. Smeeth was driving the Lembkes back to Armstrong from the town of Falkland when he lost control of the vehicle on a tight turn and it went off the road, rolling over twice before coming to a stop. A group including Mr. Lembke rushed to the scene of the accident. One look at the damage to the car—a total write-off—brought out the worst fears that someone or all had died in the accident. Thankfully, the only injuries sustained were to little Billy Lembke, who suffered a broken collarbone, and to Mrs. Lembke, who broke her arm and a leg. They made a full recovery in the hospital.[39]

In October 1917, Prohibition did come to BC, but that didn't stop the regulars of the Armstrong Hotel bar from finding a secret little bar set up for discreet drinkers in the basement of the hotel.

Despite the illegal bar, revenue was down and one way to counteract that was to build a small brick addition to the hotel solely for the use of travelling salespeople to hawk their wares.[40] George Lembke sold the Armstrong Grocery, which he also owned, to Mr. Bray in 1920, and the following year he sold the hotel to Arthur E. Whish. The Lembkes moved to Vancouver, where George sold insurance until he retired in 1955. He died there in 1957, having lived a long and interesting life.[41]

The following years saw a parade of owners as the hotel changed hands frequently. In 1933, the other major hotel in Armstrong, the Okanagan House, burned down.[42] It was closed for some time before it was destroyed, but, in its day, it gave the Armstrong Hotel a run for its money. By 1997, the reliable and aging Armstrong Hotel had seen a total of sixteen owners in its 105-year history, each making their unique contribution to the hotel and the town of Armstrong.[43] At the time of this writing, the Armstrong Hotel had been closed since 2018, but I doubt it will be vacant for long; this iconic landmark in Armstrong waits patiently for the day when the doors are reopened to welcome guests back again.

KALAMALKA HOTEL

(July 1892-Present)
3004, 30th Avenue, Vernon

FROM ARMSTRONG, our path takes us south on today's Highway 97A, past Swan Lake to the North Okanagan city of Vernon. This area was called Nintle Moos Chin by the Syilx people, translated as "the jumping over place," referring to the ease with which one could leap across the banks of the BX Creek.⁴⁴ The first European name for the area was Priest's Valley, named after Father Paul Durien, who built a cabin used as an outstation for the Okanagan Mission in the 1860s. In 1887, Priest's Valley was officially renamed Vernon in honour of Forbes George Vernon, chief commissioner for Lands and Works of British Columbia.⁴⁵

In 1892, the same year that Vernon was incorporated, the first major hotel was completed in the young town. It was named the Kalamalka Hotel, honouring a famous Syilx Chief, Hlakay, who was known as Kalamalka. There is much debate about the origin and meaning of the name, but some sources suggest it is an interesting combination of two Indigenous words, one derived from Secwépemctsín (the Secwépemc language), meaning "water," and the other from nqilxʷcn (the Syilx language), meaning "soothing" or "healing," to make "healing waters." The hotel was designed by Charles Osborn Wickenden in 1891. He was one of the first architects in Vancouver and helped introduce the Romanesque Revival style to the west coast.⁴⁶ His choice of style for the new hotel in Vernon was unique and quite striking when completed. Wickenden

The Kalamalka Hotel, ca. 1935. IMAGE F-02471 COURTESY OF THE ROYAL BC MUSEUM

would be less than pleased to see how his great design had been reduced to what is left there today.

The Kalamalka Hotel[47] was built by contractors T.E. Crowell in partnership with W.F. Cameron for owner George Grant Mackay, who founded the Okanagan Land and Development Company and was its president. A major objective of the company was to develop the area and build the city of Vernon. To achieve those goals, the company began by buying up as much land as it could. As part of the development of the town, Mackay commissioned the building of the Kalamalka Hotel.[48] The Okanagan Land and Development Company built the Kalamalka Hotel at the cost of $20,000. The company imported most of the lumber for its construction from the coast, shipping it to Enderby via the *Red Star* on the Spallumcheen River.[49] It was an attractive building and was one of the major social centres in Vernon for years, featuring a spacious billiards room, a freestone fireplace in the foyer, and the ceilings finished in the style of an English baronial ballroom. Bedrooms were furnished in oak and walnut with excellent Brussels carpets on the floor. Rates were $7 per week for board, $10 per week for room and board, and $1.50 per night for transients.[50] The Kalamalka was opened in July 1892 under the management of Mr. and Mrs. W. J. Meakin, who were well-known hotelkeepers, formerly of the Merchant's Exchange in Vancouver.[51]

The Meakins proved themselves to be excellent and very competent hosts, as indicated in their resumé for the job as managers, but Mr. Meakin didn't always see eye to eye with the hotel owners. A dispute between the two regarding hotel rates became so serious that Mr. Meakin tendered his resignation effective July 1, 1893, but cooler heads prevailed and he stayed on.[52] When it became apparent that Mr. Meakin was ill, he decided to take a trip to the milder climes of California to recuperate. In the meantime, Mrs. Meakin assumed the duties as manager of the Kalamalka Hotel until her husband returned.[53]

One day, a serious incident occurred at the hotel that resulted in a death. William Spalding, a hefty and popular thirty-year-old visitor from Dundee, Scotland, had only been staying at the Kalamalka for a few days when he had a dreadful accident. He had spent a Friday with a party of hunters searching for game in the White Valley and on their return to the hotel had enjoyed a good supper. While finishing up at the dinner table Spalding excused himself and remarked that he would only be a moment. He was searching for the lavatory door but mistakenly opened the staff door leading down a long set of stairs to the basement, where the wine was kept. Later that evening, Fouch Chau, the dishwasher, discovered a body at the bottom of the stairs, which a doctor determined was that of poor Mr. Spaulding. He had fallen down the stairs and died on impact after hitting the floor very hard with his head. An examination of the body and the facts of the case concluded that Mr. Spalding died from a concussion of the brain and spinal cord injury caused by his fall down the stairs.[54]

Mr. Meakin recovered from his illness and returned to Vernon and to his duties at the Kalamalka Hotel. The Meakins hosted a farewell dinner party for Mr. Vernon at the hotel. "Those present, among whom were competent judges, pronounced the banquet to be by far the most elaborately prepared and best served affair of the kind ever spread in the upper country." The room was decorated in bunting and fresh flowers. A peek at the menu will give you an idea of just how fine the first-class repast was for the lucky participants: "Soup—Consommé Royal and Sherry; Fish—Boiled Salmon, cucumbers, sauterne; Entrées—Fillets of Chicken with mushrooms, Lamb Chops with green peas, and Champagne; Joint—Boiled Turkey in cherry sauce, and Roast Beef, Roman Punch, Marrow Bones on toast; Cabinet Pudding, Lemon Pies, Wine Jellies; Cheese, Lettuce Salad and Ice Cream; Tea and Coffee."[55]

The Kalamalka was also known to put on fashionable balls, where participants dressed in their finest would dance the night away accompanied by a live orchestra. A unique insight into one of the many balls held at the hotel is revealed in the following diary entry by one invitee: "Nonah Pelly: There is quite a fashionable ball at the Kalemalka tonight. We were favoured with an invitation ... I believe the last ball at the Kalemalka was really not nice at all as some of the men were by no means well behaved."[56] With Mr. Meakin's frail health in mind, the Meakins retired in 1896. Fred W. Padmore and a Mr. Peer became the new managers of the hotel.

In 1896, the latest rage was tennis, and management had grass tennis courts installed on a portion of the lawns surrounding the hotel. In August that year, the hotel started hosting a number of tennis tournaments during the summer season. There was a game every Saturday afternoon until the tournament revealed an overall winner. The games drew crowds of spectators not only from Vernon but from other nearby towns such as Armstrong and Coldstream. According to the *Vernon News*, "there is no tennis lawn in the interior that will bear comparison with the spacious and well-kept grounds at the Kalemalka hotel."[57] The other popular sporting event, one that took place indoors, was billiards. The hotel continued to host billiard tournaments through the years.[58]

Fred Padmore managed the Kalamalka with Mr. Peer for the next three years, and then Padmore went to manage the CPR hotel at Sicamous. In 1902, Padmore became manager of the Phair Hotel in Nelson. George R. Raymond, formerly at the Wilson Hotel in Nanaimo, became the new manager of the Kalamalka Hotel.[59] The hotel remained popular with the travelling public, in spite of the recent changes in management, as it was the only

Postcard of the Kalamalka Hotel, Vernon, BC, ca. 1910. IMAGE COURTESY OF THE GREATER VERNON MUSEUM AND ARCHIVES

major hotel in town. But that was about to change. In the spring of 1906, Rubin Swift announced that he had secured property opposite the Kalamalka Hotel and would erect a $15,000 brick-veneered hotel that he planned to complete within two months.[60] The Royal Hotel, later renamed the National Hotel, would compete with the older Kalamalka, but there were certainly enough patrons to fill both hotels and even justify a third hotel. Rubin Swift bought the smaller Vernon Hotel in town and became part owner of the Palace Hotel in Kelowna, which was later modified to become the Royal Anne Hotel (see page 99). Manager Raymond submitted plans to City Hall to expand the Kalamalka Hotel that were accepted. It likely wasn't that the new Royal Hotel threatened to take business away from the Kalamalka, but more likely because there was more than enough business to go around and the expansion of the hotel was needed in the community.[61]

In the summer of 1910, a syndicate under the name of the Kalamalka Hotel Company purchased the hotel. "Sandy" McAuley became the new manager. First on the agenda for the new owners was to redecorate and make some marked improvements to a great portion of the existing hotel and to continue to increase the capacity of rooms.[62] Tenders were called for contractors interested in bidding to build the addition to the Kalamalka Hotel in the spring of 1911. The plan was to build a 36-by-104-foot extension on the west side of the hotel and adding a fourth storey, allowing for an additional 35 rooms to the existing capacity. The kitchen would be rebuilt into the new wing. "When these plans are carried into effect the Kalamalka will be the largest hotel in the interior."[63] The contractors winning the bid for the hotel extension were Crowell, Holland, and McMorin, who completed the job by the summer of 1912. "Few towns of the size of Vernon can boast of such an edifice as the Kalamalka Hotel, just completed by the contractors."[64] The finished hotel was a magnificent spectacle to behold and at the time was the biggest and arguably the most magnificent privately owned hotel in the southern Interior of British Columbia. The few years prior to the outbreak of the Great War in September 1914 was the golden age for the Kalamalka. Never would it be as great as it was in those halcyon years from 1912 to 1914.

The First World War was followed by the Spanish influenza outbreak in November 1918. The closure of all schools—public and private—churches, theatres, moving-picture halls, and other places of amusement also affected the hotel industry, at least for a brief time. Any lodge meetings that were previously held in the hotel were also cancelled, as gatherings of ten people or more were temporarily banned by public health notice.

In 1919, O.L. Dahl became manager of the hotel, which was still owned by the Kalamalka Hotel Company. The hotel was on the American Plan, with room rates set at four dollars per day and up.[65] The network of roads in British Columbia was improving, with more roads being constructed during the 1920s and 1930s. While passenger train service continued, the numbers of people taking the train began to drop in favour of private automobiles and bus service. The Vernon-to-Kamloops stage was particularly good for guests of the Kalamalka Hotel: a bus departed for Kamloops from in front of the hotel twice daily, at 7:30 AM and 1:00 PM, directly to the Leland Hotel and return for six dollars per adult[66]; for passengers heading to Kelowna and points south of Vernon, there was the Vernon–Kelowna passenger service, costing adults three dollars and leaving the Kalamalka Hotel at 9:00 AM and 4:00 PM, with Sunday trips departing at 10:00 AM only. "A 1923 model Big Six Studebaker seven-passenger car" would taxi passengers in comfort to their destination, operated by J. Pilkington & Son where "service is our motto."[67]

Mr. and Mrs. O.L. Dahl resigned as managers of the Kalamalka Hotel in 1922, after three years of service. During a farewell dinner for the couple held in the hotel, the staff presented the couple and their daughters with gifts of appreciation: a beautiful cut-glass bowl for the Dahls and golden pencils for the daughters.[68] By March 1928, Paddy Murphy, co-owner of the King Edward Hotel in nearby Enderby (and profiled in this chapter), became the proprietor of the Kalamalka Hotel for the next eight years.[69] The parade of proprietors continued when, in the summer of 1936, Gilbert Southwell and business partner Charles Dunsmore paid $50,000 to buy the reliable and historic hotel.[70] The new owners replaced hotelier Paddy Murphy, who then became superintendent of the Kalamalka Gold Mines Limited, responsible for bringing the old mine back into production. "It is estimated there are 1,500 tons of high-grade ore ready to be shipped to the smelter at Trail."[71]

From 1936 to 1949, five owners of the Kalamalka came and went, each adding their own changes and renovations to the long-established Vernon landmark. The exterior of the Kalamalka began to reflect those changes when it was stuccoed and the ground floor was extended to make room for the beer parlour and shops along Barnard Street, including the Nut Shop, a fur store, and a bedding store. In the fall of 1949, Valley Enterprises Limited owned the Kalamalka and the National Hotels (the National being the old Royal Hotel). Mr. M. Chechik, an RCAF war veteran from Vernon, one of the four in the syndicate controlling the hotels, was the new manager of the Kalamalka.[72]

"The Kal," as locals affectionately call the old hotel, today looks nothing like it did in its heyday. It survives without its two top floors, which were lost in a major renovation in 1980. "The hotel has now been deprived of its original beauty and has become just another of the plain square buildings which comprise most of the downtown area."[73] The Kalamalka Hotel, turned restaurant and pub, has roots reaching back in time to the beginning of Vernon and a long and distinguished history.

ELDORADO ARMS

(1927–89)
4519 Eldorado Road, Okanagan Mission

OKANAGAN MISSION was a community located at the confluence of Mission Creek where it pours into Okanagan Lake, just south of Kelowna. It was founded in 1859 by Father Charles Marie Pandosy, a missionary from France, who named it L'Anse au Sable; it grew into a religious and agricultural centre.[74] It was the first permanent European settlement in the valley and over time grew into a town.[75] Cattle ranching was the main use of the land until the early 1900s, when fruit growing became the major economic driver and much of the land was subdivided into smaller properties by the Kelowna Land and Orchard Company.[76] As the population grew, two hotels were built: the Benvoulin Hotel (1895) and the Bellevue Hotel (1907). Later, a new hotel called the Eldorado Arms opened at 4519 Eldorado Road.

The Eldorado Arms was built in 1926 on the Eldorado Ranch and was opened in the last half of the summer season by Countess Bubna of Austria. The countess was born Irene May Blair in Oxford, England, in 1876. Her fairy-tale life began when, at the age of twenty-five, she married Count Franz Bubna of Austria–Hungary at Windsor in 1901. The couple moved to Paris, but things didn't work out and they got divorced in 1908. After her seven-year-long marriage, Countess Bubna came to Canada, first moving to a ranch in Alberta and then to the Okanagan Valley in the 1920s.

The Eldorado Arms in August 1926. COURTESY OF THE CITY OF VANCOUVER ARCHIVES, CVA 1477-238

Her mother, Mary Caroline Michell, had a long affair with one of the world's richest men, the Duke of Sutherland, and received a fortune when he died. Michell spent six weeks in a London jail for burning some of the duke's documents, which branded her "the Jailbird Duchess" in the press, according to Claire Smith-Burns of the Kelowna and District Genealogical Society.[77] Upon her release from prison in 1892, Michell reached a settlement with the duke's family, receiving £500,000, a castle, and an estate in Florida.[78]

In 1926, the countess purchased lakeshore property, from Mrs. W.D. Walker, where she built her luxury hotel, the Eldorado Arms. It was to be a first-class sophisticated hotel based on European standards, just perfect for the genteel and upper-class guests that she hoped to attract. The architect was Colonel Harold Joseph Cullin[79] of Vernon, and the perfectly manicured garden was designed by the former owner, Mrs. Walker. The two-storey, twelve-room structure was done in the English style, half-timbered and gabled.[80] Just prior to the opening in June 1926, Countess Bubna ran an ad in the Vancouver newspaper the *Province*: "An Old Country Inn [in spite of being brand-new], Eldorado Arms, owned by Countess Bubna... a beautiful restful spot amid scenic splendor on the shore of Okanagan Lake... unexcelled cuisine from

An inside view of the Eldorado Arms, undated. GLEN A. MOFFORD COLLECTION

a former chef of Hotel Cecil, London... Music provided by the most reproducing instrument, the Stentophone, having the volume of a full symphony orchestra."[81] The countess had planned a week-long event in August called Regatta Week that featured various aquatic activities from swimming to sailing, in addition to horseback rides over the thousand-acre ranch during the day and dancing every evening.[82] The event was an excellent way to introduce the new Eldorado Arms to the public.

The Arms initially opened as a summer resort hotel only. Rates were five dollars per day and up, rather expensive at the time, but the luxurious surroundings, modern conveniences, and excellent service made it worth the high price.[83] The countess relied on her manager, Mrs. J. Curle, for the day-to-day operations of the hotel, and she was succeeded by Mr. and Mrs. A.G. Bennett in 1927. Perhaps the most interesting person that managed the Eldorado Arms was Major Basil Kirkland Lloyd. Born in England in 1983, Major Lloyd joined the BC Horse Division at Walhachin, BC, at the outset of the First World War and saw service with the Strathcona Horse, the Royal Irish Rifles, and the 11th Bengal Lancers. In all, he had served in France, Mesopotamia, India, and South Africa with distinction, having been awarded the Military Cross (MC) and bar for conspicuous gallantry. He worked his way up to the rank of captain by the end of the war and was later promoted to major during an appointment with the BC Dragoons. Major and Mrs. Lloyd settled in the Kelowna area, where the major was offered the position as manager of the first-rate Eldorado Arms hotel. He worked as manager from 1929 to 1932 and would have stayed on much longer had he not been severely injured in an automobile accident in May 1932. Sadly, the major died from those injuries.[84]

Twelve rooms and a red-clay tennis court were added to the hotel as Countess Bubna continued to purchase more lakeside property south of the hotel, in addition to a field to the east for further development.[85] The growing communities of nearby Kelowna and Okanagan Mission welcomed the news that oil had been discovered in East Kelowna, Okanagan Mission, and at Bankhead. The Okanagan Oil and Gas Company erected an eighty-foot derrick and support buildings and tested some sites. A new road was constructed farther back from the lake, and electricity finally arrived, operated by the West Kootenay Power and Light Company.[86]

In August 1932, the well-advertised Kelowna Tennis Tournament was held at the Eldorado Arms, attracting players from Vancouver and other corners of the Lower Mainland as well as Okanagan players. The red-clay tennis courts attracted crowds of spectators as the games proved very entertaining.[87] The hotel was as beautiful as ever, with its wide, cool verandah accessed through double French doors from the spacious lounge, "gay with chintz drapes and slip coverings." A pleasant fire blazed away each and every evening in the wide hearth, attracting guests to enjoy a pipe or a drink. Countess Bubna only spent a few months out of the year in her plush hotel, dividing the rest of her time in her other homes in England, Egypt, India, and the French Riviera.[88]

Ten days before the 1933 summer season opening, it was announced that Countess Bubna had sold the hotel to Mr. Paul H. Borradaile, former manager of the Canadian National Minaki Lodge in Ontario. Her sizable ranch was sold to Mr. W. McNair of Kamloops.[89] Friends of the countess knew about the sale in advance, but the general public was surprised to learn that the countess was leaving. Mr. and Mrs. Borradaile hired H. Angle to manage the hotel and, within two years, they sold the hotel to Mr. and Mrs. J.C. Ferguson, formerly of the Craig Lodge in Lillooet.[90]

News came of the death of Countess Bubna in the summer of 1935. Her amazing life was cut short by cancer in Montreux, Switzerland, at the age of fifty-nine (the article announcing her death got it wrong when it claimed she was seventy).[91] Her two daughters, Countess Ina in Austria and Olga Horn, who was living in Kelowna, split the inheritance, which promised to be substantial, with monies and properties accumulated by their mother and grandmother. In the 1940s, the Eldorado Arms continued to expand with the addition of comfortable cottages and was registered as a company in 1946 with assets of $100,000.[92] The hotel remained open to the public in the summer only, with Mr. and Mrs. H.T. Barrett as the owners.

The last owner of the original Eldorado Arms was Jim Nixon, who purchased the aging hotel in 1988 for $25,000, saving it from demolition as it had been sitting vacant for years. He paid to have it lifted up and put on a barge in order to relocate it three kilometres to Cook Street. This took place between March and April 1989, when, as the foundation at the new site was being prepared, disaster struck. Somehow, the vacant hotel caught on fire on April 19, 1989, and was completely destroyed.[93] Some suspected arson was the cause of the fire, but nothing was ever proven and nobody was ever arrested.

The once-elegant Eldorado Arms, build by a countess, lasted sixty-three years before it went down in flames. Those who attended functions there or stayed in the first-class rooms would always cherish their memories of the Arms.

LAKE VIEW HOTEL

(1892–1931); Mayfair Hotel (1932–48)
1561 Abbott Street, Kelowna

IN 1892 the townsite of Kelowna was surveyed. One of the earliest buildings erected was the Lake View Hotel, built by Archie McDonald. The attractive, three-storey hotel was constructed across from the city park at 1561 Abbott Street in Kelowna and loomed over Okanagan Lake. The hotel was painted white, making it highly visible to passengers arriving on the *Aberdeen* and *Okanagan* steamships that moored at nearby Kelowna dock.⁹⁴ Owner Archie McDonald contracted Crowell and Holland of Vernon to construct his hotel, which he named after being inspired of the lovely view of Okanagan Lake. "The Lake View Hotel was the first in town and the structure was Kelowna's pride and joy for many years. There was a wide veranda the length of the building facing Abbott Street. A revolving door opened onto the lobby."⁹⁵

The dining room was located in the north wing of the building while the bar was located in the south wing. Ranch hands and workers raced down the main street of Kelowna on Saturday night, anxious to wash away the week's dust from their throat. As tradition had it, the "last man to the bar pays."⁹⁶ McDonald's hotel hosted many banquets, bachelor balls, and receptions over the next few years. The backroom poker game was run by Tommy, the resident card shark, who was "prepared to take on anyone…"⁹⁷ The Lake View Hotel and Palace Hotel had the same rates: boarders $1.00 per day; tourists $1.50; single meals, 50 cents.

Mr. McDonald had a number of regular boarders and also catered to the travelling public. After operating the hotel for ten

The Lake View Hotel, Kelowna. KPA 903. COURTESY OF THE KELOWNA PUBLIC ARCHIVES

years, he then sold it to Mrs. E.J. Newsome of Vernon. Two years later, she leased it to James M. Bowes, who came from Silverton in the West Kootenays. He was immensely popular in the city, belonging to a number of local organizations. Under Mr. Bowes' capable management, the Lake View remained Kelowna's most popular hotel and the place to stay when visiting Kelowna. It was also a favourite venue for banquets and fraternal gatherings.

In 1928, Jim Bowes moved on and left Kelowna, much to the disappointment of the regular patrons of the Lake View. Mrs. E.J. Newsome became the new manager for the next few years. C.H. Jackson became manager in 1930 and there was a new proprietor, Mrs. Florence Jackson. In the fall of 1931, the hotel's name was changed from the Lake View to the Mayfair.

It was a bad omen for the newly named hotel when a murder took place in the lobby in January 1932. An undercover police officer named Genevieve Nolan (using the name Marie Lalonde) was shot in the lobby of the Mayfair Hotel in front of staff and guests. She had just realized she was being pursued by a gunman on the street when a bullet missed her head. She ran into the lobby of the Mayfair Hotel screaming for help. People standing in the lobby could only look on as a large man with his face concealed by his

The Lakeview Hotel, Kelowna. KPA 903. COURTESY OF THE KELOWNA PUBLIC ARCHIVES

hat chased after the police officer. She was finally trapped at a locked door, where the stranger confronted her and shot her seven times. She died immediately. The murderer then walked through the lobby out the hotel's front entrance and crossed the street into the park, where he disappeared.

Citizens were shocked to learn that the murderer was David Murdoch, chief constable for the city of Kelowna, and his victim, Genevieve Nolan, was a police informant on temporary assignment to the Kelowna police department. What nobody knew at that time, except for Chief Murdoch, was that the killing spree wasn't over yet.[98]

Murdoch was apparently set on killing everyone involved in what he saw as an attempt to discredit him. He arrived at the office of a lawyer named Norris but was told that Norris was in Vancouver (a fact that saved his life). Murdoch next went to the police commissioner's house, but Dr. Boyce was not home at the time. He then went to ex-constable Archie McDonald's home—the jealous Murdoch suspected that McDonald and Nolan were more than just good friends. J. Todd, a next-door neighbour, heard two gun shots and learned later that McDonald was dead. The manhunt to capture Murdoch got underway in earnest as Constable W.S. Sands decided to first check Murdoch's home, where he found the chief calmly sitting in his parlour reading the newspaper. Sands drew his revolver and arrested Murdoch on suspicion of murder.[99]

The details and motive for the killing spree came out during the trial. Apparently, the usually quiet-mannered Murdoch had fallen in love with Miss Nolan and had finally snapped, murdering two people and looking for more victims. Nolan was believed to have had important correspondence in her room between Chief Murdoch and herself that Murdoch desperately wanted back. "The fact that her room was ransacked before the killing indicates to police that someone wished to obtain these documents. Mrs. Florence Jackson, proprietor of the Mayfair Hotel, saw Murdoch outside of Miss Nolan's room at 5 o'clock the day of the shooting and overheard Murdoch mutter, "I wish to God she had never been born."[100] There was no doubt in court that Murdoch was the murderer, as a string of witnesses so did testify. (Coincidentally, the Lake View Hotel had been built by Archie McDonald, the same man murdered by Chief Murdoch.)

It took months before the talk about the dramatic murder in the Mayfair Hotel simmered down. Mr. C.H. Jackson remained as manager until the hotel closed in 1948. In 1945, Florence E. Jackson was still the proprietor of the Mayfair, but by then the old hotel was showing its age. Competition from other local hotels, especially the Royal Anne Hotel, whose owners had just finished an expensive renovation and brought in new managers, Mr. and Mrs. Jenner from Vancouver, were factors that led to the decision to finally close the historic Mayfair. Once the Mayfair was empty, it was demolished and sat as a vacant lot for years before plans to rebuild a new hotel were finalized.

THE PALACE HOTEL

(1905–28); Royal Anne Hotel
(1929–71, 1975–Present)
348 Bernard Street, Kelowna

ACROSS TOWN from the Lake View Hotel (later the Mayfair Hotel) was the Palace Hotel on Barnard Street in Kelowna. The Palace operated at this location from 1905 until 1928, when it was moved back from the road and absorbed as part of the kitchen in the larger Royal Anne Hotel. The following is a history of these two hotels.

The three-storey Palace Hotel was built by T.E. Crowell, a reputable contractor from Vernon who also built the Kalamalka Hotel and a great number of other residential and commercial buildings in the area. The Palace was built for Mr. John Milligan. It cost $20,000 when completed and opened in August 1905. Expensive English carpets covered every floor, and the furnishings were made of solid mahogany. The halls, corridors, and staircases were built exceedingly wide with customer comfort in mind: "There are two sitting rooms, and the bar has a large room to itself with a pool table for use. Mr. Milligan is an experienced hotel man and runs a good house. The hotel operates on the European plan with one large bathroom on each floor."[101] The risk of flood was also taken into account: "Unseen by guests is the four or five feet of sawdust that was packed under the Palace Hotel to prevent any rising water from Okanagan Lake seeping into the hotel."[102]

Mr. Milligan enjoyed his new hotel but must have been thinking about either taking on a partner or of early retirement, as he was

Royal Anne Hotel, Kelowna, circa. 1945. KPA 5808. COURTESY OF THE KELOWNA PUBLIC ARCHIVES

often heard to talk about his many fishing trips and how he would love more time to fish and relax. In May 1907, Milligan sold the Palace Hotel to Arthur A. Peabody.[103] Mr. Peabody was an experienced hotelier, having worked in the business for twenty-five years in Innisfail, Alberta, and for the next ten years operated the Palace with only a few hitches. He had big plans for the hotel, including an expansion, and he was determined to maintain the first-class service started by John Milligan.

In December 1907, John Weiber, a visitor from Sacramento, California, checked into the Palace Hotel. The staff and management quickly discovered that Weiber was a troublesome guest and were forced to eject him from the hotel. As he was gathering his personal items to leave, Weiber "ransacked several of the private rooms, appropriating several small articles, jewelry and clothing." He then made his getaway but didn't get far before he was arrested by Chief Constable Hidson, with aid from Constable R. Davidson. It turned out that the name John Weiber was an alias for his real name of Harry Watson, who on later investigation was found to be active in a series of burglaries all over Kelowna. He faced a number of charges that went to trial. Watson was found guilty and sentenced to twelve months' hard labour at Kamloops.[104]

As that excitement began to fade, Peabody got down to the task of managing the Palace Hotel. The Palace had been opened for a few years by this time, and the travelling public grew fond of the hotel. In early April 1909, the hotel, owner, and guests breathed a sigh of relief when a potentially serious fire that started from a fault in the kitchen chimney was quickly extinguished. The volunteer fire brigade had a stream directed on the building very quickly and received the gratitude from Mr. Peabody for the prompt and professional way in which they answered the call.[105]

The Palace Hotel was given a contract from the City of Kelowna to provide prisoners in the local jail with meals.[106] At one time, there was a large sign on the hotel's roof that ended up beside the water trough in front of the hotel, blown down on a particularly windy day. A good deal of damage was done all over town, as several other signs were torn down by the high winds along with fences and older structures such as sheds and even a barn. The ancient tree at the corner of the park was uprooted. The Palace rooftop sign was not replaced.[107]

The threat of fire was always a constant reminder to be vigilant. On a Saturday morning in November 1911, a fire caused by a defective stovepipe broke out in the Palace. It was quickly extinguished by several people waiting in a nearby bus who disembarked and helped put it out.[108]

The only time that Arthur Peabody got in hot water regarding liquor regulations in his hotel was when he was charged with selling liquor on a Sunday. According to the Liquor Act, all bars were to be closed on the Sabbath and no exchange of liquor was permitted. Peabody and his bartender, S.L. Arnot, admitted that a parcel of liquor had been handed to a customer who came to pick it up from the hotel on a Sunday, but in their defence, they claimed he had prepaid the day before. The court ruled in favour of the spirit of the law and fined Peabody $100 or four months in jail.[109]

By the fall of 1917, Peabody commented that he thought if Prohibition became law in British Columbia, some hotels would be forced to close. He calmly stated that regardless of the outcome of the vote, he intended to close the Palace Hotel on Sunday night, September 30.[110] The following day, Prohibition became law in BC. Peabody used the Prohibition argument as an excuse to close the hotel, as he was very ill at the time. After the doors were locked, he put the hotel up for sale and made plans to return to his native Nova Scotia. The hotel wasn't on the market for long before it was picked up by A.A. Ballard, who had just completed a four-year run at the CPR hotel in Sicamous. Together with a syndicate of local businessmen operating under the banner of "The Palace Hotel Limited," Ballard purchased the Palace Hotel, and Arthur Peabody went into retirement.[111] The *Vernon News* reported, "Mr. and Mrs. Ballard are well known in Kelowna and may confidently be expected to make the hotel a success, even under Prohibition."[112] Ballard reopened the hotel and with Prohibition in full swing in BC, he, being a practical and experienced hotelier, dismantled the bar and divided the space into smaller rooms to be used by commercial salespeople to sell their wares.[113] While the Ballards were getting the Palace in order, the condition of the previous owner, Arthur Peabody, worsened and he never did get back to his home in Nova Scotia. He died in Vancouver in late April of 1918.[114]

In the summer of 1922, the ownership of the hotel changed again when the Ballards sold it to another very experienced hotelier, James H. Broad.[115] Mr. Broad was the final owner of the Palace Hotel and took part in its changeover to the brand-new, modern Royal Anne Hotel in 1928. He continued as manager for years, with the hotel owned by a new syndicate of local buyers called the Community Hotel Limited.

In September 1927, there had been a call for tenders to build a new four-storey hotel on the site of the Palace Hotel. The estimated cost for the new structure was pegged at $110,000. It was to be built with reinforced concrete and finished with red-brick veneer manufactured from local Knox Mountain clay. Plans provided for fifty-six rooms and six sample rooms. The lower floor would accommodate four retail outlets, a lounge, women's tearoom, public dining room, kitchen, writing room, and the sample rooms.[116]

Named not for a member of the royal family but for a royal treat, the Royal Anne Hotel got its name from the delicious type of cherry grown in the local orchards. The Palace Hotel dining room had served cherry olives made from Royal Anne cherries that were pickled in vinegar and spices and had become a popular delicacy with hotel patrons; the Royal Anne Hotel continued that tradition.[117] The front of the new hotel was fashioned in a colonial style, using brick, beams, and stucco, and the old Palace Hotel was moved to the back of the lot and remodelled into the new kitchen.[118]

The fifty-six-room Royal Anne was designed in 1928 by Townley and Matheson, from the Vancouver firm of McCarter and Nairne.[119] The contract to build the Royal Anne hotel went to the Kamloops firm of Johnson and Company, which promised to employ local labour and purchase supplies and materials locally if possible.[120]

The official opening day was March 21, 1929, but the doors were opened weeks beforehand to show off the splendid new hotel to an appreciative public. Expensive and exotic Asian rugs were draped over hardwood floors, and priceless imported furnishings from Europe could be seen throughout. A wrought-iron and stone fireplace designed by L.A. Hutton was a special feature found in the main floor lounge that saw a lot of use during those cold fall and winter evenings. "The sum total was to give the new hotel a dignity rare in a frontier hotel."[121] Opening day activities included a formal hotel-opening ceremony conducted by Mayor D.W. Sutherland, followed by a number of short speeches and a general reception with a gala dinner and dance graciously hosted by the proprietor.[122] Practically every business and club in town wanted to hold their meetings and functions at the new hotel. Rates were set at $4.50 to $6 per day, with special weekly and monthly rates available on request. Of the fifty-six rooms, twenty-five contained an ensuite with a bath. It was owned by the Kelowna Community

Hotel Company Limited and managed by the very able James Harry Broad.[123]

Nine months after opening, on December 31, 1929, the Royal Anne was consistently busy. New Year's Eve saw the first tragic accident take place at the hotel. Twenty-five-year-old Arthur John ("Tig") Clarence of Okanagan Mission, who was attending the ball at the hotel with his brother Charlie, went upstairs to his room and tried to enter an adjoining room, but the door was jammed and he couldn't open it. Thinking the door was locked, he attempted to enter the next room by climbing out the window but missed his hold and fell two storeys to the street below, sustaining serious injuries. He later died from those injuries in hospital.[124]

In the summer of 1930, Greyhound Bus Lines of BC announced their first new bus routes that would service communities from Kamloops to Oroville, Washington, and included Vernon and Kelowna. Two of the new buses made a round trip of the new route, carrying representatives of the bus company from Kamloops and Vernon. The tour stopped in the Orchard City of Kelowna, where a complimentary banquet was held at the Royal Anne Hotel in celebration of the new service. The two new buses were described as "the last word in comfortable, speedy and safe motor travel." Powered by eight cylinders and built by General Motors, each bus had seating for twenty passengers on wicker air-conditioned chairs. There were no complaints of overheated passengers inside the buses in spite of the outside temperature exceeding thirty-two degrees Celsius as they travelled in cool comfort.[125] Year by year, the automobile gained in popularity and usage while passenger train service declined.

The new bus service was started just in time to transport out-of-town guests to the annual Kelowna Regatta held in August. As the sun set, the night sky was lit by a dazzling display of fireworks while the Ogopogo Club used their new amplifying sound system to inform the crowd of events and public messages. This innovation was clearly superior to the old megaphone method. To round off the popular two-day event, competitors were treated to a fine banquet at the Royal Anne Hotel.[126] In the fall, a large glass display

The Palace Hotel, Kelowna. GLEN A. MOFFORD COLLECTION

case was erected inside the Royal Anne lounge that contained hundreds of awards, ribbons, and trophies won by local fruit growers as well as a big basket of beautiful rosy apples.[127]

Events and activities filled the yearly calendar, with the Royal Anne Hotel usually involved by either providing a banquet, dinner, or dinner and dance. Just as the talk of the last event was dying down, a new function or event would arouse public interest. The fourth annual badminton tournament to determine the badminton champions of British Columbia was held during a three-day event in Kelowna. The previous year had seen three hundred entries, and this year was expected to far exceed that number. Participants came from all over BC, with Mr. R.H. Parkington of Vancouver, president of the Provincial Badminton Association, acting as the official referee.[128] It was a day of pure heaven for the shuttlecock set, and the weather was perfect. Reserved seating sold out at fifteen cents each, as did the magnificent "Badminton Dance" that followed at the Royal Anne, where one-dollar tickets were quickly scooped up. Following the dance, a fine dinner was served. After dinner, many took flight by their own means while others engaged a shuttle.

Boxing Day was another of the many holidays celebrated that deserved a dance at the Royal Anne Hotel. A basketball game sponsored by the Kelowna Basketball Association and open to the public was played at the local Scout Hall followed at 9 PM by the "Eskimo Jamboree," with music provided by the Kelowna High Hatters Orchestra. The dollar admission fee also included non-alcoholic refreshments.[129]

The hotel continued hosting local events and enjoying a brisk business from the travelling public over the years through the Depression and the Second World War. In October 1943, a fire was discovered in the hotel. As the guests were evacuated, thick smoke was seen for miles around coming from the Royal Anne. Firefighters managed to confine the fire to one room, where proper precautions were followed such as closing the doors to prevent the spread of the flames. The fire, although contained and quickly extinguished, reminded management of the need for vigilance when it came to fire safety.[130]

In February 1946, a significant change took place as the controlling interest for the Royal Anne Hotel, the Kelowna Community Hotel Company, was taken over by the Okanagan Investment Company. After twenty-five years spent managing the hotel, Mr. James Harry Broad and his assistant manager, J. Dunlop, were replaced with the new manager, D. Balsillie.[131] It was under the new owners and managers that a beer parlour was proposed for the Royal Anne Hotel, providing the plebiscite was accepted by the majority of the voters and if city council then approved the plans for it. The plan was to build an overhead bridge across the lane on Bernard Avenue connecting the hotel to the new beer parlour. The plebiscite approved of selling beer by the glass, and city council accepted the hotel's plan for an overpass, providing the hotel paid for the cost of removing the power lines and having them put underground.[132] By 1954, with the wave of new cocktail licences being issued to hotels across British Columbia, the Royal Anne was permitted to sell beer and wine with meals in their restaurant, along with three other Kelowna establishments.[133] Organizations and individuals who did not support liquor being sold in hotels fought the law in court but were unsuccessful. By 1956, the Kelowna police department, which was located behind the Royal Anne Hotel, was closed and torn down and replaced with a beer parlour. Times were changing, and the liquor regulations were finally relaxing.

The Royal Anne Hotel was the number one hotel in the Orchard City for forty-two years—from 1929 to 1971—but the end came quickly when fire, the bane of every building, destroyed the establishment. The fire started in the boiler room and quickly spread through the older section of wood and brick located in the rear of the hotel. Twenty-eight guests were all evacuated without injury, and the newer section, facing Bernard Avenue and connected by a walkway, only received smoke and water damage. Hotel owners Glen Belke and Verne Hogan were unable to give a firm estimate of the losses but mentioned that the hotel had sold several years prior for $600,000.[134]

It took four years, but in 1975 the new Royal Anne Hotel opened on the same site as the old one and the Palace Hotel that preceded it. While it has gone through various owners and name changes through the years, it is still in operation at the time of this writing and has again the familiar name it had since 1929, the Royal Anne Hotel, making new memories for generations to come.

SUMMERLAND HOTEL

(1902-25)
Shaughnessy Avenue at Ninth Street,
Summerland

SUMMERLAND IS a pleasant Okanagan town located approximately twenty kilometres north of Penticton along the western shore of Lake Okanagan. It was originally named Trout Creek, after pioneer George Barclay's Trout Creek Ranch, which he homesteaded in the 1890s. The name changed to Summerland in August 1902, when the Summerland Syndicate, headed by company president Sir Thomas Shaughnessy, purchased the Barclay property.[135] Among the goals of the syndicate, besides creating a townsite, was to "construct and insure a hotel for $8,000,"[136] This was the beginning of the Summerland Hotel.

The famous Sir Thomas Shaughnessy, who was also president of the CPR, also developed townsites. Together with his friend Senator John N. Kirchhoffer of Manitoba, and secretary of the Summerland Syndicate John Moore Robinson, Sir Thomas financed the building of Summerland after three years of inquiries and careful planning. The Barclay ranch consisted of 3,500 acres and sold for $44,000, including an additional 500 acres and water rights. Surveying the land and constructing an irrigation system cost a further $7,000. These and the hotel cost, estimated at $8,000, were all financed by Sir Thomas.[137] A townsite was started on the lakeshore. This later became known as "Lower Town" when the town later expanded up on the bench. Lakeshore property was limited, as it was hemmed in by overhanging cliffs.[138]

The Summerland Hotel, 1905. 1978 651 001A SM COURTESY OF THE SUMMERLAND MUSEUM AND ARCHIVES SOCIETY, SUMMERLAND, BC

The Summerland Hotel was built on the southwest corner of Shaughnessy Avenue and Ninth Street, on the left-hand side of the wharf for incoming boats. It was a comfortable, two-storey frame building overlooking beautiful Okanagan Lake and offered guests twenty-five rooms, a large dining room, a billiard room, and sample rooms, but no bar.[139] The Summerland Hotel was and would remain a temperance hotel. The manager was William J. ("Billy") Lawrence.[140]

The Summerland Development Company was incorporated on June 18, 1903, and oversaw the development of Summerland. Thomas Shaughnessy was its president, and John Moore Robinson was the manager and primarily responsible for the initial decisions on the development of the town. "The company received water, septic tanks, electricity, a post office, a school, sawmill and a hotel. Settlers from across the prairies, eastern Canada and England were drawn to the Summerland area."[141] A successful ad campaign brought tourists and settlers to the fruit-growing town, where it was promised they would find "a beautiful lake, Italic skies, fishing, pretty women and noble men." There was also the veiled warning that "no intoxicating liquors are sold here, thus the dissolute element do not care to come in contact with the abstainers."[142]

The Okanagan

In 1905, the Summerland Development Company completed the first electric light plant, bringing electricity to the town. The hotel was one of the first places to be wired up, as the small hydro-electric plant was installed in a concrete building in front of the hotel.[143] Just imagine being welcomed into Summerland aboard the ss *Aberdeen*[144] or another of the sternwheelers on a balmy summer evening and looking at the hotel lit up by electricity for the first time, the warm light reflecting off the water. A natural spring was located at the back of the hotel, and some of that water was diverted directly into the hotel by a series of pipes; the runoff continued on its way into Okanagan Lake. Business was very good even though it was a temperance hotel (some preferred it that way). The comfortable modern building was elegantly furnished, and steam heat and electricity were a definite draw for guests. A wide verandah on each of the two floors looked out onto the lake, and the view from the east-facing rooms must have been magnificent. The well-tended gardens were in full bloom from spring to fall, and the addition of a water fountain, its spray shooting skyward, added to the charm of the landscape. In the back of the hotel a spring of cool, clear water gushed straight out of the ground. Some guests had to be turned away as the Summerland Hotel became better known and popular. Proprietors Mr. and Mrs. W.J. Wallace made plans for a large addition that would double the size of the house at a cost of $10,000.[145]

On December 21, 1906, the District of Summerland was incorporated with John Moore Robinson as the first reeve. The following year, telephone service came to the growing community, and thanks to the Summerland Development Company, roads were improved and new ones built, and a reliable irrigation system was turning Summerland lush and green. A daily ferry service connected the town to Penticton, Naramata, and all points north on Okanagan Lake.

Summerland had its own twenty-one-piece band that is proudly shown off in a photograph sitting on the stairs of the Summerland Hotel. A bandstand was erected next to the hotel, for often the band would serenade the townspeople and delight

The Summerland Brass Band, on the steps of the Summerland Hotel, 1906. 2005-020-002 COURTESY OF THE SUMMERLAND MUSEUM AND ARCHIVES SOCIETY, SUMMERLAND, BC

passengers disembarking at the nearby wharf.[146] The population soon exceeded seven hundred and continued to grow.[147] These were the boom years for Summerland, and citizens were filled with optimism and unbounded confidence in the future until a disturbing event occurred in December 1908 that dampened down the celebration.

In the December 19 issue of the *Summerland Review*, the manager of the Summerland Development Company and the hotel's owner, J.M. Robinson, ran a large ad that read, "Hotel Summerland, Come for a day and stay forever. We still have some 10-acre lots left at $100 per acre and upwards..."[148] Most of the news in the paper was positive and upbeat, until a tragedy took place on Christmas Day.

During the busy Christmas season, three employees of the Summerland Hotel, cooks Arthur Wilson and Charles Blair and waiter Arthur Chapman were allowed twenty-four hours away from the hotel so they could ride into Penticton to do a little Christmas shopping and enjoy an overnight there, with the proviso that they were back at work by 2 PM on Christmas afternoon to help with the special Christmas dinner. The trio set out on horseback for the sixteen-mile trek south on the Penticton-Summerland trail. The ride south was uneventful, and they made use of the time for shopping, eating, and enjoying a few drinks when they arrived at their destination. The next morning, Christmas Day, they celebrated with a few drinks at the BC Hotel (profiled next in this chapter) and then continued with a round at the nearby Hotel Penticton. They then filled their flasks and prepared for the journey back to the Summerland Hotel. The three men, who were Black, were friends and had been hired at the same time when they had arrived from Georgia. They did not appear to suffer the same blatant discrimination that they received back home based on the colour of their skin.

They were only about a mile into the journey back when the weather took a turn for the worse. A cold rain started to fall that quickly worsened into sleet and then into snow. Two of the three, Blair and Wilson, wore only light cotton summer shirts, which absorbed the moisture, and they became soaked and were shivering. Mr. Chapman was better dressed for inclement weather. As the men rode on, a snowstorm developed and limited their visibility. One of the three was thrown from his horse in a gully and became disoriented. One of the other two lost his horse when he tried to help his companion. The third man, Chapman, lit off to recover the horses but couldn't find them and decided to continue on to get help. Meanwhile Blair and Wilson, confused and freezing, began to panic.

Chapman barely made it back to the Summerland Hotel alive, and after a short spell of recovering in dry, warm clothes by the fire, he related his tale of horror. A search party was immediately formed and a phone call placed to Constable John Tooth in Penticton. "Val" C. Haynes, stock manager for the Southern Okanagan Land Company, found Wilson's body in a gulch off the Summerland Road. Two days later, Constable Tooth found the frozen body of Blair, which he brought into Penticton.[149] Sadly, both men had died from exposure—tragically, within five miles of Penticton, which they couldn't reach most likely due to their state of panic and their advanced state of hypothermia. Witnesses who testified at the inquest that followed mentioned that all three had imbibed alcohol both the night before and Christmas morning but that they showed no signs of impairment. It was the exposure that had killed Blair and Wilson and liquor was not a factor. It was a sad reminder of just how harsh conditions could be, especially when one is unprepared. Blair and Wilson were given a funeral and buried in the Penticton Cemetery.[150]

On a lighter note, during the Naramata Regatta held in July 1909, one of the many contests was a dispatch riders' race in which a dispatch was given to each of the mounted contestants, who would race their horses the distance from Summerland to Naramata, dismount, and run up to the judges' grandstand to hand over the dispatch. Besides the prestige (and bragging rights) for whomever covered the distance the fastest, the top prize was a handsome saddle.[151]

In 1910, the Summerland Hotel had new proprietors, experienced hoteliers Mr. and Mrs. Herbert Cancellor.[152] Then in 1913, Mr. L. Race Dunrobin became manager, and his timing couldn't be worse—business dropped off severely that year and became so bad that the hotel was forced to close temporarily in October. Both Herbert Cancellor and Race Dunrobin tried to get a liquor licence approved for the hotel, but it was rejected by the licensing board each time. It was reported that "after struggling for some years to conduct a hotel at Summerland without a liquor licence, the hotel company decided to close the doors."[153] Ironically, it would be a mere four years later that Prohibition closed all the hotel bars across British Columbia. The Summerland Hotel did not languish for long before it was reopened and Prohibition was the law of the land.

From 1914 to 1919, and with the boom over in Summerland, the First World War was the biggest news and touched the lives of most people, especially those whose sons went off to fight. The Dominion Experimental Farm opened near Summerland in 1914.[154] The CPR finally had a train into Summerland arriving on May 31, 1915, and passenger service continued in the community until it was discontinued on January 16, 1964.[155] But the biggest local news story, other than the end of the Great War, was the war against Spanish influenza, which closed schools, churches, theatres, moving picture halls, pool rooms, and most places where people gathered. Gatherings of ten or more people were prohibited by law in an attempt to end the pandemic.[156]

In 1919, the Summerland Hotel was fully open again and was operated by new owner C.B. McCallum, who had purchased it from the Summerland Development Company. Meetings and gatherings were now safe, and various clubs held functions at the aging hotel, including the Player's Club from the University of British Columbia (UBC), whose members enjoyed "a scrumptious luncheon at the Summerland Hotel."[157] In 1924, a fire destroyed many of the lakeside buildings in Lower Town, but the hotel was not damaged and continued to function.

The year 1925 was not a particularly good one for C.B. McCallum. In January, he was involved in a head-on car crash on Front Street in Summerland, in which he sustained two broken ribs and several bruises.[158] McCallum spent the rest of the winter and spring recovering. By November, he had healed nicely, only to witness the end of his Summerland Hotel when it burned to the ground in a spectacular fire that was seen as far away as Penticton. All five guests and staff made for the exits as quickly as they could as the rapid fire consumed the hotel. A few days after the fire, a despondent McCallum stated that the Summerland Hotel would not be rebuilt.[159]

Gone was a piece of Summerland's history and the landmark hotel that was in business for less than twenty-three years, not counting when it closed for a time, before it was destroyed by fire.

BC HOTEL

(1905-54); Valley Hotel (1954-2012)
123 Front Street, Penticton

PENTICTON IN 1905 was a growing community with a government dock on Smith Street (later named Front Street), where passengers and freight would be loaded and unloaded from the sternwheelers that plied the waters of Okanagan Lake. Upon arriving at the government dock in Penticton, travellers could either head to the mining camps growing around the Oliver area or to a ranch. The two-storey BC Hotel was constructed at that important junction and rapidly became the cornerstone hotel when it opened in 1905. The location of the hotel was perfect, and it was built during a critical time in the city's development, according to Penticton Museum curator Peter Ord. "The perfect place to put a hotel was right at the foot of that dock. That was one of the attractions of the BC Hotel. It remained a bustling place for years and could easily be found, being the tallest structure in the community at the time."[160]

The BC Hotel was built by Percy Marks and immediately filled a void in the community. An article in the *Hedley Gazette* is the first mention of the BC Hotel in Penticton, stating that, "Penticton is beginning to wake at last. Buildings are going up and the sound of the saw and hammer is heard the weeklong. Percy Marks, hotel is being shingled. Percy seems to have a knack of catching a new place just before the rush."[161] Percy Marks was a well-known and successful businessman who had built and operated the Grand Hotel in Hedley before constructing the BC Hotel in Penticton.

Marks sold the BC Hotel in 1906 to W.H. Tapley.[162] Tapley leased Marks's hotel in Keremeos in 1909 after selling the BC Hotel.[163]

Proprietor Bill Tapley was a typical publican, portly and good-natured, who operated an honest house. His Chinese cooks kept the dining room well supplied with wholesome meals that appealed to his working-class clientele, who filled the place to capacity.[164] Despite his large physique, Tapley was active at work and play, the latter in which he recorded the fourth-best bowling score at the Claughton Brothers Bowling Alley for the winter season of 1907-1908.[165] Tapley was not immune from the occasional outbursts of anger, as witnessed by a few citizens in downtown Penticton when the proprietor took out his revolver and shot at a chicken whose clucking was annoying him. He was given a lecture about temperament from the judge and then fined ten dollars for that brief transgression.[166] In May 1909, Tapley had the hall and dining room completely renovated and the exterior of the hotel painted, and, before the year was out, he sold the BC Hotel to W.H. ("Bill") Flummerfelt and his business partner Art ("Lucky") Thompson.

Flummerfelt's and Thompson's timing of the purchase of the hotel was very good as the Kettle Valley Railway arrived in town shortly after the agreement was signed. The railway improved business for everyone. It was around this time that Smith Street was changed to Front Street after the majority of local property owners voted for the change in a petition to City Hall.[167]

A significant event took place in the BC Hotel in the spring of 1912. On a cool evening in March that year, a masked man entered the Charter and Taylor's General Store and Post Office in South Kelowna, pulled out a revolver and demanded money from the cash register. Co-owner Mr. Taylor complied as the few customers present looked on in terror, their hands in the air. While Taylor was collecting the money for the robber, almost nobody seemed to notice that a boy, Roy Randall, slipped out the back door. Young Randall ran as hard as he could to the barroom of the Bellevue Hotel, which was crowded at the time in the aftermath of a Saturday rugby game. He informed the bartender of the robbery and word was immediately sent to Constable John Tooth, a veteran

The BC Hotel, 1908. CITY OF PENTICTON MUSEUM, PMA 4949

BC Police officer stationed in Kelowna, who warned the nearby provincial police detachments. A thorough search for the armed robber ensued.[168]

The thief was identified as Walter Boyd, alias Walter Boy James, alias James Polke, a twenty-four-year-old from Goodrich, North Dakota, who was known to police. He was a labourer who had worked for the local land company and was reputed to be a crack shot with a pistol or rifle. James had seen Roy Randall flee from the store and even took a potshot at him with his .44 but missed. James knew that the police would soon be on his trail but still demanded that the safe in the store be opened. The proprietor complied, and then the desperado made his escape. It was reported that James's take was hardly worth the effort, as he escaped with $8.75.[169] The robber then met up with an accomplice, Frank Wilson, at the lakeside, where Wilson had a boat at the ready, and the two outlaws made their way south to Penticton.

The Okanagan

The BC Hotel, ca. 1920–30. CITY OF PENTICTON MUSEUM, PMA 1785

That's where the BC Hotel comes into the story. Exhausted from their journey, James and Wilson were spotted two days later by co-proprietor Art Thompson inside the lobby of the BC Hotel. Thompson immediately alerted the BC Provincial Police. Constable Geoffrey H. Ashton, accompanied by Chief Michael Roche, entered the BC Hotel with guns drawn and surprised James and Wilson, arresting them on the spot. James was carrying a loaded .44 pistol that Roche seized during the arrest, but the chief didn't notice the .22 handgun hidden underneath James's arm. James was booked into jail, and the following morning the two would be transported back to Kelowna on the sternwheeler SS *Okanagan*, which was due to depart at 5:30 the following morning.[170] Constable Ashton was assigned to take the pair back to Kelowna, where they would stand trial for armed robbery. It was during that trip on the SS *Okanagan* that the prisoners made their escape. James asked for a drink of water but couldn't drink from the cup while chained, so Constable Ashton took the handcuffs off for a moment. It was then that James went for his hidden .22 pistol, taking the constable by complete surprise. James quickly fired a shot that hit Constable Ashton in the forehead. The bullet lodged in his brain and Ashton fell to the deck, mortally wounded. Meanwhile, James fumbled for the handcuff keys and released himself and Wilson. The desperate pair waited for the sternwheeler to make its scheduled stop at Peachland, where they jumped ship.[171]

Without a real plan other than to escape, James and Wilson wandered the hills outside Peachland, most likely looking for a couple of horses or an automobile to steal to then make their getaway south to the US. Meanwhile, the whole South Okanagan was alerted to the shooting of Constable Ashton (he was in a coma and barely alive). Local farmers joined in the search for the fugitives. Percy Seeley and R.D. Ramsay, two farmers from Wilson's Landing, came upon James and Wilson and got the drop on them before James could unholster his gun. The recaptured prisoners were handed off to the authorities and held over for trial in Kamloops. James was convicted of armed robbery and murder and was hanged at Kamloops on August 9, 1912.[172]

Talk about the murder of Constable Ashton eventually calmed down, and the BC Hotel had a new owner in October 1913. Irish Canadian D.S. Riordan from Nova Scotia bought the hotel and became quite popular with locals and travellers alike. Mrs. Riordan was a charming and energetic hostess, while Mr. Riordan became a prominent businessman serving on the Penticton Council for some years before his death in 1935. Mrs. Riordan became the sole proprietor and successfully ran the hotel until she sold it in 1944.[173]

There are many stories that came out of the BC Hotel over the years, and I will leave you with this last brief but tragic event that took place in October 1921. John Jackson, day clerk at the BC Hotel, had been drinking wood alcohol most of the day and made his way into the basement of the hotel, where he laid undiscovered and very likely in great agony from a late-Thursday-night drinking spree. The poor man wasn't discovered until Sunday evening, when he was rushed to the hospital, but it was too late. He died in the Penticton Hospital that night.[174]

The BC Hotel went through a name change in 1954 to the Valley Hotel. Some readers may recall Slack Alice's and the strip bar that used to exist right up until a devastating fire destroyed the building in 2012. From its beginnings in 1905 as a modest two-storey hotel in which the top floor was a bordello, and expanded over the years through countless renovations, the BC Hotel was a landmark in the community of Penticton and its history will long be remembered.

INCOLA HOTEL

(1912–79)
100 Lakeshore Drive, Penticton

Incola, Latin for inhabitant or dweller.[175]

THE FORTY historic hotels profiled in this book all contributed to their communities, but four or five were so significant that they were deemed essential to the growth and prosperity of the town where they were built. The Incola Hotel was one of those essential hotels. The CPR was the chief stockholder in the Okanagan Land Company, which began constructing the CPR-owned Incola Hotel near the Okanagan lakeshore in August 1911. The plan was ambitious, risky, and something that could only be accomplished by a huge company with the financial wherewithal like the CPR. Once the Incola was completed, it put Penticton on the map, and the hotel became an important piece of the CPR network of hotels connected throughout BC by the railways and CPR sternwheelers.

Built on 1.23 acres on Lakeshore Drive, close to the steamship wharves and the future railway station, the Incola Hotel was a monster, four storeys tall and standing in an enclosure of 3.5 acres. The black-and-white, half-timber-patterned, mock-Tudor hotel contained sixty-two bedrooms, a sun parlour, ladies' parlour, reading room, fireplace, billiard room, and music room. Two large verandahs skirted the building on both the ground and first floors, with the main balcony 140 feet long by 15 feet wide and extending along the front and side of the building. The interior trimmings

The Incola Hotel, Penticton. COURTESY CITY OF VANCOUVER ARCHIVES, CVA 289-002.232

of the hotel were all of BC fir, and the furniture was principally mahogany and solid oak upholstered in leather. All bedrooms were furnished with brass beds, while hot and cold running water was in every room. The hotel was heated with steam throughout and lit with electricity.[176] The hotel took a year to build, with the estimated cost first pegged at $100,000. However, by the time it was finished, the cost, including furnishings, had soared in excess of $150,000.[177] Not a paltry sum in 1912. No serious accidents occurred during the building of the hotel, but in December, carpenter John B. McNaughton was doing some work in the hotel's engine room when the scaffolding he was working on gave way. McNaughton jumped to save himself but landed on a pile of rocks, breaking his lower leg just above the ankle. He was sent to the hospital in Kelowna for treatment.[178]

The Incola Hotel opened on August 19, 1912. It was the premier hotel in town and stayed number one in Penticton for decades. The CPR syndicate hired W.J. Richardson, former manager of the Queen's Hotel in Toronto, as the first manager of the Incola. "Previous to leaving Toronto to take charge of the Incola Hotel, W.J. Richardson, manager of the Queens Hotel in Toronto was presented with $1,000 in gold by patrons of that old and famous hostelry."[179] In December 1911, prior to opening, the hotel secured a liquor licence.[180]

Not only was the new CPR Incola Hotel impressive to behold, but the hotel also put on lavish balls, celebrated special events, hosted dinners and dancing, and offered guests live music every Saturday evening from 8 to 11 PM in the spacious rotunda, making the hotel the social focal point in Penticton. For a time, the Incola had Penticton's only grand piano.[181]

The hotel was well served by an aggressive advertisement campaign to make people aware that the hotel was open for business and of what it had to offer to the travelling public. A weekend stay—Friday and Saturday nights, and Sunday dinner—cost six dollars; Saturday and Sunday, the rates were half that price, a bargain when you consider that service was first-class and the meals were prepared to perfection. The dining room received its eggs, butter, cream, fresh fruit, and vegetables daily from the railway's experimental farm.[182] Guests who wandered the property at the Incola were in for a visual treat, as the hotel employed experienced gardeners who maintained the lawns and gardens that were added in the spring and summer of 1913.[183]

In July 1913, manager W.R. Richardson was forced to retire from his duties due to ill health and was replaced by Harry Vance. That was the first of many changes in management that took place in the early years of the hotel until Mr. and Mrs. W. Jackson Allerton stayed for the long term. The Allertons had worked in the CPR's first-class hotels in New Brunswick and became popular as the delightful hosts at the Incola.[184]

William Jackson Allerton was an experienced hotelier who immigrated to Canada from England in 1907 to work for the Canadian Pacific Railway's hotel service. He worked himself up to the position of manager of the Kent House in Montmorency, Quebec (a subsidiary company of the CPR), then left to manage the Brunswick Hotel in Moncton, NB. Allerton rejoined the CPR when he came west to begin his twenty-five years managing the Incola Hotel.[185]

Up until May 30, 1915, the hotel was rarely filled to capacity, but that changed when the Canadian Pacific Railway–Kettle Valley Railway's (CPR-KVR) first passenger train arrived in Penticton that day and a celebration of this momentous occasion took place that evening in the Incola ballroom. "It signalled an exciting period for the hotel and the city" and completed the transportation link with the CPR sternwheelers.[186] The railway station was across the street from the Incola, and with the regular train arriving three days per week, business at the hotel improved significantly.

The hotel not only pandered to a high-class clientele but also served the needs of the community, especially in times of emergency. Such was the case when a wing of the hotel was pressed into service exclusively for the sick during the terrible Spanish flu pandemic that plagued BC from 1918 to 1919. The hospital was overwhelmed, and when extra beds were desperately needed, the Incola Hotel manager answered the call.[187] Non-emergency use of the Incola's board and meeting rooms saw a parade of various clubs, affiliations, and organizations from unions to sports teams, book at the hotel. One advertisement from the *Creston Review* announced that the Penticton Board of Trade was now holding its regular monthly meetings "at the swell Incola Hotel," adding that "they now had an orchestra supplying music for the regular Sunday evening dinners."[188] As the Spanish flu subsided and restrictions were relaxed, the growing popularity of the Incola Hotel forced management to turn hundreds of potential guests away as the hotel often filled to capacity during the summer of 1919. An addition to the existing hotel was the solution, and planners worked toward enlarging the hotel for either 1920 or 1921.[189]

The year 1920 began with a bizarre and gruesome find on the Incola Hotel grounds. Workmen were doing some digging at the rear of the building when one of the men called his fellow workers over to show them a human skull he had dug up. It was later determined that the skull may have been buried there for years and may have been disturbed when the land was plowed a few years earlier.[190] The discovery of a human skull did not prevent the lawn bowling team from going ahead with their plans for a local tournament in the spring. Lawn bowling was a popular pastime at the Incola Hotel throughout the 1920s and 1930s.[191]

Along with daytime lawn bowling, those popular Saturday evenings with live music in the Incola Hotel also continued through the 1920s and 1930s. The house band Saxie De Blas, as well as other visiting orchestras, entertained the crowds. "The hotel had prestige, luxury and romance. It was the high-class hotel in town where five to six hundred guests in gowns and tuxedos danced the night away until six in the morning."[192] Or so they thought. The fly in the ointment came in January 1933, when a mean-spirited (righteous) municipal bylaw was narrowly passed that required all dances and places of amusement to close from midnight Saturday to six o'clock Monday morning. Magistrate Guernsey declined to make a ruling on the validity of the bylaw, but was forced to fine the manager of the Incola Hotel twenty-five dollars for violating it on New Year's Eve. The manager pleaded not guilty.[193]

On the topic of dancing at the Incola Hotel, the 1935 "Gyro" dance faced a different problem. All was going well for the first few hours of the dance: the music was fine and the crowd was enjoying themselves when manager Jackson Allerton got the news that the rising waters of the nearby Penticton Creek had overflowed its banks, causing water to spill into the streets and creep closer to the main stairs of the Incola Hotel. Within the hour, the water was rising up the hotel stairs but did not go any higher. Allerton decided to cancel the rest of the dance and find a way of getting the participants safely home.

In the summer of 1941, the ninety-room Incola Hotel was put up for sale by the Trusts and Guarantee Company of Calgary. The sale included all furniture, equipment, stock, and three acres of land.[194] The CPR had owned the luxury hotel for almost thirty years and in that time had seen its fortunes rise and fall. The golden era had ended for the hotel, but it was still a major first-class hotel that was the hub of Penticton's social life. The departure of Allerton, its manager for twenty-five years, in the spring of 1947 was a blow to the hotel and to his many friends and colleagues. Citing poor health, the Allertons moved to Trail to be close to their son. Fred Knight, former manager of the Marquis Hotel in Lethbridge, replaced Allerton as manager of the Incola.[195] In spite of retiring, Allerton's health didn't improve, and within three years, the seventy-six-year-old former manager died in his sleep at his home in Trail.

Allerton's replacements, Mr. and Mrs. Fred Knight, had not been on the job at the Incola Hotel very long when fate stepped in and cut their tenure at the hotel short. The couple were on a Saturday flight to Calgary in October 1947 with nine other people, including crew and passengers, but the plane never made it to its destination. For some reason, which remained undisclosed, the Knights were booked on a twin-engine B-25 Royal Canadian Airforce (RCAF) aircraft instead of a commercial airline.[196] Driving rain and low clouds hampered the search for the missing plane, and two search planes out of Vancouver were forced to abandon the search. A third search craft made a forced landing at Cranbrook. The last radio contact with the doomed plane was at 10:45 on a Saturday morning, when it radioed a weather inquiry, and then there was nothing afterward.[197] A few days after the plane went missing, two hunters out of Castlegar reported seeing a large silver plane flying low around the Lower Arrow Lakes area on Saturday morning. They claimed they heard the plane's engines up until about noon that day but didn't report it until they heard a plane was missing. The report from the pair concentrated search efforts from the Crescent Valley to the Lower Arrow Lakes.[198] The extensive search for the plane turned up nothing, and eventually the search was called off. All on board the plane were presumed to have died in an air crash.

Over four years went by with no news as to what happened to the plane and its passengers until the summer of 1951, when a report came in of a "bright object" seen on a mountain top near Cusick, Washington. There was speculation that this was the long-lost B-25, because the location of the object was along the normal flight path taken in 1947. A US Air Force ground party investigated, searching the area for over a week, but the piece of aluminum metal thought to be from an aircraft was not from the RCAF airplane.[199] The mystery of the missing plane was revealed almost five years to the day after it went missing when an RCMP ground search party, following a tip from a local trapper, Wilfred Gibbard, searched a rugged mountainous area fourteen miles north of Rossland, BC, at the headwaters of Murphy Creek. The search party found and confirmed that the wreckage was that of the ill-fated Canadian bomber; none of the crew or passengers survived.[200]

With the sudden disappearance of the Incola's new manager in 1947 and the realization that he and his wife most likely perished when their plane went down, a new manager, Mr. George Scott, was hired for the hotel.

In spring 1950, 65 percent of eligible Penticton voters were asked by plebiscite if they were in favour of beer being sold by the glass. Fifty-five percent in favour of the plebiscite was required for it to pass. The plebiscite passed, having received 66 percent in favour. This was significant for the hotel owners in Penticton, who realized the profits that could be made from adding a beer parlour to their hotels. Managers at the Three Gables, the BC Hotel (profiled in this chapter), and manager George Scott of the Incola all applied for beer parlour licences.[201] When the results of the vote for selling beer by the glass was released, management at the Incola Hotel announced that it planned to undertake a major alteration by adding a beer parlour to the premises and would even consider replacing the historic structure and rebuilding with a beer parlour.[202] Cooler heads prevailed, and a new owner decided not to dismantle the iconic Incola Hotel but rather to add a beer parlour onto the existing structure.

By the 1950s, the old hotel was showing its age, but the promise of a beer parlour licence made the building much more attractive to potential buyers. A number of Vancouver companies were interested, but Hencott Houses Limited of Saskatoon, Saskatchewan, under the management of John Adams, won the bid to buy the eighty-room Incola. The purchasers planned to spend $250,000 to modernize the hotel and construct an annex that would contain a "modern tavern, dining room and coffee shop."[203] Once the beer parlour licence was granted, work began to add the annex

Incola Hotel. 3546. IMAGE COURTESY OF THE PEACHLAND HISTORICAL SOCIETY

to the south side of the existing hotel. The annex jutted out to the west, which meant the removal of a few of the beautiful shade trees and the long picket fence (see photograph on page 122). A year later, the beer parlour licence was transferred from Hencott Houses to a company that knew how to operate beer parlours, Colwood Inn Limited.[204] Colwood Inn Limited operated the popular Colwood Inn and beer parlour just west of Victoria, a mock-Tudor building built by George T. Quincy in 1936.[205] The owner of the Incola remained the same, but the management changed from George Scott to George M. Preston. Three years later, Preston was replaced with Stan and Ina Guild of Incola Holdings. And, in 1955, Donald Embury of Winnipeg purchased the hotel from Mr. Adams and had the exterior of the Incola Hotel stuccoed. The parade of new managers and owners slowed for a while once Fred Donnelly and Bill Rittaller from Vancouver purchased the Incola Hotel in May 1959.[206]

By the early 1960s, the Incola had lost some of its charm, partly due to the continual renovations and changes, and partly because it was so expensive to maintain. The Penticton fire marshal was forced to order the top floor of the hotel closed in 1963.[207] John Aylward, a patron of the beer parlour wrote, "One of my most vivid memories of the Incola is playing pool in the bar during the summer of 1970 or 1971. The plumbing in the men's room had backed up and the water flowed out under the door and into the carpets surrounding the pool table. Nobody seemed to mind. It had to be half an inch deep."[208] Similar horror stories reinforced the fact that many of the short-term owners either couldn't afford or never bothered to make repairs unless it was absolutely necessary. Broken windows were boarded up rather than replaced, and a hole in the roof from a previous fire was ignored. By the late 1970s, the premises had become a gathering place for bikers, minors, and sex workers, and the hotel's reputation was destroyed. A fire broke out in the east wing of the hotel in early December 1978, and guests were evacuated without injuries. This was the third fire in the two months.[209]

On August 27, 1979, the once-grand, luxury CPR-owned Incola Hotel closed her doors. It languished for just under two years as anything of value was stripped from the inside. Then, in March 1981, the hotel was demolished.[210]

OLIVER HOTEL

(1921–99); Mesa Hotel (2000–10)
6257 Main Street, Oliver

IN 1921, the South Okanagan community of Oliver was seeing its first commercial buildings under construction, including the most prominent building in town, the Oliver Hotel. The foundation for the hotel was well underway when trucks carrying sections of the building arrived from Penticton and unloaded their cargo on Oliver's Main Street. Oliver's first hotel was originally built on the eastern edge of Lulu Island, the largest island in the estuary of the Fraser River, by Harold ("Harry") E. and Hattie Fairweather in 1912 and opened as the Strand Hotel. That section of Lulu Island was called Queensborough, the westernmost section of the city of New Westminster, in which a large sawmill provided the material to build Fairweather's hotel.

The area was thriving when Harry Fairweather invested $3,500 for his new three-storey, twenty-eight-room Strand Hotel, which included a large, 125-seat dining room. The business initially did very well and continued to prosper right up to the summer of 1914, when, in July, Canada joined Great Britain and its allies in declaring war on Germany. As a result of Canada's entering the war, many industries on Lulu Island closed or were retooled to assist in the war effort. During this transition, the hotel fell on hard times and forced Hattie and Harry Fairweather to take drastic steps in order to keep their cherished hotel. The Fairweathers joined a travelling circus in order to pay the bills.[211] Prohibition in October 1917 dealt a further economic blow that closed the hotel for a time

Hotel Oliver, ca. 1945. GLEN A. MOFFORD COLLECTION

until the Fairweathers leased it out to an American, who opened it as the Queensborough Club. Troubles continued when the club was raided by the Prohibition police and the owners fined.[212]

In desperation, the Fairweathers reluctantly had to consider selling their hotel even though that would result in serious financial hardship and a career change. A stroke of luck came at the eleventh hour when Harry Fairweather read about a government offer to persons willing to settle in the South Okanagan, where inexpensive land and tax breaks acted as incentives to draw people into a new community called Oliver. Initially the offer was restricted to returning First World War veterans, but so few veterans took advantage of the deal that the offer was extended to the general public. The Fairweathers applied and were accepted. Instead of abandoning or selling their hotel at rock-bottom prices, they paid to have it cut into pieces and shipped by railcars to Penticton. From there, the pieces were slowly and carefully transported by trucks making the final thirty-five-mile trek to Oliver, arriving there in December 1921.[213]

Despite the harsh winter weather, the Fairweathers endured, taking up temporary residence in a large circus tent that they pitched on their property while work proceeded on the foundation of their hotel. Once all the pieces arrived, the hotel was quickly assembled and arose from its new foundation on Main Street to become the largest building in town at the time. The plumbing, also sent from New Westminster, was installed on the eve of the grand opening. Oliver's pioneer druggist, R.W. Smith, who was the first guest at the hotel, had to enter through one of the windows, as the doors had not yet been added.[214] The old Strand Hotel was given a second chance: a new beginning in a new town, with a new name—the Oliver Hotel.

The Fairweathers came to love their adopted town. They were thankful for the second chance and, despite selling their hotel to T.W. and Emma Hall in 1925, they remained in Oliver, where Harry and his business partner, Joe Klieter, purchased the local sawmill and lumber yard from the Brophy Brothers.

The Halls owned the Oliver Hotel from 1926 until they sold it in 1947, operating it themselves on occasion but leasing it out to various proprietors over the years. The first few years, Mr. Hall leased the hotel to H.W. Seeley. After the hotel had been so many years in operation, Hall decided it was time to update and modernize it with new furnishings and the latest décor. Improvements, as the *Vancouver Sun* reported, also included the addition of a beer parlour in 1936:

> Keeping pace with the times and not to be outdone in giving a complete modern service to the travelling public, the management of the Hotel Oliver have lately greatly improved this house, which has given good service as the town's original and for a long time, only hotel. Its fine stucco front and ornamental glass windows add much to the visitors' first favourable impressions, which [are] enhanced by comfortable clean rooms, excellent dining room service and other modern conveniences. The hotel has recently been licensed and has a beautifully furnished and appointed refreshment parlour. Further improvements are planned, among them a beautiful neon sign.[215]

The addition of a beer parlour resulted in a healthy competition with the other hotel in town, the Reopel Hotel, which is profiled in this chapter.

It was also around this time that the front façade of the hotel was altered from the original solid-face, drop-siding to a high, ornate Craftsman-style parapet. Later that façade was removed and replaced with the current mesa-style stucco façade. "It provides a sense of time and place that evokes positive, earthy feelings about Oliver's heritage, craftsmanship and community."[216] Locals and the travelling public alike now had two hotels with their own beer parlours that helped spur on a healthy competition while providing a steady stream of revenue for them.

A serious automobile accident occurred seven miles north of Oliver at Vaseux Lake on a bright fall day in October 1939 that was connected to both Oliver beer parlours. William Sinclair and a carload of his friends decided to stop off at the Reopel Hotel beer parlour and enjoy some beverages. Then they stopped in at the Oliver Hotel beer parlour, where they continued to drink. After fuelling up, they resumed their drive, which took a turn for the worse when the car left the highway and plunged into Vaseux Lake. Passenger John Fawcett drowned in the accident. It wasn't so much the tragic loss of life that caused the Liquor Control Board (LCB) to sit up and take notice but that one of female passengers was under-aged. Once the LCB learned of the incident, they punished both hotel beer parlour owners with fines and ordered both establishments to close for an indefinite period."[217] Eventually, both liquor licences were reinstated.

In March 1947, the Halls sold the Oliver Hotel to M. Brooks and J. Atherly of Vancouver, ending their twenty-one-year ownership of the popular Oliver establishment.[218] The Halls went into retirement. Earlier in their careers, they had lived and worked in Douglas Lake in 1918 and then had moved to Merritt, where they operated the City Hotel before buying the Oliver Hotel from the Fairweathers. Two years into their retirement, Mrs. Selma Hall died peacefully in Oliver with her husband by her side. She was eighty-one.[219]

The Oliver Hotel continued in business through various owners over the years. In 2000, the name of the hotel was changed to the Mesa Hotel. Early in the morning of Sunday, May 23, 2010, flames and smoke were reported coming from the second floor of the three-storey hotel. The building was fully engulfed in flames by the time firefighters arrived, and it could not be saved. No one was injured in the blaze due to the hotel being closed—ironically because the owner had not met fire-code requirements.[220] Oliver lost its landmark historic hotel, which is still remembered fondly by its former staff and customers.

REOPEL HOTEL

(1935–82); Desert Arms Hotel (1982–Present)
6341 Main Street, Oliver

THE TWO-STOREY, Tudor-style Reopel Hotel, currently operating as the Desert Arms, is a remnant of the formative years in Oliver. "In 1932, [when] Anthony Reopel brought forward an idea to build a new and modern hotel for the growing town, little did he realize the commotion that his idea would create."[221]

On Valentine's Day in 1935, an open letter from Mr. Reopel appeared in the local newspaper addressed to the citizens of Oliver outlining his intentions to build a new hotel and licensed beer parlour. He went on to declare that if the majority of folks did not want a licensed hotel in their community, then he promised not to build it. However, if the majority of voters accepted the plan, then he would begin building immediately. He explained that his new and modern hotel would be an exciting addition to the growing community of Oliver, with its electric lighting throughout and the addition of a beer parlour. Estimated costs were pegged at $20,000. His letter must have been convincing since the results of the October 1 referendum on the question was in favour of beer by the glass and the building of a new hotel. Construction of Reopel's hotel was awarded to Harry Boone, who began the foundations the next day with plans for a May 24 completion date.[222]

The roof was completed and the windows installed by the end of April, while the first coat of stucco was being applied to the exterior walls.[223] The unfinished sixteen-room Reopel Hotel opened for business on May 24, just as the beer parlour licence was granted, but the grand gala opening would take place in another two weeks, after the finishing touches were added. An additional convenience for guests and locals was a bus-ticket booth built inside the hotel, manned by Charles Watson.[224]

The beer parlour was an instant hit as the people of Oliver and the surrounding region now had their choice of patronizing the Oliver Hotel beer parlour or the Reopel or both. Denny Bastian, a long-time customer at the Reopel beer parlour, recalls, "My gramma and grandpa moved to Oliver from Estonia, Saskatchewan. I grew up around the culture of this place. My father and Uncle Roman were both regulars in the beer parlour. I could tell many stories about this hotel, some funny and some not." Wendy Mcleod-Kreller reminisces, "Oh, what memories! It [the Reopel beer parlour] had an entrance for women and a separate entrance for men. We sure had good times there. Shuffleboard was always in use."

In early spring of 1937, while driving in Oliver, Anthony Reopel, proprietor of the Reopel Hotel, accidentally hit twelve-year-old Emanuel Suckent, who was learning how to ride his new bicycle. The report given to the police alleged that as the Reopel's car approached, the boy suddenly swung into the car and Reopel did not have time to fully stop before hitting the boy. Emanuel Suckent died from his injuries in the Penticton Hospital. This tragic event deeply disturbed Mr. Reopel and may have contributed to his decision later that year to put his hotel up for sale.[225] In July 1937, he sold the hotel to Emile Joseph Vanderpitte of Vancouver for the sum of $30,000.[226]

In December 1939, the Oliver and Reopel beer parlours were ordered closed indefinitely by the Liquor Control Board.[227] The action was taken following the conviction of Robert McNeill, beer parlour attendant in the Hotel Oliver and E.J. Vandepitte, proprietor and beer parlour attendant at the Hotel Reopel, on charges of supplying liquor to a "girl minor." The minor was a passenger in an automobile driven by William Sinclair on October 5 that had left the highway and plunged into Vaseux Lake, seven miles north of Oliver. One passenger on the fateful trip, John Fawcett, drowned in the accident. Eventually both beer parlours had their licences reinstated.

The Reopel Hotel in Oliver, 1936. GLEN A. MOFFORD COLLECTION

Less serious offences, at least without any loss of life, continued through the 1940s at both beer parlours in Oliver. These included an incident in which William Goetz, the bartender at the Reopel, was charged with selling beer after hours to undercover policemen. The bartender was charged, but Chief Justice Farris dropped the charges.[228]

The biggest news story to come out of Oliver in many years was the murder of E.J. Vanderpitte, proprietor of the Reopel Hotel. He was allegedly stabbed to death in the hotel kitchen on Christmas Eve in 1943 by William Goetz, the hotel watchman (and the bartender).[229] Mr. and Mrs. Vanderpitte had arrived in Oliver from Vancouver in 1937 to take possession of the Reopel Hotel. They had recently had adopted a four-year-old girl, and Goetz confronted Vanderpitte regarding his treatment of her. In the evening of December 24, the two were heard arguing throughout the hotel, and by the time they got to the kitchen, the argument turned physical. The sixty-six-year-old Goetz was no match for the two-hundred-pound, younger Vanderpitte. Goetz was also at a disadvantage after having suffered a crippling accident years prior that left him with a bad leg. In his rage, Vanderpitte attacked Goetz with a kitchen knife, but the wily Goetz, expecting the worst, moved out of the way and Vanderpitte managed to injure himself with the knife. Mrs. Vanderpitte saw her husband leave the kitchen with the knife in his hand and holding his left side. The proprietor later died from the wound.

The facts of the case came out during the inquiry that saw William Goetz acquitted of the charge of second-degree murder by an assize jury held in Vernon. The jury believed the defence's claim that Goetz acted in self-defence after Vanderpitte attacked him. Goetz claimed that he had witnessed Vanderpitte abusing his adopted daughter on more than one occasion. The defence also had an eyewitness, Steve Zakall, an Oliver farmer who testified that Goetz was defending himself from an attack from the knife-wielding Vanderpitte.[230] Mrs. Vanderpitte became the sole proprietor of the Reopel Hotel and immediately put it up for sale. She moved to Port Alberni on Vancouver Island, where she managed the Arlington Hotel. There is no mention of what became of the Vanderpittes' adopted daughter.[231]

In the summer of 1944, the Reopel Hotel was sold to Joseph ("Joe") C. Armstrong, who arrived in town from Dryden, Ontario.[232] An energetic and prolific hotelman, Armstrong added the following businesses under his ownership: the Rialto Hotel in Osoyoos; the Vanderhoof Hotel, of which he was part-owner; the popular Plaza Hotel in Kamloops, in which he owned shares; and a tourist camp in Sorrento, BC. Joe eventually moved into provincial politics, running for MLA under the Social Credit banner.[233]

From the late 1940s into the 1960s, a parade of new owners and proprietors leasing the Reopel Hotel came and went, including John Johnson, who managed the Stratford Hotel in Vancouver, and George Malcolm, who was fined fifty dollars by the LCB for lending money to patrons of his beer parlour so they could continue to drink.[234] Mr. and Mrs. John Hancock traded their ten-unit motel in Quesnel for the Reopel Hotel in Oliver with Mr. and Mrs. George MacMurchy. I'm not sure who got the better deal.[235] The hotel went through a series of renovations following the fashion of the time, including an impressive, streamlined Moderne neon sign installed in 1964.

Today the eighty-five-year-old hotel is still there. It operates as the Desert Arms Hotel but is an impressive landmark in Oliver with an enduring history.

RIALTO HOTEL

(1939-95)
Spartan Drive at Park Place, Osoyoos

MR. K. SAMOL and his son Victor left Penticton for Osoyoos in July 1938 to take possession of the general store that he had recently purchased from Mr. Carlson.[236] An astute businessman, Samol obtained a franchise with the Red & White grocery store chain that had stores across British Columbia. Samol also came up with a plan to open a modern hotel for the growing desert town. In September, a local plebiscite on whether to allow beer by the glass was promised, and if the results showed that a majority of voters were in favour, then Samol would build a hotel. On the evening of October 1, 1938, voters voted for beer by the glass as the plebiscite carried by a slim margin of six votes.[237] That was all Samol needed to get his hotel project going. Ground was broken the very next day on a site for the new hostelry.

Vancouver architect Thomas L. Kerr was hired to design the new hotel. His resumé was quite impressive as he had designed hotels throughout BC, including the Reopel Hotel in nearby Oliver.[238] Construction began in October and was completed the following spring at the corner of Spartan Drive and Park Place, where the Owl Pub is located today. The modest thirteen-room hotel was fashioned in a handsome Spanish style and was hailed by many as an attractive addition to downtown Osoyoos.[239] The air-conditioned rooms were up on the second floor and featured hot and cold running baths and showers in each room. A modest-sized beer parlour was added on the main floor that promised to get a lot of use. The Rialto Hotel was a big hit and remained popular long after the novelty of it wore off.

Samol didn't operate his new hotel long before he sold it to Nat Bell of Vancouver in June 1939. Bell brought in his son Jack to manage the hotel, and in turn Jack hired Barney Barron to run the beer parlour. Jack Bell advertised the Rialto as "the newest and most modern hotel in the Okanagan Valley that has a fully licensed bar and splendid fishing nearby."[240] But operating a hotel proved to be rough going for Bell and Barron as the Rialto acquired an unsavory reputation from the hijinks that took place in the bar, which reinforced the fears of those voters who did not want a beer parlour in their community. In June 1942, as a result of the many infractions that piled up under their poor management, their liquor licence was temporarily suspended and they had to pay a small fine. Seeing his investment sour, Nat Bell had had enough and, within a few months, he found a buyer for the Rialto Hotel.[241]

Harry Little was a family man from Burns Lake, BC, and it didn't take long for him to win the confidence of the townsfolk. He cleaned up the beer parlour, and subsequently the liquor licence was reinstated. Harry Little's daughter married in the local church, and a celebratory dinner was held in the Rialto Hotel dining room. Other changes saw John Vargovcsik, "the town's pioneer tonsorial artist" and the only barber in town, rent space in the Rialto Hotel. By 1946, Vargovcsik purchased a lot and built his own modern barbershop, adding a bowling alley and pool hall that he leased out.[242]

After three successful years' operating the Rialto Hotel, Harry Little sold the hotel to Joseph ("Joe") Armstrong in December 1945. Joe Armstrong had recently sold the Reopel Hotel in Oliver and was looking for a change of scenery, but within a year he, too, sold the hotel to Noel Stokes and Wasyl ("William") Yusep. Armstrong wasn't gone long before he replaced Stokes, who retired in 1947. The business partnership of Armstrong and Yusep operated the hotel under the incorporated company name of the Rialto Hotel Limited. Business was so good at the Rialto that in May 1950, the owners decided to expand the operation, adding fifteen rooms, each with a full bathroom (the so-called American Plan), to the

Rialto Hotel, 1956. GLEN A. MOFFORD COLLECTION

original thirteen for a total of twenty-eight rooms. Joe Armstrong's wife, Wandie (also spelled "Wandy") Armstrong, looked after the cleaning and management of the rooms located on the second floor.[243] The addition was well planned, built with quality craftsmanship, and filled with expensive furnishings. Joseph Armstrong entered politics in 1954, running for MLA under the Social Credit banner. He won the seat and then transferred his interest in the Rialto to Yusep, who became the sole proprietor. The Yusep family became the longest-running owners of the Rialto Hotel, operating it for the next thirty-three years in total, from 1946 to 1979.

Wasyl ("William") Alexander Yusep and Lena Yusep came to Osoyoos from Vegreville, Alberta. The couple had three sons and one daughter: Terry, Rudolph ("Rudy"), Elmer, and Gloria. When they were old enough, Terry and Rudy helped their parents with the hotel. On July 1, 1955, the Bamboo Room cocktail lounge opened in the Rialto, exactly one year to the day since the first cocktail lounge opened in BC at the Strathcona Hotel in Victoria. Terry Yusep was considered one of the greatest bartenders that ever worked the Bamboo Room.

The Yusep family continued to run the Rialto through another major makeover, completed in the early 1970s, that changed the exterior of the building away from its original Spanish theme. In

December 1975, the matriarch of the Yusep family, Lena, died surrounded by husband William and family. Four years later the Rialto Hotel was sold, signifying the end of an era for the Osoyoos landmark.

The hotel went through a succession of owners until 1992, when Terry Swityk bought the place.[244] The hotel was on the decline to the point that it was put in foreclosure and up for sale by tender in January 1995.[245] Two months later, on March 27, 1995, Osoyoos lost their only hotel when the fifty-six-year-old Rialto burned to the ground. Initially, its beer parlour was missed the most, but the community also lost a unique historic landmark. It is still remembered fondly by those who were regular patrons to the pub and in the happy memories of travellers who had stayed in the hotel over the years. Today, the Owl Pub occupies the site of the old Rialto Hotel.

CHAPTER THREE

Boundary Country

BRIDESVILLE HOTEL

(1906–52)
Bridesville

> Bridesville is mostly a farming land,
> It is the first settlement you see.
> The town is all residential now,
> Where the Customs office and G.N. station used to be."[1]

AND THEN there's Maud, a hamlet on Rock Mountain (also known as One-Eye Mountain) in the Boundary Country fifteen kilometres west of Rock Creek and thirty-six kilometres east of Osoyoos on today's Highway 3. The first postmaster, Hozie Edwards, named it after his wife, Maud Edwards.[2] This was cattle-ranching and hay-farming country that received an economic boost when the Vancouver, Victoria & Eastern Railway Line (VV&E), part of the Great Northern Railway (GNR), put tracks through the area in the fall of 1906.

Rancher David McBride negotiated with the GNR regarding right-of-way through his ranch lands for certain concessions. The year 1906 was a good one for McBride. In anticipation of the arrival of the railway, he built a modest two-storey hotel away from the present post office at Maud, close to where the railway tracks were to be laid that summer.[3] In early July, McBride married the young widow Mrs. Mary Blyth of the West Fork of the Kettle River, and they settled into McBride's new hotel.[4] He knew that the arrival of the VV&E railway would attract businesses and settlers to his nearby hotel. Others followed to the area, and the post office moved from Rock Mountain to the new location, with David

McBride as the new postmaster. The growing community would not keep the name Maud, but other names were bandied about, such as Oxford and McBride (David McBride's preference), or as someone suggested, Bridesville; that name was either a fortunate happenstance, considering McBride had just tied the knot, or a purposely clever name with a double meaning. Oxford was the name chosen,[5] but in the end, Bridesville was adopted as the official name for the new community.[6]

The paint had not yet dried and the wallpaper just recently applied at the shiny new Bridesville Hotel when a brouhaha took place in the hotel bar. McBride took pride in his new hotel, with its long, mahogany bar and beautifully ornate mirror salvaged from the Bucket of Blood saloon in the abandoned gold-mining village of Camp McKinney. While McBride was tending the bar, the first disturbance took place. One of the men working on the railroad had too much to drink and became belligerent and argumentative. McBride warned him to settle down or he'd be tossed from the bar, but that just infuriated the drunk, who pulled out a large knife and came at the proprietor. A surprised McBride defended himself the best he could but received a few ugly slashes from the perpetrator's knife before he was rescued by the quick actions of his wife Mary, who had heard the melée from the dining room and rushed into the bar to find her new husband in trouble. Mary McBride grabbed a whisky bottle and smashed it over the wild man's head, receiving a cut or two in the process. The knife-wielding madman slumped to the floor unconscious. Score one for Mrs. McBride, while a wounded Mr. McBride couldn't help but smile at Mary's swift and decisive action.[7]

The little town of Bridesville was growing, as was business at the hotel. McBride, a pioneer of Granite Creek and Rock Mountain, had come a long way in a relatively short time, and the following year he was elected mayor of Bridesville.[8] Perhaps it was because he was so busy with other duties that McBride leased his hotel to Thomas Walsh in the summer of 1909. Walsh was the proprietor of the Kootenay Hotel in Greenwood and wanted a change of scenery, so he leased out the Kootenay Hotel and came to Bridesville.[9]

The Bridesville Hotel. 293.1225.13. KETTLE RIVER VALLEY MUSEUM

Residents of Bridesville were connected by a new road west to Osoyoos and beyond in 1910, so now they had the railway and a brand-new road. Business was very good at the Bridesville Hotel, and rooms often filled up. Walsh made sure to advertise often: "Excellent accommodations for tourists and travellers; fresh eggs and butter and our special Irish Whiskey always on hand."[10] Thomas Walsh remained at the Bridesville Hotel until his lease ended in 1914. David McBride then leased the hotel to Thomas Donald; McBride was seventy-eight years old and had no intention of returning to operate the hotel. In April 1916, the eighty-year-old David McBride died with his wife Mary by his side.[11] Mary McBride became the sole owner of the Bridesville Hotel and continued to lease it out.

Tom Donald transferred the hotel to William Johns, who operated it from 1916 until 1920. Johns's obituary in July 1959 stated, "Johns, 91, died recently in Vancouver. He was a partner with Andy Salter in the Northern Hotel in Greenwood from 1901 to 1931… Johns ran the Bridesville Hotel from 1918 to 1920 then moved to Rock Creek after leaving the Northern Hotel where he ran a farm until 1943 then moved to Comox on Vancouver Island until retiring to Vancouver in 1956."[12]

A story out of Molson, located just a few miles southwest of Bridesville in Washington State, tells the story of a robbery at the Bridesville Hotel in late July 1916. A single masked gunman entered the hotel and ordered the thirteen folks inside to line up and face the wall, after which he proceeded to rifle through their pockets, demanding their watches and wallets. As if that wasn't bold enough, he then went from room to room and woke guests from their slumber, ordering them downstairs and to bring anything of value. By 2:30 in the morning, the robber had stolen about two hundred dollars from the frightened victims. He then decided he was thirsty, broke the lock to the bar, and took bottles of beer and whisky that he put into a bag; then he left town on his horse. The thief took the road south to Molson, and the local constable was immediately notified.[13] On August 6, 1916, a man answering the description of the person who robbed the Bridesville Hotel was arrested after being apprehended for another crime in which four men working for the Great Northern were held up at gunpoint near Oroville, Washington, and from whom money was taken. The robber was identified as twenty-year old Fred Huss. Okanogan County Chief Deputy Sheriff Clair Ward tracked Huss to a ranch house northeast of Oroville and surprised him at the dinner table when Ward stuck his revolver into the back of the suspected robber. He was handcuffed and driven into Oroville to spend a few days in jail. A further search found the stolen money under the pillow of a sleeping child, and a six-shooter stolen in the Bridesville robbery sealed the fate for Huss.[14] Huss was released to Constable Simpson, who took the suspect to Nelson, BC, for trial.

On the eve of Prohibition in British Columbia, which came into effect on October 1, 1917, proprietor Johns threw a huge party in the Bridesville Hotel bar called the "100-gallon dance." It was a goodbye to the wet years and hello to the new uncertain era. Patrons didn't have to be told that it was their duty to ensure that not one unopened bottle remained the following day.

The single most shocking event that took place in the Bridesville Hotel was the murder of William ("Bill") Clayton Patterson on October 19, 1922. Bill Patterson, a former logging contractor, husband, father to a family of five, and at that time the proprietor of the Bridesville Hotel, was found dead from gunshot wounds in the kitchen of the hotel. Patterson was forty years old when he died and, according to the report, there was no clue as to why he was targeted.[15] This was an era when bootlegging was active and BC had just come out of three-plus years of Prohibition (1917–21). Speculation was that someone in the district involved in the lucrative rum-running trade to the US (where they remained dry until 1933) had pulled the trigger. The conclusion of the coroner's report confirmed that Mr. Patterson died from a bullet to the head and that he was "murdered by some unknown person." The body was found in a pool of blood on the kitchen floor of the Bridesville hotel and with the victim's shirt pockets turned inside out. A bullet hole was found in the window, and tracks of an automobile were clearly discernable. "The presumption is that death was caused by persons engaged in the illicit liquor traffic between Canada and the United States."[16]

Mary McBride still owned the Bridesville Hotel when, in December 1926, she applied for a licence to sell beer by the glass and open bottle. A large beverage room was added onto the existing hotel to serve as the beer parlour.[17] Within six months, McBride had sold the Bridesville Hotel to L.C. Charleton. Although it had been leased out for the previous number of years, it was the end of an era as the last of the McBrides, original owners of the hotel for twenty years, sold it and moved on.[18]

Mr. Charleton didn't own the hotel long before he sold it to Mr. and Mrs. H.B. Purdy. It was the Purdys who breathed new life into the Bridesville Hotel, adding electricity and keeping a radio in the lobby. They also got the beer parlour licence that Mary McBride knew would give the hotel a financial boost and create a place for working men (initially just men) to drink and socialize.[19] Unfortunately, just as the party got warmed up, the railway ended freight and passenger service to Bridesville.

In 1936, the Purdys sold the Bridesville Hotel to experienced hotelier W. Roberts of Revelstoke, leaving the hotel in much better shape than when they had bought it five and a half years earlier. Two more owners came and went between 1936 and 1952. Albert B. and Evelyn Williams purchased the hotel in May 1952.[20] Their time running the Bridesville Hotel proved far too short.

Fire, the main destructive force of many a hotel, put an end to the Bridesville Hotel. Flames were seen on the roof of the hotel around one o'clock on a Tuesday morning and, despite the efforts of citizens who had little to fight the fire with, the flames quickly consumed the historic structure. The best they could do was to save as much as they could from the inside while preventing the flames from spreading to adjacent buildings. Fourteen guests escaped the fire unhurt. Besides the loss of its only hotel and the historic significance, it was a shame that the new landlords, who were working hard to improve the old hostelry, had only owned it for four and a half months before it burned down. The new neon sign and stuccoed front of the hotel collapsed during the fire, and damage was pegged at $35,000. Only a small portion of that was insured.[21] Bridesville is a ghost town today with no identifiable historic buildings left on its Main Street.

RIVERSIDE HOTEL

(1897–1933)
Riverside, near Rock Creek

FROM BRIDESVILLE, we continue east in Boundary Country to the unincorporated hamlet of Rock Creek on the Kettle River. It owes its long history to placer mining that began in October 1859 when Adam Beam discovered gold in the area.[22] Years later and a few miles south of Rock Creek was the settlement of Riverside, also on the banks of the Kettle River. This is where the story of the Riverside Hotel begins.

Called "one of the oldest hotels built in the Kettle Valley,"[23] the Riverside Hotel was built in 1897 by Malcolm McCuaig with the help of a young Swedish man, Samuel T. Larsen. The two met in Greenwood, where McCuaig enlisted him to help with the project. Later, Larsen became his business partner.[24] McCuaig was born in Glengarry, Ontario, in 1842 and came to BC in hopes of finding his fortune during the Cariboo gold rush. He later travelled south, making his home in Fairview before spending time in Rock Creek, Camp McKinney, and Midway.[25] In all these places, he was involved in the hotel business.[26] In 1896, McCuaig worked in partnership with Thomas McAuley at the Boundary Hotel in Midway and before opening his own hotel in Riverside.[27] Initially there wasn't much in Riverside except for the hotel, but it survived and soon flourished as a stage stop between Penticton and Boundary Creek points. The beginnings of a small settlement materialized with seven additional businesses opening there in the late 1890s, including the Canadian Bank of Commerce and the Rock Creek Implement Company.[28]

On May 4, 1899, Malcolm McCuaig died at the age of fifty-six from pneumonia. Samuel Larsen became the sole owner of the Riverside, but he insisted that his friend and business partner's name continue on advertisements and in the directory in his honour. Just over two months after McCuaig died, on July 6, 1899, the Snodgrass Stage, which had operated between Rock Creek and Penticton, was robbed. Two masked men on horseback waited for Joe Snodgrass's stagecoach on a steep grade near Kennedy Creek, and, when the stagecoach appeared, pulled out their handguns and ordered Joe to stop. At first, Joe thought they were fooling, but he soon learned they were serious and stopped the stage. The thieves looked nervous and uncertain when they demanded the express box but were told that there was none. The bandits settled for the mail bags and told the stagecoach driver to move on. Their take must have not been much as only one of the mail sacks was opened and only half the mail was tampered with by the would-be thieves.[29]

When that excitement had passed and was forgotten, another robbery took place, this time inside the Riverside Hotel. According to the *Greenwood Weekly Times*, two masked men, with guns drawn, entered the parlour of the Riverside Hotel early on a Saturday evening. One of the robbers barked orders to those in the room to stand up against the wall with their hands up. Initially, Sam Larsen and a few of his friends and family thought the robbers were kidding but realized that they meant business when they pointed their guns at the proprietor. One held a gun on the group while the other went through their pockets, finding the largest amount of cash in Larsen's pocket. Stories differ on exactly how much they stole from Larsen that night; the amount varies from at least $400 to as much as $950 in cash and cheques. The cheques were useless to the robbers, who certainly seemed to know what they were doing, and they promised to leave the cheques in a bag about a half mile out from the hotel. The robbery took little time before they were gone, riding out on horseback. Sam Larsen eventually ventured outside with a lamp, walking in the direction that the robbers escaped and indeed did find a small bag containing all the stolen cheques.[30]

The Riverside Hotel. 041.978.19.5.4.2. KETTLE RIVER VALLEY MUSEUM

Fortunately, we have an eyewitness to the robbery. Gladys Bell Burlton (née Larson) wrote of the robbery at the Riverside Hotel that night. Gladys was the daughter of Laura Bell, who had lost her husband and later married Sam Larsen, making Gladys his stepdaughter. As she was being tucked into bed by her mother, they clearly heard the commotion downstairs in the parlour when the robbers arrived, demanding money. Mrs. Larsen took a number of gold coins from a drawer and placed them under her daughter's pillow explaining that the robbers would most likely not look for them there. But the robbers never came up the stairs. The closest constable was sixteen kilometres away at Midway, and there being no telephone, it wasn't until the following day that the robbery was reported and the pursuit of the bandits began. Being so close to the American border, it seemed an impossible task to apprehend them, and the culprits were never caught.[31] One drawback of having a tavern and hotel a mile out of a larger town is that the isolation makes a good target for would-be robbers, but as the hamlet of Riverside grew, that became less of a potential problem.

The communities of Rock Creek and Riverside are surrounded by ranches, mining camps, and a sawmill. Most of the workers from these industries looked forward to the Saturday night dances held at the Riverside Hotel.[32]

Sam Larsen worked tirelessly to improve his hotel. He had a gasoline lighting system installed in the hotel—the cutting edge of technology in 1905.[33] Around that time, the automobile became the newest and most interesting invention. Very few people could afford them, but as time went on and technology improved, they became more common and accepted by the public. Sam Larsen was not going to be left behind. He saw the practical need of having an automobile in his personal life and for his business.

His stepdaughter Gladys Bell Larsen relates the story of when her dad bought the first family car:

> It was a red letter day for me when my Dad bought our first car. It was an International Harvester. Purchased in Spokane.[34] [It was a] brass trimmed touring style which required the popular duster and cap for women with the addition of a flowing veil. A trip to Greenwood from the hotel at Riverside [thirty-three kilometres] now took under an hour under normal circumstances but the number of flat tires experienced during the trip usually was a factor in the time limit.[35]

Larsen bought two vehicles, one for personal use and convenience and the other a six-seater wagon, also manufactured by International Harvester, intended to pick up and drop off hotel guests at the CPR train station in Midway, twenty kilometres away. The latter "bus" didn't quite work out as planned. The chain-driven, six-passenger vehicle needed constant attention and proved impractical for the journey to Midway and back, as Gladys Bell Larsen explains:

> Milt, the chauffeur, had a keen ear for engine knocks and would often slide under the vehicle to make minor adjustments. [Apparently, these adjustments would take place often along the route to Midway] ... passengers, fearing they'd miss the train, would slip off the bus one by one to seek a ride with anyone else making

"All aboard!" A postcard mailed in 1917 from Rock Creek, showing a typical touring car of the time. GLEN A. MOFFORD COLLECTION

the journey to Midway. When Milt came up from under the car, he'd find most of his passengers gone.[36]

In March 1919, Samuel Larsen put the Riverside Hotel up for sale. He needed to sell his beloved hotel, which he had helped build and had operated for twenty-two years, because his wife, Laura, was ill. Larsen hoped a change of location and a rest would help his wife recover. Along with the turnkey hotel, included in the sale was a garage, large stables, a granary, chicken, root and preserve houses, all on five acres of land for the bargain price of $3,000.[37]

On September 15, 1920, Laura Bell Larsen died in hospital at Spokane, Washington, from an undisclosed ailment. Sam Larsen drove to Spokane to collect his wife's body for burial and service at Rock Creek.[38] The funeral took place on a Saturday, which

> residents of the entire Rock Creek district attended to pay their last respects... the concourse was the largest ever seen in the district, 42 motors and conveyances being in the procession. The very popular Mrs. Larsen was 48 years old and leaves behind her loving husband Sam T. Larsen and a daughter from a previous marriage, Gladys Bell Larsen.[39]

The Riverside Hotel did not sell in 1919, so Larsen continued to operate his hotel after his wife's death. That had changed by 1922, when the Wrigley-Henderson Amalgamated British Columbia Directory listed H. Snell as proprietor of the Riverside Hotel.[40] Larsen retained ownership of the hotel but had decided to lease it out.

The directory lists William Johns as the proprietor of the Riverside Hotel at Rock Creek from 1924 to 1925.

The *Vancouver Sun* reported that in April 1933, S.T. Larsen bought the Pacific Hotel in Greenwood and would also manage it.[41] In June 1934, the Riverside Hotel was "to be reopened by Mrs. H. Whiting and her daughter Mrs. Thompson."[42]

The *Gazette* in Grand Forks reported on June 28, 1934, that "Mr. and Mrs. A.C. Thompson of Vancouver have moved into the Riverside Hotel opening a restaurant there."

Five years later, on June 1, 1939, the *Gazette* reported on its front page that the Riverside's former owner Sam Larsen had died in a Seattle hospital.

The Riverside Hotel did not last much longer than Larsen. The hotel was demolished in June 1940, according to the *Vancouver Sun* on June 3.

BEAVERDELL HOTEL

(1925-2011)
Fourth Street, Beaverdell

BEAVERDELL IS a settlement in the Monashee country of BC, midway along the West Kettle River, between Kelowna and Rock Creek along today's Highway 33. The Beaverdell Range is on the settlement's east side, lying between the West Kettle River and the Kettle River. The settlement was created in an amalgamation of the adjoining Beaverton and Rendell townsites in 1901 (although the Beaverton post office was not renamed until 1905).[43]

Mining and logging kept the community alive for over ninety years. "In 1897 rich silver ore was discovered on Wallace Mountain and gold was discovered in Carmi, a few kilometres from what is today known as Beaverdell. The Highland Mine on Wallace Mountain produced continuously for over ninety years before the mine was closed and the site sold to the provincial government. At the time of its closure, the mine held the record for being the longest-operating in BC and had kept the community going through many hard times. Two hundred attempts were made to locate high-grade silver ore on Wallace Mountain, of which seven were successful. As a result, three small towns sprung up: Beaverton, Carmi, and Rendell."[44]

An article in the *Boundary Creek Times* on March 29, 1899, states that "Beaverton is already on the market and another townsite is to be surveyed at the junction of Beaver Creek and the West Fork. This latter townsite is owned by Messrs. Smailes and Bell.

Messrs. Olson and Phelan of Greenwood have decided that Messrs. Smailes's and Bell's is the most advantageous spot. Mr. Olson is already on the ground superintending the erection of a large store and hotel which will be run by the firm."[45]

Years before the Beaverdell Hotel was built, a hotel known as Smith Hotel was constructed around the turn of the century. An article on September 28, 1900, on the first page of the *Greenwood Miner* states that "Smith's hotel is nearly completed. It is a large building and would do credit to a much larger place than Beaverdell. Benson the packer has established a record of four days packing doors and windows between Westbridge and Beaverton [the former name of what is now Beaverdell]. Evidently the trail is not designed for that class of freight."

The *Greenwood Weekly Times* reported on the progress of the Smith Hotel construction on November 14, 1900: "The Smith Hotel is completed. It is furnished and provides as good as accommodation as can be found in Greenwood. D.W. Smith is the proprietor and transients will find him a gentleman in every way."

Smith placed an advertisement for his hotel on page three of the *West Fork News* on November 16:

> Smith's Hotel, D.W. Smith, Proprietor—The Best Furnished House in the West Fork District... Being located in the centre of the West Fork mineral belt, the hotel will be found the most convenient for mining men wishing to visit the properties of the district; Excellent hunting and fishing. Comfortable parlours for Ladies.

There are differing historical accounts concerning when the Beaverdell Hotel was opened. Michael Kluckner, in his book *Vanishing British Columbia,* wrote, "The Beaverdell Hotel was built in c. 1900 and looks like a roadhouse [with] its fine period interior, especially in the beer parlour."[46]

Meanwhile, according to the Kelowna's *Capital City News* staff reporter, writing on March 29, 2011, after the Beaverdell Hotel burned down:

The Beaverdell Hotel, ca. 1950s. IMAGE COURTESY OF LUMIN MCCUTCHEON

Constructed in 1897, the Beaverdell Hotel opened in July 1901 under trapper D.W. Smith's name as Smith's Hotel. Roughly 1,000 prospectors were living in the area at the time.

The town grew with the opening of the Bell Mine, which transferred hands several times before becoming the first large mine Teck Corporation (later Teck Cominco) owned in BC.

The mine closed in 1991, and the hotel was one of the few remaining attractions and anchor for the Beaverdell town site.

Michael Kluckner describes Beaverdell and its hotel thus: "Beaverdell provides a bit of a break on the long run from Kelowna down Highway 33 to Rock Creek, with a couple of cafés and stores and the venerable Beaverdell Hotel, which its owners claim is the oldest continuously operating one in the province, leading, as Rosemary Neering quipped in her *Traveller's Guide to Historic BC*, to 'some very tired bartenders.'" [47]

While the precise year Beaverdell's eponymous hotel became commonly known as the Beaverdell Hotel remains unknown, articles in the regional newspapers, city directories, and interviews with former residents tell us who owned and looked after the hotel in the years that followed.

The *Hedley Gazette* tells us on May 13, 1909, (page two) that Mrs. Joan M. Smith of Beaverdell, BC, applied for the renewal of her liquor licence for Smith's Hotel.

The *Ledge* of Greenwood, BC, records on page two of its November 26, 1914, edition that Joan M. Smith had transferred the licence of the Smith Hotel to F.F. Ketchum, until recently "a mining recorder."

(Although in the BC Directory there is no evidence of a hotel in Beaverdell, I suspect that Frank F. Ketchum converted all or at least half of the hotel into a general store that he operated for well into the 1920s.)

In 1918, the population of Beaverdell was approximately fifty people. Over the following years a number of names were found to be associated or involved with the Beaverdell Hotel in various capacities:

On August 20, 1925, the Greenwood *Ledge* reported that "Mrs. Bjorkman, who has been employed at the Beaverdell Hotel, left for home in Rock Creek last week."

In the directories for 1925 through 1929, Mrs. Augusta Lutner operated the Beaverdell Hotell, and in 1925, she ran the Beaverdell Café.

The *Gazette* (Grand Forks) reported on July 30, 1926, that "A.W. Lunter [sic] and family of Vernon, were guests of Mrs. A. Lutner at the Beaverdell hotel for ten days..." There may have been a change of ownership for the Beaverdell Hotel from Lutner to Moran this year. The *Gazette* on May 23, 1939, reported that consent from the Liquor Board was being sought to transfer the beer parlour licence from Augusta Lutner to Patrick J. Moran and Alice Gwendolen Moran. Directories from 1930 through 1937 listed Patrick J. Moran as proprietor of the Beaverdell Hotel.

According to the *Gazette*, on September 13, 1934, William Youngson was the proprietor of the Beaverdell Hotel. Youngson may have been leasing it from the Morans.

A Mrs. George Burns arrived from Kelowna to work at the Beaverdell in July 1935, although the *Gazette* does not mention in what capacity.[48]

According to the directories from 1938 through 1946, Mrs. P.J. Moran was proprietor of the Beaverdell Hotel. Mrs. Moran was visited by her parents, Mr. and Mrs. H. Davis of Smithers in August 1936 and in August 1946 by her daughter, Miss C. Moran of Vancouver, reported the *Gazette* of Grand Forks.

Mrs. Moran may have sold the Beaverdell Hotel around 1946. The *Gazette* reported on September 26 that "Mrs. A. Moran, who has been ill for some time, is getting on very well and is able to be around again under Doctor's care." On February 20, 1947, the *Gazette* reported that "an application for transfer of licence from Alice Gwendolen Moran to Peter and Elizabeth Mildred Murie was filed."

The Muries only owned the Beaverdell for six months. In 1947, "Mrs. E. Rushworth and son arrived... from Vancouver to join her husband who has recently purchased the Beaverdell Hotel. Mr. and Mrs. P. Murie and family left on Thursday for Vancouver having sold out the Beaverdell Hotel to Ernie and Cecilia Rushworth."[49]

In 1948, the Rushworths applied to transfer their beer parlour licence to Laurence Erle and Kathleen Richards of Vancouver.[50] The Richardses continued to operate the Beaverdell through 1950 and received a visit from their son, Harry Richards, in October of that year. The *Gazette* reported that in September 1951, Harry Richards was "taking care of the Beaverdell Hotel while his father, Mr. Laurie Richards, is in Vancouver on business..."[51]

A fire broke out in the wee hours of March 18, 1953, in the Beaverdell Hotel. Finding and fighting the fire early saved the hotel from destruction. The *Gazette* reported the next day, March 19, 1953, under the headline on the front page, "Beaverdell Hotel Has Close Call From Fire." "Practically the whole town turned out to assist in combating the blaze... damage is estimated at around $500... Mr. Richards wishes to express his gratitude to all who assisted and rendered the service they did."

The *Gazette* reported on January 14, 1954, that "Mrs. Kay Richards is ill and requires hospitalization in Oliver."

The M.K. Williams family purchased the Beaverdell Hotel in 1954 or 1955. Their grandson, Russ Williams, described in 2011 some of his recollections from their time running the hotel:

My grandparents Mervin and Delia Williams owned the hotel in the 50s and 60s. My dad purchased the hotel circa 1954. I lived in the hotel residence and on occasion stayed in the rooms. I never saw a ghost—not once! I did see a lot of heavy drinking, brawling, singing, banjo playing, loving, laughter... in other words, full of life. To the sourpuss who said the food was bad—not on the Williams watch. The food was excellent and the beer must have been fabulous, 'cause we sold the hell out of it.

In the years from 1958 through 1963, three former owners of the Beaverdell passed away.

An obituary in the *Province* reported that Laurence Erle Richards, aged seventy-seven years, died on July 31, 1958: "Mr. Richards operated the Beaverdell Hotel in that community until he retired in 1951, moving to New Westminster, BC."[52]

The *Gazette* ran an obituary in its April 30, 1959, edition: "Beaverdell Hotel owner M.K. Williams Died Suddenly on Friday: Mervyn Kyle Williams died early Friday morning. He had been owner of the hotel for the past four years since coming from the Fraser Valley."

Four years later, the *Gazette* ran the following obituary on October 10, 1963: "Former Hotel Owner Mrs. A. Moran, Dies. Mrs. Alice Gwendolen Moran died on September 27 at Penticton at the age of 67. Mrs. Moran was born in India and came to Canada at the age of nine... she owned and operated the Beaverdell Hotel for 22 years, from 1926 to 1947."

In the fall of 1964, the Beaverdell again changed hands: "Mr. and Mrs. Lu Shulaike of Creston, BC, are the new owners of the Beaverdell Hotel. It was sold on August 17 by Mr. and Mrs. Lassard, owners of the hotel for many years."[53]

In 2011, a former employee, Barry Zettergreen, who worked at the Beaverdell Hotel in 1967, recalled some of his experiences:

> In 1967, at the age of 19, I was working in the Beaverdell area running loader for the Department of Highways on a chip seal job of 70 miles. One night while in the small bar section of the

hotel, one of our truckers came in and said he was hauling his holiday trailer behind [a] dump truck to [a] new location 20 miles down the road when a black bear ran across the road and hit his trailer. The bear died. The four of us got in an old Land Rover with no top at 10 at night and drove 3 miles down the road where we found the bear. We dragged it onto the hood of car then drove back to the hotel. There, we put a large blue jean jacket on it and a poke [polka] dot baseball cap, took it in the bar, and sat it in a chair with a glass of beer in front. Two elderly women in their later sixties owned the hotel at that time but said nothing... True story.

(This story would be cute if the bear didn't really die.)

On March 28, 2011, the Beaverdell Hotel burned to the ground. Kelowna's *Capital News* reporter Cheryl Weirda wrote about it under the headline "Lawsuits and ownership battle plagued lost historic landmark. Lengthy investigation expected into cause of fire that burned down Beaverdell Hotel." Arson was suspected, particularly as the fire came in the month following owner Tyrone Daum's home in Beaverdell also being burned. About a year before this incident, Daum had been embroiled in a legal battle with the Beaverdell's previous owners, Mary Ellen and Eugene Katchin, over the hotel's title. According to Daum, the Katchins—who bought the hotel on a mortgage in 2001—entered into an lease-to-own agreement with Daum in 2005 after they accepted a $20,000 down payment from him and an understanding that he would pay the rest at a later date. The details seem murky as to whether this was a written or oral agreement, but Daum assumed ownership and ran the hotel. As Cheryl Weirda reports, things went sour after a few years:

> According to the court documents, Daum indicated he was in a position to pay the parties out in 2008, around the time he received two offers on the property—one for $700,000 and the other for $800,000—which were more than double what he had agreed to pay the Katchins.

But the documents allege Eugene Katchin then broke into the hotel, changed the locks and started to liquidate Daum's belongings from the property, although Daum had sunk $100,000 into the building to run it as a tourist attraction.

It was also reported that in 2009 the Katchins had defaulted on their mortgage and their guarantors had requested a foreclosure order, though further details on this were not forthcoming. Ultimately, the hotel title was granted to Tyrone Daum in January 2010 then transferred to a numbered company in November; the Katchins all allegations of foul play after the devastating fire and criminal charges were not brought against them.

Meanwhile, Beaverdell residents are wondering how they will cope with the heart of the town gone. The hotel was well-known as a tourist stop for cyclists along the Kettle Valley Railway and motorcycle enthusiasts who would line their bikes up out front for a picture before visiting the few remaining shops in town. "People are just crying," said Lorna Hollingsworth. "When the town was active, it was like everybody's front room. Weddings, birthdays, you went to the hotel."

In 2011, Russ Williams, grandson of former owner M.K. Williams, commented: "The big surprise is that the hotel never burned down sooner—everyone smoked! Inebriated miners and loggers would pass out in the rooms with lit cigarettes. Maybe God does love a drunk. There are a lot of memories... mostly good ones. While the hotel may be gone, the memories are not.[54]

M.K. Williams's granddaughter, Coral Fife, commented:

It is a sad day for the Williams family. My grandparents Mervin and Delia Williams owned the hotel in the 50s and 60s. My parents were helping after my grandfather passed and lived there with my sister. It has been the last link to my grandfather for most of us. Five generations have had their photo taken on that porch. And many family weddings and parties took place there.

The hotel was closed for the season when the fire broke out and no one was in the building. It was one of many historic buildings to tragically meet its fate in this way.

WINNIPEG HOTEL

(1900–2012)
Central Avenue at Fourth Street, Grand Forks

ON JANUARY 4, 1901, the newest hotel in the bustling town of Grand Forks had its grand opening. One couldn't miss it—the three-storey, thirty-room Winnipeg Hotel, painted bright white, loomed over the corner of Central Avenue and Fourth Street.[55] It was constructed in the Queen Anne commercial style, which included an impressive corner tower complete with bay windows that made the structure look more like a huge residential mansion than a hotel. The timing of the opening could not have been better as the Granby Company copper smelter was working at full capacity and accommodations for its workers were in high demand.

"The Winny," as it was affectionately called by regular customers, was built by William Logie Bonthron, a local contractor who had arrived in Grand Forks to construct section houses for the CPR in 1889. Bonthron also built the Yale Hotel and the Bonthron Block in town as well as many bridges in the region. The interior walls of the Winny were pure white with blue and gold touches, and the floors were carpeted in velvet with a Japanese theme. Some rooms were furnished with carved chests and antique tapestries.[56] The hotel featured modern conveniences of the day, such as electric bells and lights. The following year, a hotel carriage was purchased to pick up and drop off guests in style from the train depot and hotel.[57]

Dr. and Mrs. J.H. Murray were the first owners, and they operated the hotel for a short time before they leased it out. In the first seven years, no less than seven short-term proprietors managed the hotel until November 1908, when Mr. and Mrs. Samuel J. Miller of Victoria purchased the hotel and ran it for the next thirteen years, with the exception of a few years when it was leased to Mr. J. McBride Shively.[58] Previous owners had added their personal flair in decoration and furnishings, but the Millers had extensive improvements and additions made to the hotel, including repainting the building in the latest metropolitan colours.[59]

The same year the Millers bought the Winnipeg Hotel, the city of Grand Forks had its first major fire. The July 10, 1908, fire reduced two blocks of downtown Grand Forks to ashes. In all, six hotels and two banks were destroyed.[60] Luckily, the Winnipeg Hotel was spared. A second major fire followed in August 1909 that destroyed an entire block, including the Queens and Eagle Hotels. On July 25, 1911, the third major fire swept through Grand Forks, and again the Winnipeg Hotel was unscathed. Fire was the single most destructive force to threaten the early towns as most buildings were built of wood that became quite flammable after years of long, dry summers. The Winnipeg Hotel competed well with the hotels in town before the fires, but naturally saw an increase in business while new hotels were being built to replace those destroyed by fire. Most, but not all, owners rebuilt their hotels, and when the buildings were completed, offered guests brand-new accommodations. The Millers had plans to expand the capacity of the Winnipeg Hotel before the fires, and what better time was there than now, as some of the competition had to start over again. Besides enlarging the hotel, the Millers could update and modernize at the same time, keeping their hotel on the competitive edge.

The Millers' tenure at the Winnipeg Hotel was a successful one. They continued to make improvements to the hotel as technology progressed and fashion dictated, while providing first-class service.[61] No major incidents occurred in their tenure at the Winnipeg, but a minor incident kept the proprietors on their toes. On a warm July afternoon in 1911, fire box number 14, located near the Winnipeg Hotel, set off an alarm warning that a fire had broken out. The panic-stricken Millers and other concerned citizens were

The Winnipeg Hotel. IMAGE COURTESY OF BOUNDARY MUSEUM AND ARCHIVES. 1986_130_001_01

relieved to find out that the small fire, which had started in the ice-house for the hotel, was quickly brought under control, resulting in minimal damage. Apparently, a spark from a rock-crushing machine had ignited the fire.[62]

The following year, in June 1912, saw Mrs. Miller in a Vancouver hospital. Mr. Miller had taken his ill wife to Vancouver, where she was admitted to hospital for an undisclosed surgical procedure. The surgery went well, and the couple returned to Grand Forks, where Mrs. Miller spent the next six weeks recovering from the ordeal.[63] Recovery was slow, so Mr. Miller decided to sell his beloved Winnipeg Hotel in order to reduce the stress on his wife and allow them time together as she recuperated. It looked as though the hotel would be sold to a Vancouver couple, but the deal fell through. Mr. Miller continued offering the hotel for sale. In November 1913, it was announced that the Millers had sold the Winnipeg Hotel to J. McBride Shively of Lethbridge. At the time of the sale, Mr. Miller mentioned that his wife taking ill and her long recovery was the major reason they sold.[64]

The new proprietor of the Winnipeg was an experienced hotelman. Mr. Shively had operated hotels in Lethbridge, Alberta, for years before buying the Winnipeg. He continued where the Millers left off, making improvements to the hotel. In April 1914, Shively was granted permission from the City of Grand Forks to drain the "cesspool" located at the south end of the hotel property. It had been a constant nuisance to the public, not to mention an assault on the sense of smell for both guests and local residents.

In 1916, the Millers, who had moved to Victoria three years earlier after selling the hotel, returned to visit friends and relatives at Grand Forks. Their visit resulted in a surprise announcement: the Millers were buying back the Winnipeg Hotel. Past guests, friends, and relatives were jubilant, and in July 1916, the Millers' ownership of the hotel was made official.[65]

Mrs. Miller had fully recovered from her surgery and was fully rested, while Mr. Miller was only too happy to be back to the hotel he loved. All was right in their world. In 1917, Prohibition came to British Columbia. Like a dress rehearsal of things to come, in March 1917, Sam Miller was ordered to pay a fine of fifty dollars after he was charged with keeping the hotel bar opened after regular hours.[66] Apparently, the bar door was opened on a Sunday. It was necessary to go through the bar in order to access the cellar, where the proprietor was going to get some fruit. On his return, two men and the chief of police were waiting for him in the bar. No liquor had been served, but this was the year that authorities were cracking down on even the most minor infractions. Within six months, Prohibition in British Columbia would put an end to the hotel bar and saloon business, at least for the foreseeable future.

The Millers continued to do well, however, operating the Winnipeg Hotel in spite of Prohibition and the loss of revenue from liquor sales in the bar and restaurant. The couple had a stellar reputation as hosts of one of the oldest landmark hotels in Grand Forks. In April 1920, the Millers walked into the Grand Forks Garage and drove out in their new McLaughlin automobile purchased with cash.

In December 1920, the Millers sold the Winnipeg Hotel to William Rainey of Swift Current, Saskatchewan. Rainey took possession of the hotel on New Year's Day in 1921. Rainey, born in the township of Fullerton, Pell County, England, had operated the

Empress Hotel in Swift Current. His hotel experience allowed him to operate the Winnipeg Hotel successfully for the next twenty-five years.[67] Sam Miller, meanwhile, retired from the hotel business. While visiting Los Angeles on May 12, 1929, Miller was involved in a freak accident: he was hit and killed by a streetcar while crossing a street.[68]

Like most new proprietors, Rainey made some adjustments to the Winnipeg Hotel to suit his style in décor and management. Rainey could not have picked a better time to purchase a hotel in Grand Forks. The economy was booming as the town benefitted from the CPR and the extension of the Kettle Valley Railway, making the growing city a divisional point with a link to the coast. With most of the devastating fires behind it, Grand Forks took on an air of confidence and permanence as new brick buildings replaced older wood structures and the population grew.[69]

Grand Forks was a thriving city, not only attracting workers for the massive Granby smelter; farmers and ranchers were also attracted by the rolling, productive landscape of the region. Merchants were attracted by the prospects of a bright future, and visitors were not disappointed when staying at the sophisticated and attractive hotels, including the Winnipeg Hotel. Prohibition of alcohol ended in 1921 in British Columbia, and by 1925, beer parlour licences were granted to some Vancouver and Victoria hotels. South of the border, things were quite different. Prohibition in the US began in 1920 and would last until it was repealed in 1933. In the meantime, with government liquor sales legal in Canada and the US dry, demand for Canadian liquor was at an all-time high, which gave rise to rum-running.

Rum-running between Canada and the US was serious business in the 1920s and 1930s. In early October 1924, a woman named Mrs. Murray checked into the Winnipeg Hotel in Grand Forks. Her husband had been admitted to the Grand Forks Hospital a few days prior to her arrival, and she had been notified as to his whereabouts and condition. Her husband, George D. Murray, was an American Prohibition police officer. Officer Murray had been attempting to stop a vehicle suspected of carrying illegal booze in the small Washington State town of Curlew, approximately fourteen miles southwest of Grand Forks, when the driver refused to stop and instead produced a revolver and shot Officer Murray. The bullet entered the right side of Murray's abdomen and exited to the left, leaving him bleeding profusely on the ground—but not before he fired at the speeding car and caught one of the men inside with a bullet to the neck. Murray was rushed to the closest large hospital, which just happened to be across the border at Grand Forks. After a week in hospital and still quite weak, Murray, with the support of his wife, was able to walk out and return back to the States.[70] Rum-running continued until 1933, when the Volstead Act was repealed in the United States.

In British Columbia, most hotel proprietors were anxious to get back the bar revenue they lost during Prohibition. It wasn't until 1929 when the hotels in Grand Forks could apply for a beer parlour licence. Only four licences were available for Grand Forks hotels initially, and in November 1929, three hotels were inspected by Sergeant King of Penticton, with Corporal McKay of Grand Forks, on behalf of the Liquor Control Board, to ascertain if the hotels met the criteria to be granted beer parlour licences from the BC government. The Province Hotel, the Grand Forks Hotel, and the Winnipeg Hotel were inspected, with a possible future visit to the Yale Hotel. These four hotels received the first beer parlour licences in Grand Forks.[71]

By 1945, the Raineys had owned and operated the Winnipeg Hotel for twenty-four years. In August, Rainey contracted Ed Beliveau to paint the exterior and part of the interior of the hotel.[72] Mr. Rainey was getting tired, and at age seventy-one, he planned to retire soon, so he wanted the hotel to look its best.

On October 31, 1946, the Raineys sold the Winnipeg Hotel to Michael and Rose Warman, who took possession on November 23.[73] Within three months of selling the hotel and going into retirement, William Rainey's health took a turn for the worse and he was admitted to Grand Forks Hospital. He was eventually released but never quite regained his health. In April 1948, William Rainey died.[74]

For the next sixty-four years, a succession of owners came and went. From the Warman family, who purchased the hotel from the Raineys and added new siding to the old hotel in the summer of 1950, giving it a different look, to Fred Wilson from Hope, to Norman and Jim Gower from Penticton, who arrived in 1965, each contributed their personal touch while helping to maintain and sustain the landmark hotel of Grand Forks.

On the evening of March 7, 2012, the Grand Forks Hotel was destroyed by fire. On that same fateful night, the Winnipeg Hotel was burned and sustained considerable fire and water damage. Several people who called the hotel home lost everything they owned. What made the news equally devastating was that the fires were suspicious and believed to be deliberately set. "It's believed that the fiery night began after a patron was tossed from the Winnipeg Hotel and then pinned a note to the front door. Former hotel employee Dane Elliot described the note as threatening: 'The bar is going down, I'm angry' it read."[75] A short time after the fires, an arrest was made and a suspect was charged with arson. But the damage was done: the Grand Forks Hotel was utterly destroyed, and although the Winnipeg still had some sections of the building standing, a decision was made to demolish it. The Winnipeg Liquor Store stands on the site today, its name an homage of the hotel that preceded it.

CHAPTER FOUR

West Kootenay

Part One

CROWN POINT HOTEL

(1895-1929, 1929-2016)
1399 Bay Avenue at Spokane Street, Trail

THE WEST KOOTENAY city of Trail was originally called Trail Creek Landing, named for the old Dewdney Trail that followed down from the Columbia River. In 1897, the name was shortened to Trail. The community began to develop around the nearby Le Roi mine, when Colonel Eugene Sayre Topping surveyed the townsite at the mouth of Trail Creek. Fritz Augustus Heinze, a wealthy young smelter owner from Butte, Montana, established a copper smelter in 1895, the same year the original Crown Point Hotel opened, and the town grew from there.[1]

Hotelman Simon F. Petersen came to Trail with his family and two brothers, Frederick Julius and John Peter. Petersen purchased three lots at the corner of Bayview and Spokane near the steamboat dock and erected the Crown Point Hotel with his brothers, using lumber from Pete Genelle's portable sawmill. The hotel was named after the Crown Point Mine operation located between Trail and Rossland. The three-storey wood-framed Crown Point Hotel, with its gabled roof studded with dormer windows lighting the upper floor, became an early social centre for the rapidly growing town. In time, the hotel would be fitted with attractive Brussels carpets and bathrooms built in marble.[2] The Crown Point Hotel was guaranteed to receive business from workers constructing and employed at the smelter. "The three-storey hotel had all the modern conveniences with 40 bedrooms, a large dining room, a bar and sample rooms. The dining room was reputed to be the

The Crown Point Hotel, 1906. COURTESY OF THE TRAIL HISTORICAL SOCIETY

largest and finest in town and was often the centre of Trail's social life in the early days."[3]

The Petersen brothers were constantly updating and improving their establishment.[4] In 1897, electric lights made an enormous difference for the hotel and the town. Residents marvelled as they went for their first evening stroll with streets lit by electricity that was generated in a small power station from the water of three streams, producing 400 horsepower.[5] It was a nice change from coal-oil lighting, which was soon phased out. In the winter of 1897–98, while children enjoyed sliding down the Spokane Street hill in the snow and to the front of the Crown Point Hotel, smelter owner F.H. Heinze was finalizing a deal with the CPR that saw the Montreal-based company purchase the smelter, railroads, and one-half of Heinze's land for $800,000.[6] Trail would remain a smelter city, but with a new owner.

In the summer of 1900, with the hotel not yet five years old, an attempt to burn the structure down was thwarted by Henry Boss. As reported in the *Nelson Tribune*:

> An attempt to burn the Crown Point Hotel was foiled when a guest, Henry Boss, extinguished the flames and gave in the alarm.

Boss occupied one of the rooms off the back parlour when he was awakened by light and smoke. He found evidence that someone had made a deliberate attempt to burn down the building from a pile of shavings whittled from a piece of wood found on the floor. The owner notified the police who investigated the arson attempt.[7]

Further attempts to burn down the Crown Point and other Trail hotels continued for the next few years until they finally succeeded.

The City of Trail was incorporated on June 14, 1901, and five years later, three major mines, along with the Rossland Power Company, were amalgamated to form the Consolidated Mining and Smelting Company of Canada (CM & S).[8]

A fire started across the street from the Crown Point Hotel on October 24, 1911, destroying the Klondike and Central Hotels as well as the Goddu Brothers grocery. Guests of the two hotels fled the rapid flames clad only in their nightclothes while citizens and the fire brigade worked furiously but in vain to save the structures. Two guests received severe burns in the fire, while others escaped with less serious injuries. The fire was so intense that the front of the Crown Point Hotel had to be watered down to prevent it from catching on fire. An arsonist was suspected as the cause of the fire.[9]

Between 1907 and 1909, the Petersen brothers had the Crown Point Hotel up for sale with no takers.[10] Nor was there any interest in buying it for several more years. After having their hotel on the market for years, the Petersen brothers finally sold the Crown Point Hotel to Mr. Z.D. Bray of Taber, Alberta, in 1912.[11] Bray sold to well-known local "old-timer" Ike McLeod in 1914, who didn't own the Crown Point long before selling to W. Thompson in 1915. Thompson made improvements to the aging hotel and built a ten-room addition.[12] These short-term owners gave the hotel their personal touch, but it was the following owner, Ambrose ("Andy") McDermott who was determined to stay and operate the hotel for the long haul.[13]

McDermott was a popular, well-known hotelman who had worked on both sides of the border, having operated saloons in Oroville and Republic in Washington and the Similkameen Hotel in Hedley. He was born in Ottawa, Ontario, in 1875, the son of Mr. and Mrs. Patrick McDermott. He headed west in 1899, mining in the Hedley area and then leasing the Similkameen Hotel in October 1904, where he stayed for a few years. McDermott then moved south into Washington State and ran a saloon in Oroville before moving east to the town of Republic, where he continued in the saloon trade.[14] The fates were not so kind to him, as he was eventually arrested along with three other non-Americans and charged with operating a saloon without a licence. Mr. J.W. Mathews, new prosecuting attorney in Ferry County for the town of Republic, took it upon himself to "clean up" the county. Mathews caused the arrest of the four businessmen, Ambrose McDermott, Sam McDonald, John Ludlow, and William Maddaugh, by invoking a seldom-used provision of the local option law of 1909, which prohibits a non-citizen of the United States from holding a liquor licence. Consequently, the four were charged under the act and their premises were seized, as were their stocks of liquor and saloon fixtures. It was the first time this law was enacted and, added attorney Mathews, "Under the law these men are guilty of maintaining a nuisance which can be abated by the courts."[15] It's no wonder McDermott was relieved to cross back into Canada, where he could continue the work he enjoyed. His last acquisition was the Crown Point Hotel in Trail in 1916.

The 1920s was a watershed decade for the Crown Point Hotel, as three major events took place that greatly altered the hotel. Mr. and Mrs. A. McDermott were still operating the hotel on March 31, 1925, when they received word that their application for a beer parlour licence was granted along with thirty-three other BC hotels. This was a game changer because it meant a substantial boost in revenue from the beverage room receipts.[16] Since Prohibition was enacted in October 1917, those hotels that had bars were forced to close or remain open by selling a watered-down product. It was a dry seven-and-a-half years before liquor was permitted to be sold in BC hotels under strict provincial government control. Three years after opening their beer parlour, Andy McDermott died at his home in Trail. The pioneer hotelman died on a Saturday of heart failure. He was survived by his wife and two daughters, five brothers, and six sisters.[17]

The third significant event was that the Crown Point Hotel went up for sale. Normally, the sale of a hotel wasn't too significant, despite the fact that the McDermotts had run it longer than the previous four owners. It was the fact, announced shortly after the sale of the Crown Point, that the new owner, Mr. James Hanna of Drumheller, Alberta, decided to demolish the thirty-three-year-old hotel and build a brand-new one on the same site.[18]

The new owners, James Hanna and Associates, formed Trail Hotels Limited. The demolition of the Crown Point Hotel would be followed with the construction of a brand-new, modern, three-storey brick hotel. "Mr. Hanna decided that the progress and future of Trail warranted a new and modern hotel,"[19] and the Trail Board of Trade wholeheartedly agreed.

Ernest T. Brown was chosen to design the new Crown Point Hotel. Born in Brighton, England, Brown trained as an architect in Guelph, Ontario, and then moved to Regina in 1906, where he remained until 1914, when he moved to Alberta, mainly in the Calgary area. In 1926, Brown applied to join the Architect Institute of British Columbia and began taking on projects in Kamloops, designing the Kamloops Lodge 44 of the Benevolent and Protective Order of Elks building and the Spanish-influenced style of the Plaza Hotel, from 1927 to 1928, that is still in operation as a first-class hotel to this day.[20] In July 1928, he and his family moved back to Calgary, but not before designing one more important building in British Columbia, the Crown Point Hotel. When completed in 1928, the Plaza was the number one hotel in Kamloops, and the Crown Point Hotel was the equivalent in Trail when it opened in 1929.

In September 1929, while the old Crown Point Hotel was closed and being stripped down ready for demolition, a contractor was found to build the new hotel. Lazareff and Company had been awarded the contract, chosen by James Hanna, manager and president of Trail Hotels Limited, with a bid of $80,000. The plan was to begin building as soon as the old hotel was demolished, hopefully before the cold winter weather arrived.[21] Between September and October, changes were made. The original Crown Point Hotel was demolished and the site was prepared for the rebuild, but now the three-storey hotel would be a four-storey concrete building containing between sixty and sixty-five rooms, to be built by contractor A.H. Green. The extra floor and other expenses raised the estimated total for completing the hotel to $150,000. Due to these changes, the completion date was extended to sometime in early 1930.[22]

The new Crown Point Hotel opened in late 1929, before it was completed, but the grand opening was held on August 11, 1930. The imposing, modern, four-storey hotel was described by the *Daily News* as rising fifty feet above the street, making it the tallest building in Trail and visible for miles around. It occupied seventy-five feet on Bay Avenue, where the beer parlour entrance was located, and a hundred feet along Spokane Street. The pillared lobby off Bay Avenue was sixty feet long and forty-four feet wide, with the red-tiled floor hidden under soft carpeting. The ornamental tile fireplace and attractive light fixtures in the form of lanterns had a stalactite effect. Receptions and meetings were already booked in the Blue Room and the Palm Room. The seventy-five-by-forty-foot reception hall was in the basement of the hotel. Sixty-three guest rooms and some suites were on the top three floors, and every room was self-contained with a bath or shower and a toilet. [23]

The next long-term manager of the Crown Point was John ("Jack") A. Kerr of Nelson. Kerr earned his hotel experience from managing the Occidental (1922–23), moving on to the Queens (1924–25), and then to the Savoy (1926–35), all Nelson hotels.[24] Mr. and Mrs. Kerr moved from Nelson to Trail in 1935, when Jack Kerr took up his position of manager at the Crown Point Hotel.

The first owner of the original Crown Point Hotel, Simon F. Petersen, died on his ranch at Blueberry, BC, at the age of seventy-six in January 1940. As mentioned earlier, Petersen, a native of Denmark, had arrived in Trail with his brothers John and Julius in 1895. "Mr. Peterson was the last surviving member of the

Trail chapter of the Knights of Pythias Lodge No. 23 and the oldest member of the Fidelity Lodge, A.F and A.M."[25] Mrs. Laura H. Petersen passed away sixteen years later in Trail at the age of ninety-two. Also a native of Denmark, she arrived at Trail aboard the paddlewheeler *Nakusp* in 1895, when Trail was little more than a landscape of tents. Mrs. Petersen was survived by her daughter, Mrs. J.H. Young of Trail, two grandchildren, and three great-great-grandchildren.[26]

J.A. Kerr managed the sixty-five-room Crown Point Hotel for twenty-two years, from 1934 to 1956, and commented that the hotel business was better now than in the old days: "It takes a lot of beer to make a man troublesome," he said, referring to the beer parlour system, when compared to the wide-open saloon days before Prohibition.[27] On May 2, 1955, Jack Kerr was honoured by the directors of the British Columbia Hotel Association at a banquet in the posh Plaza Hotel in Kamloops. Kerr received a lifetime membership in the association and was praised for his outstanding service managing hotels in Nelson and Trail, which had earned him a reputation as a "clean and proper operator with high principles." It was noted that Jack Kerr appeared surprised but delighted.[28]

Just before Mr. Kerr stepped down from his job as manager of the Crown Point Hotel, a potentially serious incident occurred when the hotel was picketed by fifteen members of the Mine Mill Local 480, Trail. The row involved a confirmation for certification of the union for Cominco's smelter workers. Charles Millard arrived in town to survey the damage done during the process, and police were called to calm the opposing parties. Word got out that Millard was staying at the Crown Point Hotel, and immediately pickets went up in front of the hotel, waving banners that read, "Get out of town, Millard." The *Vancouver Sun* reported, "However the picket line broke up when the paraders learned the person registered at the hotel was not Charles Millard but A.J. Millard of Vancouver, a spark plug salesman."[29]

In April 1952, J.A. Kerr sold the Crown Point Hotel to a Vancouver syndicate consisting of Leon Pari, his son George Pari, and

Ken McKinnon. Pari had owned and operated the Canford sawmill in Merritt, his son was manager of the Western Pine Lumber Company of Princeton, and McKinnon had operated the Russell and the Premier Hotels in New Westminster. The sale price was just shy of $500,000.[30] Karen Robinson, granddaughter of Leon Pari, recalls that "there was a rat infestation that required a complete renovation of the dining area and basement prior to serving the public." Robinson goes on to say that the hotel was a "grand beauty" and that the family retains fond memories of living in Trail. They eventually sold the Crown Point and moved to Port Moody, where they built the Leon Hotel.[31]

The historic Crown Point Hotel continues today as the Crown Columbia boutique hotel. It was renovated in 2016, and its guests have come to expect excellent service and first-class accommodations like generations of guests have enjoyed at this site going all the way back to 1895.

ST. LEON HOTEL

(1902–45); Gates of St. Leon (1945–56)
St. Leon Hot Springs

TWENTY-SIX KILOMETRES north of Nakusp by sternwheeler, on the eastern shore of Upper Arrow Lake, we arrive at St. Leon Hot Springs. St. Leon was named by a French hunter whose relatives came from Saint-Pol-de-Léon in Finistère, France.[32] The hamlet of St. Leon, located at the mouth of St. Leon Creek between Nakusp to the south and Shelter Bay to the north, was founded by Michael O'Grady (also known as Mike Grady) while he was prospecting with a trapper. Grady was entranced by its sheer beauty and natural hot springs and saw the potential for a community built there with a hotel for guests arriving by boat.[33]

Mike M. Grady arrived in British Columbia from Ontario when he was working for the CPR. In 1892, he left the company and, with other partners, began purchasing various mines in the Silverton area. Grady was a shrewd investor and perhaps a bit lucky as some of his mine investments paid off handsomely. In June 1892, partners Mike Grady, Charles Flaatz, and another unidentified man "struck it rich between Red Paddie Creek and the Slocan Star Group."[34] Fortune continued to smile on Grady and his company of investors, now formally called the Grady Group, when they sold the Alpha Mine for $70,000 to another group of investors, an incredible amount of money at the time. The Grady Group still owned five other mines, with the best payout yet to come.[35] In October 1894, Grady purchased the Standard Mine, which promised to pay off handsomely.

The Gates of St. Leon. COURTESY OF THE TRAIL HISTORICAL SOCIETY

In 1894, Mike Grady built a crude log structure at St. Leon Hot Springs. The main guests were loggers, prospectors, and miners; there were no provisions for women at the time. In 1898, Grady advertised that baths were free, but an overnight stay was $1.25. He hoped that St. Leon would be developed along the lines of how their close neighbour, Halcyon Hot Springs, was. He tried to interest the CPR in his idea, but the company turned him down.[36] Undaunted, Grady was determined to develop a resort at St. Leon, so he bided his time and kept investing in gold mines on his own and with the Grady Group.

By 1901, Grady felt he had enough money to finally build the hotel of his dreams at St. Leon. He began by advertising for tenders in the Nelson newspaper.[37] By July, he had selected Andy Wallace of New Denver to construct his first-class hotel, which would include nine thousand feet of pipe that would bring a portion of the hot springs into two pools inside the hotel.[38] Grady's St. Leon Hotel rose above the bush and trees, an impressive three-storey structure almost entirely built with clear cedar that, when weathered, had a reddish-brown appearance. It contained a pillared entrance and arched balcony and featured a sweeping staircase, lofty dining room, and generously proportioned bar.[39] The pools, which were centered near the lobby, were made of cedar, with the ladies' pool directly above the men's pool. The mouldings and banisters were also made of wood, with no paint or varnish applied. Molly and Louise Smith, Mike's nieces, scrubbed this woodwork clean daily.[40] It is unclear whether the Grady Group sold the Standard Mine at Silverton at this time or held off until 1904, but whatever was the date of the sale, Mike Grady's share was a small fortune that guaranteed his financial independence for many years to come.

The official gala opening of the St. Leon Hotel was February 28, 1902. Curious, excited crowds braved the cold weather to see the magnificent palace in the bush for themselves.[41] Except for a close call with a small stubborn fire in July that was quickly extinguished, the first year of for the new hotel was a huge success. A few things required some adjustments. The pipes leading from the natural hot springs to the ladies' and men's pools inside the hotel were a problem, as the hot water cooled substantially along its journey and entered the pools either too cool or tepid, depending on the weather. The building itself looked amazing, towering over a landscape that included a pleasant sandy beach and the natural hot springs.

It was an excellent resort and became a very popular picnicking spot. Sternwheelers plying the waters of Upper Arrow Lake made St. Leon one of their regular stops. The CPR built the SS *Bonnington*, launched in 1911, which travelled on the Arrow Lakes, bringing passengers and freight to the waterfront communities. Most communities had a wharf, but St. Leon did not, relying instead on smaller boats to ferry people to the sandy shore.[42]

There were few problems in those early years at the St. Leon. A few of the more refined guests complained about noise coming from the bar, especially when the loggers were visiting on their time off, but there was nothing of a serious nature until Mr. McMinn checked into the hotel in the fall of 1905. For reasons not divulged, McMinn, in a fit of despondency, attempted to take his own life, taking a large knife and slashing at his throat. He was subdued and held until Constable George Campbell of Arrowhead arrived and took McMinn to Revelstoke for some help.[43] Lesser problems occurred on occasion that included a charge and fine when Mike Grady overlooked renewing his liquor licence.⁴⁴ Grady was still involved in his mine investments and had other business concerns that required his attention, so he leased his hotel to Mr. Herbert Cousins of Revelstoke for a brief time.⁴⁵

The summer of 1914 was the last good season at St. Leon. The First World War was declared in August, and Prohibition was just around the corner. The steady stream of customers, especially during the summer months, slowed considerably until Grady was forced to close his hotel, except for a few active months in the summer. His hotel sat on 230 acres, so he decided to have a series of cabins built on the property and by 1915, there were ten self-contained cabins that proved popular with guests.⁴⁶ An area was set up for those guests that wished to pitch a tent for their stay. Sternwheelers continued to stop regularly at St. Leon, allowing passengers to refresh themselves until the boat whistle beckoned them back to continue their journey. Loggers and sawmill workers from nearby Pingston and Arrowhead would often drop in at the St. Leon hotel bar up until (and very likely beyond) October 1917, when Prohibition became the law of the land.⁴⁷

By 1921, Mike Grady, by now aged and grey, was the lone occupant at his hotel more often than not. He remained a recluse in his large rambling hotel, with the occasional guest or a friend checking up on him from time to time. Sometime in the 1930s, his friends Mr. Olson and his son Peter Olson, dropped in on the aging Grady and took him in at their home at nearby Galena Bay until it was later agreed to send Mike to a seniors' home in Kamloops.⁴⁸ Mike Grady spent his last few years in Kamloops, no doubt telling stories about his amazing life. He died there in 1944.⁴⁹

In 1933, the St. Leon Hotel had a new owner, Miss Grace Goodworth Rixon. Rixon was an experienced hotel manager, having operated the Revelstoke Hotel from 1931 to 1941.⁵⁰ Miss Rixon also owned the ten-room Rixon Court Apartments at 720 Jervis Street in Vancouver from 1941 to 1944.⁵¹ Rixon bought the St. Leon Hotel on speculation, assuming that the much-talked-about Nakusp–Arrowhead road would be constructed into the isolated area, but it did not happen until years after she sold it.

In 1945, Rixon sold the hotel to an American chemical engineer, Edwin B. Gates, who changed the hotel's name to the Gates of St. Leon. Gates and his wife took possession of their new hotel in August and hired two workers to help make repairs to the building. The couple had elaborate and costly plans that included tourist and hunting lodges in the woodland trails at the back of the hotel.[52]

Mr. and Mrs. E.B. Gates advertised the Gates of St. Leon Hotel as a "year-round vacation spot for the sportsmen and their families. Rainbow and brook trout; new fishing-boat fleet; swimming from the beach; water sports; campgrounds; hiking trails; hot springs; big-game hunting and winter sports; plus all the food you can eat cooked by our noted chef Bill Swain."[53]

Regular columnist for the *Vancouver Sun* Lee Straight gave the Gateses a plug, writing, "Mr. and Mrs. Ed Gates are developing the hot springs and resort on Upper Arrow Lake, midway between Arrowhead and Nakusp. Catering to all pocketbooks, it will be known as the Gates of St. Leon."[54]

The first five or six years looked promising for the Gateses in their new hotel. Their goal was to develop it as an all-year-round resort similar in scope to the Halcyon Hot Springs without the sanitarium, but on year nine of their ownership of the St. Leon, they received the worst news possible. The CPR announced that their paddlewheeler service on the SS *Minto*, a vital lifeline for the hotel's success, would come to an end, with the final run on April 24, 1954. "For the three to four thousand people along the Arrow Lakes it dealt a damaging blow," and to some, like the Gateses, it was a death stroke to their business. While the CPR was willing to make concessions on Lower Arrow Lake, no such deal was available for the Upper Arrow Lake. The news went from bad to worse as the British Columbia government announced that work would begin on a one-billion-dollar dam project in the Columbia Basin, with a joint US–Canada massive hydroelectric project.[55]

The final run of the SS *Minto* was a bitter moment for those who relied upon the service as they realized that it was an end to an era. Gone was the only major link to both St. Leon and Halcyon Hot Springs, and now the only way in or out was by private boat or seaplane. It dawned on the Gateses that the question was not *how are we going to survive* so much as *how to do we lessen our losses before the hotel is closed, perhaps permanently*.

In the early 1960s, it was announced that a series of dams would cause the water level to rise in the Arrow Lakes. Many properties, including the St. Leon Hotel, would be under water due to the construction of the Upper Arrow Dam (later renamed the Keenleyside Dam). The owners of these properties negotiated with BC Hydro for compensation for the loss of their land, and many ended up disappointed. Gates would not buckle under the pressure during negotiations from BC Hydro to accept their paltry offer. Instead, Gates paid $8,000 for an independent appraisal of his 110 acres with the hotel. He also toyed with the idea of moving the hotel to higher ground and spending a fortune to further develop the hot springs, which would remain untouched by the rising waters. Gates felt that his investment at St. Leon was currently pegged at $300,000. BC Hydro commented that it might be impossible to move the old Gates of Leon Hotel, but Gates disagreed, mentioning that it could likely be done at the cost of $55,000.[56] The two parties were miles apart.

In March 1967, BC Hydro crews were clearing land along the banks of the Arrow Lakes while Ed Gates continued to negotiate with the giant company. Gates owned 2,000 feet of waterfront on his hotel property and 500 acres in the whole vicinity, of which all but 20 acres would be submerged, so there was a lot to be resolved yet.[57] The Hydro crew kept at their work through 1967, preparing for the flood waters to come and spending money to move townsfolk into new towns away from the flood plain. Ed Gates, now quite ill with arthritis, had seen the writing on the wall and was in the final negotiations with BC Hydro to receive fair compensation for all his hard work and his magnificent old relic, the Gates of St. Leon Hotel. The once-stunning hotel, stripped of all its carpets, doorknobs, and windows, sat forlorn, waiting for the end that was soon to come. The magnificent mahogany bar inside the hotel saw its final use as a bullcook's workshop to feed the crews making the final preparations for the coming flood.[58]

On November 2, 1968, it was announced that an auction would take place on Saturday, November 16, in the Royal Canadian Legion Hall in Nakusp that would feature a variety of items from the Gates of St. Leon Hotel. Here was the chance for some lucky bidder to own a piece of BC history. Some of the major items of significance was a box grand piano, manufactured in 1898, twin maple spindle beds, antique iron bedsteads, dishes, kitchenware, pictures, and chandeliers.[59]

The magnificent cedar hotel burned to the ground on November 9, 1968.[60] Some people blame BC Hydro for setting fire to the sixty-six-year-old historic hotel, while some point to a despondent Ed Gates for lighting the match. The RCMP never came to a solid conclusion on just who burned the hotel down, but by then the point was moot, as it was doomed either by fire or flood. It is probably best instead to remember those pleasant sunny summer picnics at the St. Leon Hotel all those years ago.

HALCYON HOT SPRINGS HOTEL

(1894–1955)
Halcyon

F ROM ST. LEON, we board the CPR steamer for our next stop at the small community of Halcyon to visit the world-renowned Halcyon Hot Springs Hotel and Sanitarium. (Note the variant spelling of "sanatorium.") It's a mere nine kilometres between the two communities, as the steamer hugs the east shore of Upper Arrow Lake and the resort hotel, perched high on a mountainside, soon comes into view.

The natural springs were first experienced by several Indigenous Peoples, including the Ktunaxa and Sinixt, who in time fought for its ownership.[61] After one hostile encounter between the two tribes, Chiefs negotiated a peace agreement, and to endorse it, warriors fired several arrows into rock crevices by the lake, which were visible to the white men who later passed by. It is said this is how the Arrow Lakes received the name that endures to this day.[62]

By the 1890s, a small community grew around the hot springs after riverboat Captain Robert Sanderson purchased four hundred acres of Crown land there. Sanderson had the foresight to realize the potential of the area for a resort hotel attracting tourists to its natural, pleasant, and healing waters. He built a modest structure that included wooden "plunges" for visitors to soak in.[63] Captain Sanderson also came up with the name Halcyon Hotel Springs,

The Halcyon Hot Springs Hotel. ALHS 2014.003.6020, IMAGE COURTESY OF THE ARROW LAKES HISTORICAL SOCIETY

meaning "calm, tranquil, and peaceful."[64] On September 22, 1894, the Halcyon Hot Springs Hotel had its gala opening, complete with fiddle music, dancing, and feasting.[65] The following summer saw "a good many" visitors arriving at the resort, quickly filling up all the rooms provided in the small hotel. By this time, Captain Sanderson had leased his hotel to experienced hoteliers Dawson and Craddock, who had made plans to double its size.[66] The Halcyon Hot Springs was fast becoming a tourist hot spot, not only for the natural springs, where one could recuperate and get relief from all types of ailments, including rheumatism, but also for the plentiful game and the excellent trout fishing in the area.

In 1897, Captain Sanderson and his business partner Nathen Lay sold the improved and expanded Halcyon Hot Springs Hotel for just over $20,000 to Robert Brett, a doctor from Ontario, and his business partner, David McPherson, a politician from Alberta. (It seems only appropriate that the healing power of the hot springs should be partially owned by a doctor.)[67] Captain Sanderson went back to running his steamer, the *Marion*, which had plied the waters of the Columbia River. He had his boat brought down to Kootenay Lake, where he had a contract making regular runs on the Duncan River for the following season.[68]

New owners Brett and McPherson launched the Halcyon Hot Springs Sanitarium Company and began adding additional outbuildings and doubling the size of the hotel. One of the new additions contained a bottle works where the mineral waters from the hot springs was bottled and shipped for the market. The partners promoted their mineral water with a massive advertising campaign. They found a chemist from Edinburgh, Scotland, J. Falconer King, School of Medicine, to endorse the product in their ad campaign: "This water is remarkable chiefly for the very large proportion of silica and alkaline salts which it contains... a very considerable amount of sulphuretted hydrogen and also the rare substance LITHIA..."[69] A similar advertisement for Halcyon Hot Springs mineral water was aimed at those who enjoyed an alcoholic beverage on occasion: "Halcyon Natural Mineral Water mixes well with spirits."[70]

In the summer of 1898, the hotel owners, who were financed by the British-American Corporation, realized there was money to be made in selling the local mineral water and supporting a health resort, which was growing in popularity. The company comprised president C.R. Hamilton, secretary Thomas McNaught, medical director Dr. R.G. Brett, treasurer H.M. Ellis, and director Chas. H.L. MacIntosh. They hired experienced hotelier E.E. Phair, owner of the successful Phair Hotel in Nelson, as temporary manager at the hot springs.[71]

There were no roads leading into the community of Halcyon, so the town and hotel relied on the CPR steamer, which added Halcyon Hot Springs onto its daily schedule of stops on the Arrow Lakes. A round-trip ticket for an adult on the CPR steamer from Nakusp to Halcyon Hot Springs cost $9.75 and was good for thirty days.[72] A secondary road was eventually built along the east shore of Upper Arrow Lake that included Halcyon Hot Springs, but until then, supplies and visitors arrived by boat.

In 1901, the hotel had grown to a large and attractive four-storey resort and sanitarium more than double the size of the original. There were now three owners of the Halcyon Hot Springs: Harry ("Governor") MacIntosh, Dr. Brett, and Thomas McNaught, who was also the manager. Several cottages were added, and the expansion of the hotel contained the baths considered "the most complete and substantially built in the west." Baths were separated by gender, with the ladies' baths on a separate floor. Tennis courts were constructed that saw a lot of use. A series of trails were developed that led in all directions within the large hotel grounds. One trail led to the popular "gorge," while another took visitors and guests to two natural waterfalls—thirty and forty feet high respectively—and the main trail led up to the source of the hot springs.[73] The Halcyon Hot Springs Resort and Sanitarium became more and more popular as word got out of the magnificent views, the beauty of the hotel, the natural landscape, and the healing waters of the hot springs. Its popularity continued to grow right up to the outbreak of the First World War and took a further setback when Prohibition became law in BC on October 1, 1917.[74]

Prior to Prohibition, the health resort benefitted greatly from its very popular bar and the revenue it generated. "A barroom located out of earshot from the hotel saw many all-night parties with heavy drinking and gambling."[75] Closing time was determined when the last person left the bar. "Halcyon hosted numerous extravagant banquets and balls at a barroom near the hotel, where attendees would drink, gamble and dance until sunrise. If you were looking for a good time, Halcyon was the place to be."[76] In spite of Prohibition, party goers in the hotel bar managed to find enough liquor to keep the party going, but, in 1924, the party ended abruptly when the new owner of the Halcyon Hot Springs Hotel arrived in town.

Two significant events in the history of the hotel took place in 1924. On September 10, Captain Robert Sanderson, pioneer pilot, steamboat builder, skipper of his own steamboat that plied the waters of the Arrow Lake, Kootenay Lake, and the Columbia River, and creator of the Halcyon Hot Springs, died at the age of seventy-five. The captain was buried at Halcyon, as per his last request. "Old-timers from all over the Arrow Lakes attended, including three steamboat masters."[77] In March of that year, the hotel got a new owner, who took the hotel in a new direction.

A rare view inside the Halcyon Hot Springs Hotel Dining Room, 1934.
2014.003.3396. IMAGE COURTESY OF THE ARROW LAKES HISTORICAL SOCIETY

Brigadier General Frederick William E. Burnham bought the Halcyon Hot Springs Hotel and Sanitarium and moved in with his wife and children.[78] For the next thirty-one years, Brigadier General Burnham ran the hotel as a sanitarium and hospital on the strictest of terms. Gambling, drinking, and smoking were banned, the barroom was closed and repurposed, and the nonsense ended. The gaiety and excess of the previous owners was replaced with the discipline and art of healing. It was a new era for the hotel, and it proved to be its final chapter.

Burnham had an extraordinary life. Born in 1870 in Peterborough, Ontario, Burnham eventually moved to Emerson, Manitoba, where he studied to be a physician at the Manitoba College. He did post-graduate work at Leeds, England, and in Germany. Upon graduation, he practised medicine at Morden, Manitoba. Doctor Burnham travelled extensively and was in South Africa when news of the start of the First World War reached him. Doctor Burnham set sail for England to enlist.[79] He was commissioned with the rank of Colonel and appointed chief staff surgeon of the Pljevlja Military Hospital in Montenegro, but had to flee before it was captured by the Axis powers. After a year on the Western Front,

Burnham was assigned to operate a hospital in the city of Vodena in the Balkans. It was on this return trip to the hospital at Vodena that Burnham decided to establish a Canadian branch of the White Cross of St. John. He started the Canadian branch in 1918.[80]

At the close of the war, Burnham, decorated by several countries and given high honours and gratitude by the Montenegrins for his service in their country, where he had saved countless lives on the operating table, returned to Canada and organized the Canadian War Hospital Fund under the White Cross of St. John. The purpose of the fund was to assist the people suffering in the war-torn countries of Serbia, Montenegro, and Macedonia by sending much-needed medical supplies. The Burnhams returned to the newly formed country of Yugoslavia in 1919 to ensure the flow of medical supplies reached their destination and to assist hospitals with organization and funding. They stayed for fourteen months and did not charge any money for their services.[81]

The Burnhams were dedicated to the ideals of the White Cross of St. John, and they brought this attitude and dedication to their new hotel, sanitarium, and hospital at Halcyon. It didn't take long to settle in and begin the task of implementing their agenda. The first noticeable change, after the bar was closed down, was noted by Captain Fitzsimmons on the paddlewheeler *Bonnington* as it neared the dock at Halcyon. The large hotel sign had been replaced with a sign that simply read "White Cross."[82] Within days of their arrival, the general, along with his wife, Anna (née Bartle), and two sisters-in-law began renovating the four-storey building. All the mattresses were burned, old carpets were ripped up and discarded, new beds replaced the old, and new paint was added.[83] Old pictures were taken down and replaced with Japanese etchings and watercolours from Burnham's vast collection. "West meets East" was the theme; there was an odd mix of French furnishings, Viennese vases, and Chinese porcelains. Later on, two bronze statuettes of the brigadier general and Anna Burnham were added at the foot of the stairs. These were gifts from the Albanian government in thanks and appreciation to the couple who gave so much to ease the suffering of their people, both during and after the war.[84] In addition, a marble bust of Burnham was lovingly created by Yanko Braovitch, the best known sculptor of southern Europe at the time, who came to Halcyon from Montenegro to create it in person.[85]

Under the direction of Dr. Burnham and Anna Burnham, who was a registered nurse, Halcyon Hot Springs became known internationally as a place of healing. The emphasis for the resort hospital was for healing and relaxing. Guests checking in were told that breakfast was at 7:30 in the morning and that it was lights out in the public areas at 10:00 in the evening. The preferred beverages included a choice of fresh goat's milk, Halcyon mineral water, or tea. Burnham had a series of cottages built and hot baths, where arthritis and rheumatism sufferers could find relief and be treated.[86]

Burnham believed in the principle of *mens sana in corpore sano*: a healthy mind in a healthy body. Not only did he preach it, but he lived it too. On Sunday mornings, those up early enough would occasionally see the good doctor running the trails near the hotel as part of his exercise regime, after which he would shower and bathe in the buff in the men's mineral pool.[87] What seems like the peculiar peccadillos of Doctor Burnham, especially using today's standards of behaviour, was common practice for some that stretched back in time to the ancient Greeks and Romans.

A variety of animals could be found at the Halcyon Hotel that included caribou, monkeys, canaries, peacocks, chickens, goats, goldfish, and a donkey. The pet bear cub, Joey, was the bear whose image was used on the bottled water label after he was given a bottle of it and promptly tipped it up and drained it. There was a thriving poultry business there for a while, supplying Halcyon and the CPR steamers. The goats were milked, the donkey pulled a cart from the dock to the hotel, and the goldfish added lively colour to the ponds.[88]

In 1945, Anna Burnham died. The couple had successfully run the hotel, spa, sanitarium, and hospital together for over twenty years; now Doctor Burnham ran it alone with a Chinese cook and a small staff. The grieving Burnham built a small wooden chapel and resting place for Anna upon a hill near the hotel as a shrine in memory of his life partner. A copper plaque was erected on each side of the front-door entrance. One read, ""To Anna Burnham, 1945. My dear old sweetheart and companion of life's joys and adventures." The other, "Sometime, somewhere in the great unknown we shall meet again, and I shall have a happy, happy smile for you."[89]

Doctor Burnham continued his important work, and through the years, thousands of people benefitted from the treatment and healing mineral waters at the Halcyon Hot Springs Sanitarium. By 1954, Doctor Burnham was eighty-two years old but felt healthy enough to continue running his health spa until bad news came in April that the sternwheeler *Minto* was to make its final voyage on the Arrow Lakes on April 24 as the CPR was taking it out of service.[90] Halcyon had only one regular way by land in and out of the small community by a tortuous circular route that took days to complete before a more direct road was finally completed years later. No longer would Burnham, with his two black spaniels by his side, greet guests when the *Minto* arrived, and the final visit of the ship was a bittersweet moment for the doctor and his guests. Two hundred people crowded the dock on that last day, with about a hundred cars strung out toward the town. It seemed that everyone in Halcyon came out for the last visit of the *Minto*. It was a sombre occasion, as Brigadier General Burnham, in full uniform and wearing his seventeen medals earned during and after the Great War, doffed his service cap to Captain Manning in the *Minto* pilothouse in a gesture of final farewell as the boat slowly backed away from the Halcyon dock for the last time.[91] Burnham watched it go out of sight, wiping the tears from his eyes. The old general would have to soldier on, and so he did just that, but within a year the final blow came in the form of a devastating fire.

On a cold morning, February 19, 1955, Burnham put a match to the oil-fuelled stove in the kitchen when oil spilled on the floor and caught on fire. The general died while attempting to extinguish the rapidly moving fire, and in no time, the kitchen and then the entire hotel was engulfed in flames and thick black smoke. Irma Schram, a waitress in the hotel, and Umoto, the Japanese cook, were unable to save the general, who had collapsed onto the floor.[92] Schram made a desperate plea for help on the telephone, but by the time help had arrived, the $80,000-four-storey hotel and sanitarium was a total loss.[93] The general was the only casualty in the disaster.

A hydroelectric project in the 1960s saw many small communities on the Arrow Lakes disappear beneath the waters of the rising lakes including St. Leon, West and East Demars, Pingston Creek, Fosthall, Arrowhead, Beaton, and the lowest portion of Halcyon. Saved from the lake flooding were the hot springs themselves, and, among a grove of silver birch trees, the modest little wooden chapel survived, built by Doctor Burnham, where he and his beloved Anna would rest together for eternity.

The Halcyon Hot Springs resort opened in 1999. Although there is no hotel, guests may rent a cabin or stay at one of the many campsites.

KING EDWARD HOTEL

(1910–95)
112 Second Street East, Revelstoke

THE CITY OF Revelstoke, incorporated in 1889, was originally named Farwell, after A.S. Farwell, who surveyed the original townsite in 1880. For six years, the settlement of Farwell slowly developed, waiting for the coming of the CPR and the prosperity the railroad would bring, but Mr. Farwell got greedy. As the CPR tracks approached the town, Farwell tried to sell land for the CPR station and maintenance yard at inflated prices in a vain attempt to make money out of the deal. The CPR, knowing that they had the upper hand and the final word, bypassed Farwell and surveyed their own settlement on higher ground, and in June 1886 named the CPR station Revelstoke in honour of the First Lord Revelstoke of the Baring Brothers banking firm in London, England, which bankrolled a portion of the CPR. Farwell was left out in the cold as the small population moved to where the railroad was located.[94]

The CPR established Revelstoke as its main operations and maintenance centre (railway divisional point). The CPR, along with mining and logging operations, were initially the three biggest employers in town, and the new town quickly grew as the supply centre for the West Kootenay District.[95]

In 1897, Mrs. A.J. Lapworth managed the Rhodesia Restaurant and Boarding House on Second Street at Orton Avenue in

Revelstoke. A fine advertisement in the *Revelstoke Herald* read: "Rhodesia Restaurant and Boarding House, English cooking under the supervision of Mrs. Lapworth. Dining room attached attended personally by the proprietor. Cleanliness and civility our motto."[96] In March 1898, Lapworth's restaurant and boarding house was used for quite a different purpose. Mr. James Durign, a visitor from Iowa, was laid up in one of the rooms at the Rhodesia after both his feet were badly frostbitten from walking from Arrowhead to Revelstoke, a distance of approximately twenty-eight miles through the snow and ice. He was in serious condition awaiting transportation to the hospital.[97]

In 1901, William H. Caldwell changed the name of the business from the Rhodesia Boarding House to the Queen's Hotel. The following year, it was leased by John H. Robinson, who operated the hotel for a few years. Then came the McSorley Brothers—John and Henry J. McSorley—who purchased the hotel in 1910 and planned sweeping changes to the structure to make it into a larger, modern hotel. Prior to purchasing the Queen's, Henry McSorley dabbled in politics. A staunch Conservative, McSorley ran for office in the 1907 election in municipal politics and won in Ward Three.[98] In December 1909, he was appointed as one of the delegates representing Revelstoke in the Conservative convention in Kamloops.[99] Politics would remain a part of Henry McSorley's life, and his brother John McSorley would also become involved at the local level.

In April 1910, work commenced on removing a portion of the Queen's Hotel and following the design drawn up by architect William King. King's other projects included designing the Selkirk School in Revelstoke and the Court House in Kaslo.[100] The new hotel for the McSorley brothers was King's largest project to date. I didn't find evidence whether the brothers intended to keep the Queen's as the name for their newly modified hotel or if they planned to change it, but they could have been influenced by the death of King Edward VII on May 6, 1910, while the Queen's Hotel remodelling was in midstream. The name was changed to the King Edward Hotel in honour of the late king.

The Queen's Hotel, ca. 1905. COURTESY OF THE REVELSTOKE MUSEUM & ARCHIVES, P561

A new wing measuring sixty by sixty-two feet was added to the existing structure, covering a whole city block from the alley on Second Street behind the city hall to the corner of Orton Avenue and down to First Street. A large steam-heat furnace was built in the basement, and on the ground floor, a finely fitted and spacious twenty-four-foot-by-forty-six-foot bar complete with tiled floor was added. An additional six-foot-by-twelve-foot liquor room was built off the back of the ornate oak bar. Three card rooms were constructed off the main barroom, and no self-respecting hotel would operate without a billiards room—the King Edward's being twenty feet by thirty feet. The second and third floors contained a total of fifty-five rooms, fifteen of those ensuite. There was a large, shared bathroom on each floor. The roof was made of tin with handsome cornices and ornaments. The walls were lined inside and studded with felt to deaden the sound and to keep out the cold.[101] This was just the beginning of their hotel makeover.

The job was completed in the summer of 1911, and the new King Edward Hotel was an amazing, first-class hotel. The location was perfect; away from the bulk of the hotels on Front Street, the King Edward was one block away from the retail-business heart of Revelstoke and a mere three blocks from the CPR station. A free bus operated by Joe Farmiloe was made available for guests to get from the station to the hotel and back. High ceilings, spacious halls, two excellent fire escapes, writing rooms, and a spacious rotunda, finished in Mission-style oak with tooled leather in the frieze, were added.[102] The *pièce de résistance* was the exterior and basement concrete blocks that, with the addition of protruding bay windows and a distinct tower placed in the corner of the hotel at Second Street and Orton Avenue, gave the King Edward its unique look of beauty and permanence.

During renovations, the hotel remained open. At one point, James June, a railway brakeman who was a guest at the hotel, had not been seen in a few days. The manager went to check on him in his room and found him deceased. June had been ill for some time, and the coroner determined that he had passed away due to heart failure.[103]

Patrons of the King Edward Hotel bar could enjoy fine French wines, imported spirits, and local beer brewed at the Enterprise Brewing Company (which took pride in their new brewhouse, completed in the spring of 1907 on Charles Street) or from Allan's Brewery.[104] German Humbser beer, imported from Bavaria through H.W. Kostenbader in Victoria, proved to be a popular choice for customers at the King Edward Hotel until the weekly shipment ran into a problem due to the beer in a few of the kegs having turned sour.[105] The argument over who was to blame and who would compensate whom became moot when the outbreak of the First World War put an immediate halt to all German imports.

When discussing Revelstoke and its historic hotels, one cannot overlook the town's long history with skiing. In 1915, Revelstoke became a world-class ski-jumping destination that attracted many Scandinavian families and produced the world-champion ski jumper Nels Nelsen.[106] Skiers from around the world visited Revelstoke, many staying at the local hotels like the King Edward.

Prior to the start of Prohibition, the King Edward Hotel underwent extensive repairs and upgrading that proved to be quite expensive. The McSorley brothers were aware that Prohibition could come to British Columbia in late 1916 or 1917 and ran the following advertisement in a number of newspapers: "Compensation... where men [hotel owners specifically] are threatened with financial ruin should a Prohibition bill without compensation be approved by the electors." The brothers argued that they had followed the new regulations (the Liquor Act of 1911) governing the class of buildings necessary to secure a renewal of their liquor licence and had paid over $50,000, much of it borrowed, to fulfill those requirements. Should Prohibition prevail without compensation, then he argued they could lose all that they worked for.[107]

Prohibition in British Columbia did become law on October 1, 1917, to the brothers' chagrin. To compound the problem, John McSorley's young wife, who had just returned from visiting relatives in Vancouver, contracted a severe case of influenza and died. She was only twenty years old, and the couple's baby daughter was without a mother at four weeks old.[108]

The McSorley brothers managed to survive Prohibition, although with the revenue from the popular hotel bar gone, it took longer to maintain the hotel. In a strange twist of fate, H.J. McSorley decided to sell the hotel. In November 1924, a major real-estate transaction took place when the McSorley brothers sold the hotel and property to Bert McCallum, reportedly for $100,000. An old rival in the hotel business, Paddy Murphy, was now the new proprietor of the King Edward Hotel and co-owner of the King Edward Hotel in Enderby (see Chapter Two).[109] But this wasn't the end of the story for Henry J. McSorley and Paddy H. Murphy.

In 1927, Chief Justice Hunter in the BC Supreme Court appointed A.J. Waskett of Revelstoke receiver of the King Edward Hotel when the owner was unable to make his payments. Murphy, who had a lease agreement with the former owner, claimed possession of the hotel, which was allegedly agreed to in his contract.[110] The

The King Edward Hotel, Revelstoke. COURTESY OF THE REVELSTOKE MUSEUM & ARCHIVES, 1100

dispute had gone on for almost two years when the court finally allowed the King Edward Hotel to revert back to the McSorley brothers.[111] John McSorley sold his portion of the hotel, making H.J. McSorley sole proprietor. H.J. McSorley hired his son, Cecil P. McSorley, as manager.

In March 1939, the pioneer railway and hotelman Henry J. McSorley died at the age of seventy-three. At the age of eighteen, he had come west from Peel County, Ontario, and worked for the CPR as a locomotive fireman before moving up to train engineer. He had then moved to Revelstoke, where he and his younger brother John had purchased the Queen's Hotel, making it their own and changing the name to the King Edward Hotel. His wife Katherine (née Coughlin) and two sons, Cecil and John, were by his side when he died. Stores in Revelstoke were closed on the day of his funeral, which most of the townsfolk attended.[112]

The King Edward Hotel survived for another fifty-six years, allowing future generations to enjoy the business while making their own unique memories. On Thursday, January 12, 1995, near midnight, a kitchen grease fire got out of control and the flames spread rapidly through the kitchen. By the time firefighters could control the blaze, the King Edward was destroyed. A fitting eulogy was written by one of the regular customers that reflected the sentiments of many:

> Dear old Hotel, we will miss you! Like Mount Begbie, even if we haven't looked at you lately, we knew you were always there and hoped you always would be. You were home, decent shelter, good food and lively company in all kinds of small town mischief. Watching you burn we became as refugees on a snowy night, remembering so much we cannot return to. Losing you we all became older. Memories of the King Edward Hotel will follow much farther than the soot and ashes we tracked around downtown on that black Friday.[113]

ST. PANCRAS HOTEL

(1897–1905); King George Hotel (1911–53)
Front Street, Kaslo

THE BEAUTIFUL VILLAGE of Kaslo hugs the west shore of Kootenay Lake in the West Kootenay. The origin of the name "Kaslo" is disputed. Some maintain the settlement was first called Kane's Landing, after brothers George and David Kane, who pre-empted land in the area, but that the name was changed to Kaslo, taking the name from the Kaslo River, when the local post office opened. Others say that Kaslo is an anglicized spelling of the French name Kasleau, after John Kasleau, a prospector and one-time Hudson's Bay Company employee.[114] Historian and writer Greg Nesteroff suggests that the name is more likely derived from an Indigenous word, but whether it might be from Ktunaxa or Sinixt isn't well established.[115] We may never really know for sure where the name originated, but suffice it to say that the name "Kaslo" represents one of the most beautiful locations in the West Kootenay.

The three-storey King George Hotel was built with American capital at Kaslo in the summer of 1897 and opened as the St. Pancras Hotel. It was owned by a group headed up by Dr. D.M. Linnard called the Rossland Syndicate, which hoped to cash in on the influx of miners seeking to make their fortunes during the rush of 1897. The hotel contained forty rooms and featured a conical tower topping a bay window. The rooms were filled for months during the height of the gold rush, but once that simmered down, the Rossland Syndicate put the hotel up for sale.[116] Along came

King George Hotel, ca. 1940. IMAGE E-05345 COURTESY OF THE ROYAL BC MUSEUM

Charles Franklin Caldwell, a local mining broker and owner of the Franklin Mine, who purchased the St. Pancras. He hired Mrs. J.C. Davies to manage it while Caldwell attended to his many business ventures.[117]

The St. Pancras Hotel wasn't in operation for long, closing in 1905, but there was one event worth mentioning. A pretty summer wedding took place in one of the parlours at the St. Pancras when Miss Catherine Graney of Kellogg, Idaho, married Cyrus Poyntz of the Maritime Mining Company, New Denver. The happy couple began their honeymoon by taking the steamship *Kaslo* to an undisclosed port.[118]

The hotel was forced to close, and from June 1905 to August 1911, the hotel became the private residence of the Caldwell family.

In 1911, Charles Caldwell put his residence, the old St. Pancras Hotel, up for sale, and it was purchased by John Reuter and his business partner, Edward Latham.[119] Reuter and Latham had been running the Maze Saloon for a few years and wished to branch out into the hotel business. The new owners announced that the hotel would be redecorated, refurbished, and updated from a residential home to a hotel. The business partners felt that there was a need for a large hotel in Kaslo as the area was growing and the future seemed rosy.[120]

The coronation ceremony of King George V took place at Westminster Abbey on June 22, 1911, and the new hotel was named in his honour.[121] The King George Hotel in Kaslo opened on August 10, 1911, with curious Kaslovians crowding into the refurbished building for its gala opening. Reuter and Latham had done a remarkable job restoring and renovating the hotel. Their business partnership would continue for an unprecedented thirty-nine years until Reuter retired in 1945.

On Monday, March 11, 1912, a special luncheon was held at the King George Hotel. Attending was Mayor A.T. Garland along with Premier Richard McBride, the premier's private secretary, and the attorney-general of BC.[122] The premier was on the stump looking for votes in the West Kootenay, with his next stop at Nelson. Later that year, Latham was elected fire chief for the city of Kaslo and had political aspirations.[123]

Edward H. Latham was born in England. His family had immigrated to Canada, arriving in Moose Jaw, Saskatchewan, in 1883. Latham travelled west in the early 1900s, arriving in Kaslo and forming a partnership with Mr. Reuter to open the Maze Saloon before they bought the St. Pancras Hotel. Sebastian John Reuter was born in Formosa, Ontario, on September 8, 1873. He had come to Kaslo in 1892 and had worked for Perdue and Wilson as manager of the local butcher shop. He left that business when he partnered with Latham in the Maze Saloon. In 1914, Reuter fell in love with an employee at his hotel, Miss Christine McDiarmid, and the couple married.[124]

During the Great War, the people of Kaslo did their part to help in the war effort. The Kaslo War Workers sent 344 parcels to the soldiers at the front that contained socks, tobacco, candy, gum, towels, cakes, tea, Oxo, notebooks, and pencils. Recovering soldiers from the Balfour Sanitarium were entertained by the war workers during a luncheon held at the King George Hotel.[125]

The 1920s and 1930s saw a different type of clientele arrive at the hotel. While commercial men continued to hawk their wares in special rooms provided by the hotel owners, tourist families began replacing prospectors and promoters, especially during the warm summer months. Children ran up and down the wide halls of the

King George, scattering sand over everything, while at the end of the hallway was the fire escape—a coiled rope to be flung out the window in case of an emergency.[126]

New roads were opening up as automobiles became more prolific, but the railway was still in full service. It was a time of transition, and the King George adapted to the changes, although its outward appearance hadn't changed in over forty years, until the exterior walls were stuccoed.

The King George was still the popular choice for out-of-town travellers, as well as a place for locals to hold their meetings, banquets, and dances. The Kaslo Liberal Party held its big banquet at the King George.[127] Edward Latham was on the board of directors of the golf and country club and supervised the construction of the club's building. Both Latham and his business partner, Reuter, were elected to the city council numerous times through the years and were very involved with their community.

A few disturbing events took place at the King George in 1929 and in 1933. A family man, Jacob Teigen, far from his home and family in Norway, worked in one of the local mines and was rooming at the King George. When he hadn't been seen outside his room for a few days, the manager when up to check on him and found that Teigen had hanged himself in his room. No note was found, nor were there any clues as to why he had taken his own life.[128] Another sad event took place in the hotel when the night clerk at the King George, Louis Riesner, aged sixty-six, was discovered dead from what was later determined to be heart failure.[129]

From 1943 to 1944, Edward Latham served as the mayor of Kaslo. As the Second World War ended, so, too, did the long, successful business partnership between Latham and Reuter when Reuter decided to retire. Presiding over the King George, John S. Reuter and Edward H. Latham had greeted Kaslo visitors with kindness and forbearance for the best part of thirty-four years.[130] Mr. B. Albrect became the new proprietor of the King George Hotel in the spring of 1945.[131]

Having had a full and productive life, Edward H. Latham died at the age of seventy-seven at his home in Kaslo on December 11, 1950. He was buried in the Kaslo cemetery.[132]

The sixtieth anniversary of the incorporation of Kaslo took place in 1953, but the afterglow of the celebration turned sour when, on September 26, a fire started that quickly grew out of control and destroyed the landmark King George Hotel. Only a dozen guests had been staying at the hotel that Saturday night, and they all managed to escape, most wearing their night attire, without serious injury. The fire was believed to have started in the furnace room but rapidly raced through the old wooden timbers. The last proprietors to own the hotel, Garry L. Laughton and John Staudacher, put the cost of their loss at between $75,000 and $100,000.[133] After the smoking remains of the hotel cooled, the site was cleared and the old King George vanished without a trace from the beach where it had held sway for so long.[134]

When the King George burned down, it left Kaslo without a hotel, and the promised twenty-four-room replacement that was to be built by S.A. Bishop of Vancouver in 1954 never came to fruition.[135] It is probably fitting that the SS *Moyie* was placed on the site of the King George Hotel in 1957 as a dryland museum that, at one time, had brought its fair share of customers to the old hotel.[136]

CHAPTER FIVE

West Kootenay

Part Two

RECO HOTEL

(1898–1900, 1900–54)
Reco Street, Sandon

THE MINING TOWN of Sandon was founded by Jack Sandon, who, with his partner, Eli Carpenter, discovered mineral ore in the area in 1891.[1] The following summer, John ("Johnny") Morgan Harris purchased the Reco mine and, once that was established, he set out to pre-empt a townsite in the valley below. Word got out of the rich silver ore discovered in Sandon, and the rush was on. Seaton and four of his Irish friends quickly staked a claim called the Noble Five that turned a great profit for their investment. Eli Carpenter and Jack Sandon also staked a claim, and others who arrived followed suit, until there were approximately two hundred men working their claims and hoping for that big silver strike.[2]

Five men arrived in the spring of 1893, pitched their tents in a section of the townsite, and built a hotel. As the hotel was nearing completion, the five held a meeting to try and come up with a name for the town and subsequently for the hotel. The name "Sandon" was suggested for the new town, after Jack Sandon, who had drowned earlier that year. They all agreed, and the new town was called Sandon.[3]

Sandon was doomed from the beginning. The town was built deep in a gulch over Carpenter Creek which, in hindsight, was probably not a great location. Sandon was plagued by avalanches in the winter, floods in the spring, and fire in the hot summer months, yet most of the citizens endured these hardships, at least initially, when it was worth the pain and trouble. The fortunes of the town, like most typical boom-and-bust economies, was based on the availability of silver in the ground for the mines to extract and process, and the price of silver on the world market. Those halcyon years between 1892 and 1900 saw the fluctuating price of silver dip in the fall of 1893 and again in July 1897. These dips lasted for brief periods before rebounding each time.[4]

Essential for transporting the silver ore from the mine to the smelter and beyond was the railroad. Initially, the nearby town of Three Forks was the terminus of the Nakusp and Slocan Railway (N&S). It was an arduous journey to transport the silver ore by wagon to Three Forks, and thankfully the need for that journey ended when the competing Kaslo and Slocan Railway (K&S) passed Three Forks and carried right on into Sandon in October 1895. With the arrival of the train service, Sandon really took off. "During the winter of 1896 and throughout 1897 Sandon was the scene of phenomenal growth... Sandon boasted 17 hotels,"[5] and the Reco Hotel was the largest of them all, owned by the founder of Sandon, John Harris.

John Morgan Harris was Sandon's wealthiest and most prominent citizen. He owned the Reco mine, and that's where he got the name for his hotel on Reco Street. He also owned a few other buildings and properties in Sandon as well as the waterworks and power plant. Born at Vernon Mills, Virginia, in 1864 as John Morgan Davis, he decided to change his name after his older brother Arthur fatally shot a rival storekeeper and fled to the Pacific Northwest. Arthur adopted the surname Harris, and Johnny, who later joined him, appears to have followed suit. Johnny Harris worked for a time in Wallace, Idaho, in a variety of jobs before settling as a realtor. He bought up parcels of land but ran into trouble in January 1891 after shooting and killing a squatter on his property named Zach Lewis and wounding Lewis's son Charles.[6] Harris and a co-accused were brought before a grand jury that resulted in a hung jury, with most believing Harris acted in self-defence. In 1892, Harris caught wind of the silver strike north of the border and made his way to the West Kootenay to join the Slocan rush. In

Sandon, BC. COURTESY OF THE CITY OF VANCOUVER ARCHIVES, CVA 2-33

addition to staking several claims, he and some partners bought a promising property called the Rueceau (later renamed the Reco) that paid out handsomely.[7]

The Reco Hotel was a large, handsome, four-storey wooden building facing Reco Street and conveniently located next to the train station. The hotel was built at an earlier time, opening as Black's Hotel, owned by Ira Black.[8] On May 14, 1898, it reopened with a new name and a new owner.[9] The opening of the hotel was commemorated with a dance held at the nearby Virginia Hall, with music provided by the Sandon Orchestra followed by a delicious dinner served in the large Reco Hotel dining room. Approximately fifty couples attended the celebratory event.[10]

Sandon was incorporated in January 1898, with a population of over two thousand. The business section was the envy of rival towns. Sandon boasted twenty-three hotels and eleven saloons, with more opening daily. The town even had an opera house. It was served by not one, but two railroads, the K&S and the CPR. Sandon was the major town in what was dubbed the "Silvery Slocan."

West Kootenay, Part Two 215

It was an exciting town; brash and boisterous and down its crooked streets came a curious medley of humanity—the tinhorns, drifters, parsons, promotors, outlaws and prostitutes and Sandon took them all in stride for this was their type of town. Its main street ran wide open twenty-four hours a day, seven days a week and in the backrooms, fortunes were made and lost by the buying or selling of a claim or by the tune of a car in Stud Horse [poker].[11]

Liquor flowed freely as saloons and hotel bars made money, only to be outdone by most of the 115 "ladies of ill repute." Men came down from their claims seeking yellow liquor, green gambling cloth, and women in red, and after days of wild spending, they usually sobered up and perhaps regretfully returned to their claims swearing off drink until the urge struck them and the whole process would repeat itself.[12]

Near midnight on May 3, 1900, the party came to an abrupt end. A fire began on the outside of the opera house and then quickly spread through the tightly packed wooden buildings that made up the business section. The citizens of Sandon, led by the volunteer fire brigade, did all they could to slow the fire. Buildings were blown up, but the strategy failed to stop the wall of flame intent on destroying all in its path. Hundreds of men, women, and children were forced to flee for their lives with whatever they could carry. The inferno continued until dawn, when there was not much left to burn. Atherton's brick warehouse, a shop or two, and some residential houses were spared from total destruction. Johnny Harris had the most to lose, as his handsome, four-storey Reco Hotel lay in ruins at the cost of $30,000. He did not have insurance. Other hotels destroyed in the blaze included the Sandon ($18,000); the Exchange ($11,000); the Clifton ($9,000); the Klondike ($4,500); the Palace ($4,500); the Miner's Exchange ($3,000); the Star ($3,000); the Kootenay ($2,000); the Vancouver ($2,000); the Balmoral ($1,500); and the Thistle Hotel.[13]

The devastation caused by the fire was a sad sight to behold by the light of day. The whole upper portion of town was entirely wiped out. Once the news of the fire reached other towns, relief aid in money, material, and basic needs began flowing toward Sandon.[14]

Now the long process of recovery and rebuilding began. By the summer of 1900, Sandon's business area was rebuilt, including the new Reco Hotel. Harris's replacement for the original Reco Hotel was almost as large as the original, being sixty by eighty feet with well-lit spacious rooms.[15] One of the barns not destroyed in the fire provided some of the material in the rebuilt Reco Hotel.

The fire had forced some to leave Sandon, and the population took a slight drop, but rebuilding continued through 1901. The last thing the fragile town needed was another disaster.

Late spring and early summer of 1901 were unusually hot, leading to a rapid snowmelt. The creeks began to swell until a log jam dammed Sandon Creek, where the water built up, forcing it to find a new route down the back streets of Sandon. This flooded the cellars on Reco Avenue. The Denver House fell victim to the roaring river as a log knocked out the central support. The building was sure to follow, but that was prevented by the quick actions of citizens who made a makeshift breakwater.[16]

In 1906, Sandon was ravaged by yet another fire. Although that summer was unusually hot, Mother Nature had nothing to do with starting it. A four-year-old boy was playing with matches in one of the houses in Upper Sandon when he managed to light the lace curtains on fire. The window was half open and the wind caught the flame, forcing it onto the wallpaper and igniting the wall. The frightened little boy crawled under the bed. His sister, mother, and father became aware of the fire and rushed out of the home. As they watched their house and their personal possessions burn, the young girl realized that her brother was not with them. She rushed into the blazing house and found her little brother whimpering under the bed; she crawled under and dragged him to safety. She paid for her bold rescue with badly burned hands and feet but had saved her little brother's life.[17] In all, some twenty buildings were lost, including the hospital. The Reco Hotel was untouched.

Harris leased the Reco Hotel to William Bennett, who was the proprietor of the Filbert Hotel until the 1906 fire burned that hotel

Sandon Station and the Reco Hotel, 1900. IMAGE C-05207 COURTESY OF THE ROYAL BC MUSEUM

to the ground.[18] Bennett ran a large ad in the *Slocan Mining Review*: "The leading hotel of the Silvery Slocan, Reco Hotel in Sandon. Headquarters for mining and travelling men; meals first-class, warm the best; rooms large, clean and cozy—William Bennett."[19]

Misfortune continued to plague Sandon as the spring of 1908 saw snowslides followed by landslides that destroyed roads, bridges, and railway tracks in and out of the town. The K&S railway decided not to rebuild, leaving Sandon with the CPR. One slide took out the water main at the powerhouse, plunging the town into darkness. In addition to the slides, a smaller fire destroyed the New York Brewery, which was owned by Twogood and Brunder. Poor W.M. ("Billy") Bennett, who was leasing the Reco Hotel, was ill for a week with the grippe (the flu) as that ailment made the rounds through town.[20] When Bennett eventually recovered, he tried to find someone to buy out his lease at the Reco; he had had enough. With no takers, he simply closed the Reco Hotel and moved into a room near the post office.[21] The Reco remained closed while regular ads in the newspapers sought someone to lease the hotel; Finally, Mrs. McKinnon of Ainsworth reopened the Reco in mid-August.[22] The population of Sandon was on a slow decline as tired citizens wondered what to expect next.

Harris continued to lease out the Reco Hotel, as Norman Hurlburt and C. Stewart became the new proprietors. They hired Tom Trenary as head bartender.[23] In the meantime, Harris, who had been residing south of the border in Spokane and was very active in his mining and other interests, received news that his brother, E.M. Harris (nicknamed "Spokane,") was found dead in his cabin on Sproule Creek just northwest of Nelson. Two bear hunters had dropped in to see him and were met with a disturbing sight. A gun lay nearby in what looked like a suicide, as the trigger was tied with a string that led to the dead man's hand. Dried blood was found on the floor. "The unfortunate man was an old-time prospector and had a number of claims on Bear Creek."[24]

In late spring 1911, J.M Harris, manager of the Reco Mine, celebrated his good fortune when mine workers discovered two rich veins of silver ore.[25] Harris made his fortune from his mine investments, which allowed him to invest in other businesses like the Reco Hotel. Harris had no intention of ever selling the hotel, although from time to time interested parties approached him with offers. In the summer of 1916, there was talk about the possibility that Prohibition would come to British Columbia. Most hotel owners were appalled at the idea of closing their bar and cutting off a main source of revenue, but Harris had a different opinion. Harris said he was certain that most hotels would survive Prohibition, as there was always the revenue from renting out rooms. There was no indication that the travelling public would not continue to require hotel rooms. Harris's surprising answer regarding bar patrons was that with the bar closed, "hangers-on around bars can get out and do a real day's work." Harris went further, noting, "I am selling whiskey and have been selling it for quite a number of years, but I am going to vote for Prohibition." Perhaps speaking more as a mine owner than a hotelman, Harris added, "When Prohibition carries, and it will carry just as sure as snooting, then you will have true prosperity in British Columbia and particularly through the mining sections of the province." Harris also quipped, "If we can't get enough men to run the hotels once Prohibition carries, then there are plenty of women who can do it ... and the men that can't get work around the hotels following the passage of the act can get out and do a real man's work in this province."[26] On October 1, 1917, Prohibition did take effect in British Columbia and Harris's Reco Hotel did survive and continue to operate.

In May 1919, Johnny Harris sold his interest in the Reco Mine. Just as interesting as Harris selling his number-one money-making venture was who he sold it to: James Dunsmuir, who had inherited his father's coal empire on Vancouver Island and was a past premier of British Columbia. Harris and his business partner Fred Kelly were said to have sold the mine for $250,000. Not a bad investment, when Harris purchased it back in 1892 for $2,800. Dunsmuir had recently purchased the Noble Five mine and other property adjoining the Reco with plans to erect a new mill.[27]

In 1926, at the age of sixty-two, Johnny Harris married his secretary, twenty-six-year-old Alma Lommatzsch.[28] The marriage would last until Harris's death at the age of eighty-eight in December 1953.

The 1920s were the last good decade for Sandon, as 37,895 tons of ore were mined in 1923 alone and silver prices were relatively stable.[29] An odd incident took place in the Reco Hotel in February 1930, when Steve Danisovsky, a Slovakian miner a long way from home, ran amuck one evening and had to be arrested for going on a rampage. Danisovsky worked for the Noble Five Mine and was in the Sandon hospital when he suddenly he jumped up and caused about seventy-five dollars' worth of damage. He left the hospital and ended up at the Reco Hotel, where he grabbed an axe and immediately began using it on the furniture. He then chased a guest of the hotel with the axe, forcing the terrified customer to dive out of the front door of the hotel. It took five men from the bar to hold the demented man down so he could be arrested.[30]

The 1930s and the onset of the Great Depression saw silver prices fall, resulting in an exodus out of Sandon until, by 1940, there were very few people left. Two people that remained

Amie Egan at the front desk in the Reco Hotel. IMAGE G-00828 COURTESY OF THE ROYAL BC MUSEUM

steadfast in their large Reco Hotel were Johnny Harris and his wife Alma. The couple had been growing oranges and lemons as well as tending their large garden on the property where the old Filbert Hotel used to stand.[31]

By 1950, of the twenty-three hotels that were built in the silver-rush days of the 1890s and rebuilt in 1900, only the Reco Hotel remained. On December 6, 1953, Harris died in the New Denver hospital with Alma by his side. Although he remained in Sandon for over sixty years, at his request, his body was returned to Virginia for burial.[32] The gravestone simply read, "John Morgan Davis 1864–1953." Two years later, the town of Sandon received its final blow when the spring runoff swelled Carpenter Creek, forcing it to rage through what was left of the downtown. There were eleven families still living in Sandon when the flood finished off the town. "The historic and empty Reco Hotel, once the mining capital of the Slocan, caved in at the height of the storm."[33]

NEWMARKET HOTEL

(1893-1973)
New Denver

LOCATED ON the eastern shore of Slocan Lake at the mouth of Carpenter Creek, the small village of New Denver is in the West Kootenay region. Like many places in BC's Interior, New Denver got its start with the lure of possible riches to be found underground, in this case, silver.

In his book *Gold Creeks and Ghost Towns*, BC historian N.L. Barlee wrote, "First known as Eldorado until they found no gold there, it became New Denver when it was believed it would eclipse its namesake. Although never as large a town as Kaslo or Slocan City, New Denver had a great location... at the mouth of a flat and pleasant delta of Carpenter Creek that served as a natural water route into the silver country. By 1893, it claimed 250 permanent residents and a transient population of nearly twice that. Silver mines close by like the Mountain Chief, Alpha, California, Idaho-Cumberland and the Alamo contributed greatly to the town's prosperity."[34]

Before 1900, hotels such as the New Market, Denver, Central, St. James, and Windsor served the miners who came to the area to try their luck at prospecting, and a town grew up around the mines. Boats made daily trips on Slocan Lake, and the CPR built its line into Sandon and Three Forks. For nearly twenty years, wrote Barlee, "the fluctuating silver excitement made for a spirited town."[35]

G.P.V. and Helen Akrigg, in their book *1001 British Columbia Place Names*, also wrote of New Denver's optimistic beginnings and the story of its name changes:

The Newmarket Hotel. IMAGE B-05350 COURTESY OF THE ROYAL BC MUSEUM

[New Denver was] originally called Eldorado by a prospector who hoped he would find enough gold to justify conferring the name of the legendary city of gold. When gold wasn't discovered but in its place silver, lead, zinc and other base metals, a meeting was held to decide on a more suitable name. Thomas Latheen, who came from Denver, Colorado, let know that he believed the town would be even greater than Denver and persuaded the citizens to adopt the name New Denver for the settlement.[36]

Plans to build the hotel in New Denver that would become the New Market Hotel became public in 1893. A paper called *The Tribune* on May 18 reported that "S.M. Wharton plans for a hotel in New Denver." The *Kaslo Claim* on May 12 provided more details under the headline "Hotel for New Denver":

S.M. Wharton, one of the owners of the Ruceau mine, who recently sold an interest in that property for $30,000, arrived in Kaslo last Saturday from Spokane on his way to New Denver.

He was accompanied by five carpenters who will build for him a hotel in the thriving little town at the mouth of Carpenter creek. The building will be 50 by 80 feet in size, three stories in height and contain 40 rooms exclusive of the first floor. Work will be commenced immediately, the lumber and necessary material being now on the ground and the structure will be ready for occupancy as soon as the skill of the builders can make it. Mr. Wharton is an enthusiastic admirer of New Denver, and never loses an opportunity to speak on its behalf with polished rhetoric and delightful diction. He is demonstrating his faith by practical works, being a prime mover in all enterprises that will tend to benefit his adopted town. Mr. Wharton is also owner of a sawmill on Slocan Lake that is in successful and continued operation.

The location for the new hotel was prime, across the street from the main wharf at New Denver, which was handy for guests arriving by paddlewheeler.

One account suggests the builder of the New Market Hotel was possibly Cornelius ("Neil") Gething, who had also built the Slocan Hotel in New Denver in 1890. The *Province* reported on January 13, 1929, that "in the summer of 1890, Cornelius "Neil" Gething built the Slocan Hotel in New Denver... afterwards and only a short distance away, came the New Market Hotel, proprietor Henry Stege..."

Around 1893, the name of the hotel began to be spelled as one word, "Newmarket." The Nakusp *Ledge* recorded on November 2, 1893, that "Mr. Teesdale, one of the proprietors of the Newmarket Hotel, New Denver, is in town and will remain for a few days."

On December 7, the same paper tells us that "Mr. Teasedale [*sic*] of the Newmarket Hotel, New Denver is very ill with pneumonia." (Evidently, he survived through the ordeal, as his name continues to appear in local newspaers.)

The New Denver *Ledge* on February 28, 1895, reported that

> Mr. Teesdale [or Teasdale] has retired and J.M. Winter late of the Windsor restaurant is the new partner with Stege at the

Newmarket hotel... In April a two-storey addition will be erected to the rear of the barroom, which will then be removed thither. A pool and billiard table will also be put in. The present barroom will be furnished with desks and other furniture suited for an office and sitting room.

The dining room is being looked after by Mr. Winter, who moved over from the Windsor yesterday afternoon He will give that his chief attention, while Mr. Stege looks after the hotel proper, thus ensuring success in every department. Invitations have been issued for the formal opening on Saturday, when the patrons of the hostelry will be served with a free lunch in the evening. Both men understand their duties and having the confidence of the businessmen and travelling public, they should and undoubtedly will meet the expectations of their many well-wishers.

In September 1895, Stege and Winter were co-proprietors (Winter managed the restaurant). The dining room was redecorated and reopened in March 1896.[37]

The following year, the entire hotel was renovated. Stege was still the proprietor. He placed a wonderful ad for the Newmarket Hotel in the October 28 issue of the New Denver *Ledge*, stating that the building had been enlarged and all the rooms plastered, and new carpets and furniture would make "the house a marvel of comfort and elegance." The refurbished hotel had twenty-eight rooms, and its "beautiful situation amidst the finest scenery in America, [made] this hotel unsurpassed in all Kootenay."

Thomas Avison joined Henry Stege as co-proprietor sometime around 1898. An ad placed by them in the *Province* on June 18, 1898, reads, "The Newmarket Hotel in New Denver is one of the best hotels in the Slocan. The house is plastered, new and elegant. Furniture has been put in and everything possible has been done to make the hotel a pleasant place for the traveler plus good boating and fishing."

By early 1899, Thomas Avison had left the partnership, making Henry Stege the sole owner of the Newmarket Hotel.

Various events unfolded over the next few years: a wedding took place in the hotel in 1900, and in 1902, a tourist association was formed with a membership of over fifty and Henry Stege as president. Oddly, in January 1903, an owl was shot at the hotel.

In March and April of 1903, the spectre of fire came to New Denver, but does not seem to have destroyed the Newmarket Hotel, although it may have sustained some damage. A 1908 ad for the Newmarket in the *Slocan Mining Review* indicated that Henry Stege was still around as proprietor.

In January 1912, Stege appealed a cancellation of the hotel's liquor licence for "past infractions," claiming that the information that led to the decision to cancel his licence was incorrect and misleading.[38] However, on January 18, the Greenwood *Ledge* reported the happy news that "the government has cancelled the embargo against the New Market hotel and Henry Stege can again sell booze legally in New Denver."

The *Vancouver Sun* reported on March 21, 1912, that the provincial government was proposing to help fund a bridge that would connect the CPR and the Newmarket Hotel, a move that would be good for business.

Other events of note occurred in 1912. On April 18, the *Ledge* reported that "H.O. Sait [sic] has been granted a licence for the Newmarket Hotel in New Denver." Sait leased from Stege. Then, on May 30, the *Ledge* reported that "A. Jacobson recently bought the New Market from Henry Stege for $8,000. He is adding bathrooms and making other improvements ... Stege intends to go north and start a brewery at Fort George." Andrew Jacobson would remain the owner of the Newmarket Hotel for decades to come. The *Calgary Herald* reported on June 5, 1912, that Jacobson was selling a thousand acres of land close to the lake and railroad that was "well watered and free from stones."

The *Nelson Daily News* on October 14, 1912, informed its readers of the latest improvements to the Newmarket Hotel:

> With the installation of a furnace, the improvements to the Newmarket hotel here will be practically completed. Since taking over the property from Henry Stege several months ago, Andrew

Jacobson remodelled the whole structure, making it the largest and best appointed hotel in the Slocan district. A two storey wide veranda has been built around three sides of the hotel and baths installed, the dining room changed and greatly enlarged, a comfortable downstairs sitting room installed, rooms all newly papered and painted and next week the painters will be at work giving the exterior a renovating. With a fast launch at the disposal of the guests, etc., the Newmarket hotel should soon attract numbers of tourists to this part of the beautiful Slocan district.

New Denver, by virtue of its lovely location on the shores of Slocan Lake, earned the nickname "Lucerne of America." (It should be noted that Kaslo was also at times referred to as such.) Historian Greg Nesteroff shared the following information from the Greenwood *Ledge*, which on June 19, 1913, praised the efforts of Newmarket owner Andrew Jacobson in helping New Denver merit the comparison to the idyllic location in Switzerland:

> It is 20 years since Andrew Jacobson came to New Denver, and in that time, he has through his own industry become a rich and influential citizen of the Lucerne of America, since he became proprietor of the Newmarket hotel. He has made that house one of the best hotels in the province. The hotel is now heated by steam, lit by electricity, supplied with flush closets, bathrooms, and many other modern conveniences. The dining room is one of the largest in the mountains and even epicures can find no objection to the cuisine. A long verandah halfway around the building provides a delightful place for tourists to sit and watch the magnificent sunsets that have made the Slocan famous. From its balconies can be seen the unrivalled scenery that will yet make the Lucerne of America one of the greatest resorts for tourists on the continent. The hotel has recently been painted by that famous house painter, John Roche, who hails from the county of Cork, and knows how to paint a building so that it will harmonize with scenery. Mr. Jacobson deserves great credit for providing that beauty spot, the Lucerne of America, with such an excellent and up-to-date hostelry."

The Newmarket continued to draw tourists over the years. The Greenwood *Ledge* on June 5, 1919, noted that "Tourists and others will find the Newmarket Hotel at New Denver one of the best places in the west to stop at for a few weeks. Under the management of Andrew Jacobson, this famous old hotel is a delight to all who travel in the Slocan."

The hotel was burgled in May 1930, with the robber (or robbers) making off with sixty dollars from two registers after breaking into the bar from a cellar.[39]

In the summer of 1932, the *Vancouver Sun* noted on June 4 that Andrew Jacobson, proprietor of the Newmarket Hotel, was making improvements to the hotel building and had installed a putting green for the use of guests and local golfers.[40]

BC directories for 1934, 1936, and 1939 continued to list Andrew Jacobson as the proprietor of the Newmarket Hotel.

The opening of the Big Bend Highway in the spring of 1942 along with local road improvements boded well for the business at the Newmarket Hotel.

During the Second World War, New Denver became a Japanese Canadian internment camp. Not long after the outbreak of hostilities and Japan's attack on Canadian troops in Hong Kong in December 1941, men of Japanese descent between the ages of eighteen and forty-five were sent to labour camps in the Interior of British Columbia or farther into Eastern Canada. Additionally, approximately 1,500 women, children, and elderly men were sent to the "Orchard," a small section of New Denver set up to house them. New Denver's Nikkei Internment Memorial Centre, a National Historic Site, is dedicated to the history of the 27,000 Japanese Canadians who were interned by the Canadian government.

The 1945–47 British Columbia and Yukon Directories continue to list Andrew Jacobson as proprietor of the Newmarket Hotel in New Denver, but on January 22, 1948, the *Calgary Herald* noted in the classified ads that "Mr. Taffrie is selling the 29-room New Market Hotel at New Denver. It is a licenced hotel with a full basement, garage and coal shed. Owner retiring."

He must not have been able to sell the hotel quickly as a near identical ad appeared in the *Province* on April 6, 1948, again mentioning Mr. Taffrie as the owner. Then, on July 2, 1949, the Edmonton Journal ran an ad stating that J. Mikita, who perhaps had bought the hotel from Mr. Taffrie, was selling the Newmarket Hotel.

The BC Directory for 1955 lists a C.N. Uphill as proprietor of the Newmarket and Janet Ono as a waitress. Mrs. Clifford Uphill was still on hand in 1962: "Mrs. Clifford Uphill, of the Newmarket Hotel in New Denver, admires the painting hanging on the beer parlour walls of a huge mural of a steam-wheeler [the SS *Slocan*] of 1897 vintage." The artist, Jack Lines, had painted it with ordinary house paint over top of the old wallpaper.[41]

The *Nanaimo Daily News* on September 11, 1967, ran an article on the Newmarket Hotel in New Denver, saying it was "one of the last-standing hotels of earlier days with its large verandah and fancy wood scroll-work. There is much history and beauty in the Slocan and Kootenay country."

BC historian N.L. Bill Barlee wrote in *Gold Creeks and Ghost Towns* in 1972, "Today the mining activity has lessened and New Denver isn't the busy centre it once was but it has retained much of its old atmosphere; the Newmarket Hotel is still there down by the waterfront."

On October 5, 1973, the venerable Newmarket Hotel met the fate of so many other pioneering hotels, burning to the ground. The *Vancouver Sun* on October 6 wrote: "Hotel Razed—The 80-year-old Newmarket Hotel, home to generations of miners, loggers and travellers in this West Kootenay town, was destroyed by fire early today. No one was injured in the blaze."

An obituary appeared in the *Calgary Herald* on September 14, 1992, for the long-time cook at the Newmarket Hotel in New Denver, Irene Sylvia Enokson.

The *Silver Standard,* the newsletter of the Silvery Slocan Historical Society, in its Spring 2014 issue (Vol. 1, No. 4), discusses the fire that destroyed the historic New Market Hotel in New Denver.

Until 1973, the historic Newmarket Hotel continued to operate near the waterfront on Slocan Lake, and a visit inside brought a sense of the excitement when New Denver and the whole of the Silvery Slocan ran with the excitement of "silver fever."

OUTLET HOTEL

(1896–1966)
Procter

FROM SLOCAN CITY, we head east to the unincorporated hamlet of Procter, located on the south shore entrance to the West Arm of Kootenay Lake approximately, approximately thirty-five kilometres east of Nelson. Previously called Kootenay City, the community received its name from Thomas Gregg Procter (1862–1913), who managed the Kootenay Valley Company, which was active in real estate in the area.[42] A townsite was planned in anticipation of the coming of the BC Southern Railway from Crowsnest Pass to Nelson, which was never built.

In 1891, Procter bought land at the outlet of Kootenay Lake, where he built his home and tried his hand at farming. Procter soon expanded his house, adding a hunting and fishing lodge that five years later became the Outlet Hotel, which opened in 1896.[43] Thomas Gregg Procter was one of nine siblings that included a twin brother, John; all were born in England to Gilbert Procter and Mary Gorton. He served in the Royal Navy for five years joining at the tender age of fourteen, and then, upon his release, immigrated to the United States, where, in 1881, he became a cattle dealer. On a visit home to England in 1888, he married Beatrice Arrowsmith, and in 1891, the couple moved to the Kootenay, where Procter became involved in a variety of real estate, mining, and industrial promotions.[44]

The Outlet Hotel was opened by Thomas Procter and business partners Busk and West in the spring of 1896. The first

The Outlet Hotel. 988.040.1348. KOOTENAY LAKE HISTORICAL SOCIETY

advertisement was placed in Nelson's The *Miner*, which read: "Outlet Hotel, opposite Balfour, Best fishing in Kootenay Outlet, lawn tennis, sail and rowing boats. Specially suitable for dancing and picnic parties."[45] (The community of Balfour was on the north side of the entrance to the western are of Kootenay Lake.) The Outlet Hotel grounds became recognized over the years as an ideal spot for summer picnics; pleasant memories of frolicking in the sun and on the beach would remain with its guests for a lifetime.

The Outlet was open to the public during summer season only, from about June 1 to the end of September. In May 1897, Procter and partners leased the hotel to J.C. Blandy for two years.[46] In the meantime, Procter kept busy with his real estate business, and one property high on his selling list was his own Outlet Hotel: "An investment as good as a 'Klondyke Claim' and for sale at a bargain, the Outlet Hotel... hotel contains 18 rooms, 13 bedrooms, bar, storeroom, kitchen, sitting room and dining room; lawn tennis grounds, summer houses (cottages), with steamboat landing on grounds—price $5,000."[47] Until the hotel sold, Procter continued to lease it out. When John Blandy's lease expired in May 1899, Mr. and Mrs. R. Daniels became the new lessees. The Danielses completely remodeled and updated the Outlet Hotel, advertising that "special attention will be given to ladies who wish to spend a few weeks holidays" at the hotel.[48] Meanwhile, the Procters moved to Nelson, where Thomas had his real estate business and also worked as a mining broker.

Once the Outlet Hotel opened again to the public for the summer season, a tradition began that was to last for as long as the hotel was in operation. The hotel began to enjoy an ever-increasing popularity once the word got out. Not only was it a fine hotel to book for a week or more, but it soon proved to be the place to go for a summer picnic, dance, or similar event for individuals and organized social events. One group that visited in the summer of 1898 were treated to a first-class orchestra, a dance, dinner, and round-trip fare for one dollar.[49]

That October, the SS *Moyie* was launched from the CPR dock at Nelson and would serve communities on Kootenay Lake for the next fifty-nine years. Besides being a working boat, picking up and dropping off goods, freight, and passengers, the sternwheeler would ferry excursionists to resort towns. On Wednesday afternoons during the summer, the *Moyie* would cast off from the Nelson wharf, crowded with excursionists dressed in their best holiday attire, bound for the hot springs at Ainsworth or the picnic grounds at the Outlet Hotel at Procter. On Sundays, the *Moyie* was available for charter and often used for trips to Procter filled with picnickers. Excited children would often scurry around while the parents enjoyed the moving scenery as they relaxed on deck chairs or enjoyed a promenade on the deck. Once the boat docked at Procter, everyone would disembark and head to the Outlet Hotel grounds, where the fun was waiting. "The rest of the day would be full of sporting activities and games, like sack races, football games, diving and swimming contests. Best of all were the big kegs of ice cream packed in slated ice and plenty of peanut and candy scramers."[50] As the sun set, the day-trippers would head back to the boat, which departed in the gloaming of the day. Sometimes an impromptu singsong would start up while the children began to nod off one by one with memories of the day's festivities fresh in their dreams.

After having the hotel on the market for years, Procter finally sold it to Mr. and Mrs. Gilbert Snow in 1906, and for the next twelve years, they operated the hotel as a summer resort.[51] Gilbert Snow knew a good thing when he saw it, and while making renovations, he made sure they didn't tamper with the successful formula that the Procters started. In March 1908, the Snows more than doubled the size of the Outlet Hotel by adding a large two-storey extension to the west of the original hotel. Business was very good at the hotel. Sports fishermen couldn't believe the fine fishing to be had at Procter, so the attractive addition to the hotel came at the right time. The new owners made sure to get plenty of photographs of their guests' catches and also made sure to mention the fine fishing in their advertisements. Summer excursions to the Outlet Hotel continued with the *Kuskanook*, the *Kokanee*, or the *Moyie* making round trips from Nelson. The evening sailings were particularly popular; the cool breeze was refreshing after a day of fun in the summer sun. Adding to the enjoyment of the trip was live music provided on board by Mrs. McIntyre's orchestra. Arrangements were made beforehand at the Outlet Hotel for dancing in the dining room, spilling out onto the lawn, which was illuminated for the occasion.[52]

At the start of the 1913 summer season, the Snows accepted an offer from the CPR to buy the place. The CPR offered $34,000 and would pay them to stay on and manage the hotel for the company.[53] In 1915, the CPR had telephone and telegraph poles and lines connected from Nelson through Procter to Pilot Bay. Now it was possible to phone in telegrams.[54] A bit of excitement took place in August 1916 when Premier William John Bowser and his entourage stayed overnight at the Outlet Hotel during the premier's swing through the Kootenays.[55]

In April 1917, the licence for the Outlet Hotel was transferred from Mr. and Mrs. Snow to H.H. Pitts,[56] but it was William Ward, who bought the hotel the following April, who owned the hotel longer than anyone else. William ("Billy") Arthur Ward, with his wife Anna, purchased the Outlet Hotel in April 1918 and they would operate it for the next twenty-three years.[57] The Ward name goes back to the pioneer days of Nelson, where William's father, Thomas M. Ward, ran the Ward & Corning Saloon on Vernon Street as early as June 1890.[58] Billy Ward followed in his father's footsteps, operating either the same or a nearby saloon by 1897. By 1905, Ward was bartending at the prestigious Hume Hotel and, by 1912, he was the proprietor of the Nelson House.[59] Billy Ward had the experience and the temperament to operate a hotel successfully and jumped at the chance to buy a resort hotel for a pleasant change of pace.

Summer seasons continued to draw guests to the Outlet Hotel into the 1920s. Incredible fishing, lazy summer days on the beach, and picnicking on the grounds were as popular as ever, and the Saturday evening dances resumed each June.[60]

In January 1929, the CPR faced a major calamity when the Surprise Creek bridge, a few miles east of Glacier near Rogers Pass, collapsed, putting the main railway line out of commission for several weeks and killing train engineer Bert Woodland and fireman C. Gibbons.[61] All vital east-west traffic was diverted south to the Kettle Valley route until the bridge was rebuilt. All available tugs and sternwheelers were put into use to transport passengers and express freight by boat. Freight railcars were ferried on barges over the thirty miles from Procter to Kootenay Landing, near Kuskonook. Normal service returned when the Surprise Creek bridge was replaced, but the managers at the CPR were now aware that an alternate east-west route was necessary to avoid any future disruptions.

Little did the Wards know that the summer seasons of 1929 and 1930 were to be the zenith for the Outlet Hotel. The CPR opened a new, thirty-mile rail line from Procter to Kootenay Landing in January 1931 that put the sternwheelers out of business. After the line opened, only the weekly boat to Kaslo, Lardeau, and Argenta remained in operation.[62] Although there was a road from Nelson to Procter, the Outlet Hotel relied heavily on the sternwheelers to bring boatloads of guests to the hotel. With that now ended, the hotel took a serious financial hit. In spite of the downturn in business, the Wards soldiered on until that fateful day in January 1941 when news came of the death of Billy Ward.

William Arthur Ward died at the Outlet Hotel at the age of seventy. Ward worked in the hospitality industry for forty-four years, first as a bartender in a Nelson saloon. But he wasn't limited to saloons and hotels: "His many talents included construction worker, teamster, prospector, miner, survey worker and sportsman."[63] Mrs. Ward became the sole owner of the Outlet Hotel and in the summer of 1942, she put it up for sale.[64] The new proprietor changed the name to the Holiday Inn in 1944. It was an end of the era.

The Outlet Hotel continued to operate under its new proprietor, William Klein, who also ran the general store in Procter. Tom Lymbery, author of *Tom's Gray Creek: A Kootenay Memoir, Part I: The Early Years, Gray Creek, BC*, mentioned that he and a few friends attended a wedding in the church at Procter in December 1948. Afterward, the groom treated the guests to a beer at the Outlet Hotel beer parlour. "To get to Procter we caught the Greyhound [bus] across the ferry to Balfour where we rented a rowboat to Procter."[65]

By 1966, the Outlet Hotel was a memory. The furnishings were auctioned off and the old historic resort hotel was demolished to make way for residential houses.[66]

PHAIR HOTEL

(1891-1903); Strathcona Hotel (1903-55)
Southwest corner of Victoria Street
and Stanley Street, Nelson

AT TIMES it is necessary to go beyond the borders of British Columbia to learn more about those great entrepreneurs that helped shape BC's social history. This is the case with the following extraordinary hotelier, Mr. Edwin Ernest Phair (1851-1929) and his Phair Hotel in Nelson, BC, which was later renamed the Strathcona Hotel.

Phair was born in Fredericton, New Brunswick, in 1851. As a young man, he worked his way up to the position of manager of the Kent Northern Railway, which operated throughout Nova Scotia, New Brunswick, and Quebec. An extension of the Kent Northern went into the resort town of Richibucto, New Brunswick.

> At Kent Junction the Kent Northern RR may be taken for the quiet little town of Richibucto, the capital of Kent County, near the mouth of the Richibucto River. The neighbourhood is interesting to tourists chiefly for the typical Acadian town of St. Louis, with its sacred well and grotto, 7 miles by rail from Richibucto. The fine summer hotel of Richibucto, known as "The Beeches[67] [sic]," is now closed [for the season]. The name Richibucto means "the river of fire."[68]

Phair learned his trade as a hotelman in New Brunswick in his formative years before moving to British Columbia and becoming an important figure in BC social history.

The Strathcona Hotel. TN-83.169.29. NELSON AND DISTRICT MUSEUM, ARCHIVES, ART GALLERY AND HISTORICAL SOCIETY

Chris Bradley, the great-grandson of Edwin Ernest ("Pop") Phair, confirmed in an email to me that before his great-grandfather built the Phair Hotel in Nelson, he was proprietor of the Beaches Hotel in Richibucto, New Brunswick. In his lifetime, Edwin Phair operated at least five hotels over the years: the Beaches Hotel in New Brunswick; the Phair Hotel (later the Strathcona Hotel) in Nelson, British Columbia; the Grand Hotel in Spokane, Washington; the Prince George Hotel in Prince George, British Columbia; and, for a brief time, the Halcyon Hot Springs Hotel.

In the spring of 1891, Phair came to Vancouver after negotiating a deal with a group of Vancouver investors keen to build a large hotel in Nelson. The investors wanted an experienced manager for their new, as yet unnamed hotel and heard that the popular resort town of Richibucto—one of the best known resorts in Canada—was where proprietor Phair gained much of his esteemed reputation as a most capable hotel man.[69] The group of investors consisted of Mr. Dan McGillivary, H.F. Keefer, Captain Tatlow, R.C. Ferguson, and Mr. Vicker of Vancouver, along with H. Selous of Nelson and E. Phair of New Brunswick. They visited the hotel site in Nelson and were satisfied. Next, they looked for a contractor, as Phair had agreed to manage the hotel. In June 1891, construction began, and Phair left Vancouver for Nelson to begin his tenure as manager.[70]

To the new manager's delight, the unnamed hotel's planned opening was for October 15, 1891, and it would be called the Phair Hotel. It cost $12,000 to build, plus the cost of furnishings and supplies ordered from Winnipeg.[71] The hotel was grand, offering thirty-five comfortable rooms with hot and cold running water, steam heat, flush (water) closets, and electric bells. "The Honeymoon Suite could not be rivalled anywhere in the Interior." The dining room was spacious and beautiful, described as

> the finest in the Kootenays with the most up to date cooking stoves and staff. Beautifully engraved menus graced each table, and the servers clad in spotless uniforms were at your elbow at a moment's notice. The linens were crisp, the crystal fine and the sterling silverware heavy and polished. The separate parlours offered exquisite furnishings, with fine Persian carpeting for the comfort of both male and female guests alike. No expense was spared, and no amenity was missed.[72]

Chef Robinson, late of the Adman House of Boston, was in charge of the culinary department at the Phair, and a fine new carriage met the trains and sternwheelers.

Prior to the gala opening of the Phair Hotel, the assize court held a session in the hotel as a temporary location, with Mr. Justice Crease presiding.[73]

The new hotel was perched on a hillside, prompting one happy customer to comment on the commanding view of the Outlet River.[74] Furnished rooms were available for overnight stays or up to a month or more if required.

In 1897, the same year that the city of Nelson was incorporated, Phair planned to build a large addition to the hotel at a cost of between $2,800 and $7,000. "The town is alive and the hotels are full."[75] With the hotel addition completed, Ernest Phair was asked if he would fill in as temporary manager at the Halcyon Hot Springs for a limited time until a new manager was found. Phair accepted, bringing his excellent managerial skills to that fine holiday resort hotel.[76] Perhaps it was the change of scenery, temporarily leaving Nelson and the Phair Hotel to be acting manager of the Halcyon Hotel Springs Hotel, but Phair enjoyed the change and began looking at other prospects. By 1903, Phair would sell his popular hotel in Nelson.

In June 1900, a fire broke out in the basement of the Phair Hotel. It was extinguished quickly, and the water caused more damage than the flames. This was the first of a series of fires that would plague the hotel over the years, leading up to a major fire in 1938 and followed by the most devastating fire in 1955.

Back around the turn of the twentieth century, business at the Phair Hotel couldn't be better. In order to celebrate the opening of the Nelson Tramway, a huge banquet was held at the Phair Hotel "where a corps of pretty waitresses fitted [sic] about serving steaming and tasty soup, delicious morsels of fish, appetizing entrees and savory joints, while a company of white uniformed boys kept the glasses of the guests full."[77] An important political figure arrived for an afternoon reception at the Phair Hotel in the fall of 1901. Months earlier, in February 1901, Mr. Robert Laird Borden had been nominated by the aging Sir Charles Tupper to take over as leader of the Conservative Party of Canada. Tupper, dubbed the "Cumberland war horse" and loved by his party, had rallied behind the young nominee, and the Conservative Party was showing off their new leader with a cross-Canada tour.[78] Borden and his entourage left Rossland by train for Nelson, where they were met by fifty important Conservatives of the city. Borden later gave a speech at the Phair Hotel that was very well attended.[79]

In 1903, Ernest Phair made an application to the BC Chief Commissioner of Lands and Works for a licence to prospect for coal and petroleum on the Flathead River near Elko, BC. He also mentioned to friends the possibility of opening a new hotel in Morrissey, BC.[80] So it didn't come as too much of a shock to most people when, two weeks later, Phair announced that the new manager of the Phair Hotel was Mr. B. Tomkins.

Colonel Belville ("Ben") Tomkins was born in New York City on New Year's Day in 1852. As a young man, he became a printer's apprentice but for reasons unknown had decided to change careers and went to sea. By 1891, the seafaring life saw Tomkins employed as a steward upon the CPR steamship *Lytton*, which plied the Arrow Lakes between Revelstoke and Northport, Washington. A while later, the *Lytton* was assigned to towing barges of iron ore to the smelter at Trail.[81] In 1893, Tomkins met and married the love of his life, Miss Margaret Hutchinson of California.[82] It was that same year that Tomkins decided to change careers yet again and got some direct hotel experience when he was hired as bartender at the Crown Point Hotel in Trail. Tomkins worked at the Crown Point in Trail until 1901, gaining valuable experience about the hotel and bar business.

The Tomkinses moved to the mining town of Phoenix, BC, in the Boundary Country after the manager of the Victoria Hotel hired Ben Tomkins as a desk clerk. Within a year of arriving at the Victoria Hotel, Tomkins worked his way up to manager.[83] Tomkins's star was rising, as he kept his options open for other opportunities in the hotel business within BC. He had proven to be a successful hotel manager and had gained considerable experience in various positions within the hotel business. "He is distinctively American in spirit and actions, possessing the marked enterprise and foresight which have been the dominant factors in the rapid settlement, improvement and development of this great western hemisphere. He possesses marked individuality, strong resolution and reliability, and he is enrolled among the best citizens of the Kootenay district," wrote the contemporary historian R. Edward Gosnell in 1909.[84]

In March 1903, the Tomkinses were on the move again, from Phoenix to Nelson, where Ben Tomkins took over the management of the Phair Hotel. This was a giant career move forward for Tomkins, and the larger urban centre of Nelson gave him the challenge he needed.

Ernest Phair was moving on too. He left the Phair Hotel after twelve years of successfully managing the popular hostelry. The Phair Hotel and the more recently built Hume Hotel were the best built and managed hotels in Nelson at the time and arguably the best hotels in all the Kootenay.[85] Phair was offered a position to manage the Grand Hotel in Spokane, Washington.

With a new manager came a new name: the Phair Hotel became the Strathcona Hotel by September 1903,[86] very likely named for Lord and Lady Strathcona.[87]

An important banquet was held in November just prior to the annual Christmas celebration at the Strathcona, the sixth annual celebration of the founding of the Nelson Caledonian Society, in which copious amounts of whisky and haggis were consumed. The clans gathered around the festive board and savoured the good things provided by their amicable and capable host, Ben Tomkins, and his hard-working staff. The toast list was read, with speeches and songs backed by a mandolin and piano that continued into the wee hours.[88] Tomkins managed the Strathcona Hotel for four years until March 1907, when the hotel was sold to an Australian buyer.

Reginald G. Webb, from Perth, Australia, purchased the Strathcona Hotel for $40,000 with plans to expand and improve it.[89] Webb intended to manage the hotel himself, so Ben Tomkins was out of a job and wondering what to do and where he and his wife would eventually wind up. As time wound down to Tomkins's last day as manager, a group of people were planning a surprise farewell event for the couple, as the Nelson *Daily Times* resported:

> Surprised Mine Host ~ Presentation to Belville Tomkins by Strathcona Guests. A large and representative gathering witnessed the pleasant little ceremony in the Strathcona dining room at 9 pm last evening when friends of Mr. and Mrs. B. Tomkins made a surprise presentation to the couple who ran the Strathcona Hotel these past four years and won the hearts of many who regret their decision to retire. Mr. Belville Tomkins was presented with a diamond ring and the following letter that read, "Dear Sir... [we] beg you accept the accompanying ring as a slight token of our

esteem appreciation of the winning geniality you have shown towards all those that have had the pleasure to meet you during the years you have been associated with the public in the Kootenays. It is with sincere regret that we learn about your departure from Nelson"... In addition to the diamond ring, a large cut glass rose vase was given to Mrs. Tomkins.[90]

In June 1907, the liquor licence was transferred from Ben Tomkins to the new owner. Mr. and Mrs. Tomkins then received some welcome news. G.P. Wells, the new owner of the other major hotel in Nelson, the Hume, asked Tomkins if he would become his new manager. A grateful Tomkins accepted the offer.[91]

Things didn't work out for the new owner of the Strathcona Hotel, and a year to the day that he had bought it, Reginal G. Webb was forced to sell the Strathcona Hotel by auction through the Mortgage Act. A familiar face returned to the Strathcona Hotel after the sale. Edwin Phair was hired by the new owners to manage the Strathcona Hotel.[92] Meanwhile, Tomkins managed the Hume for a few years and then went on to manage the Allan Hotel in Rossland, and after that, the Leland Hotel in Kamloops.[93] The Tomkinses retired to California around 1913, where it was reported that Ben Tomkins died in San Francisco some years later.[94]

About the time of Tomkins's death, Edwin Phair left the management of the Strathcona Hotel, for good this time. He was replaced by Frank B. Whiting, who managed the Strathcona for just over a year before passing the job on to James Marshall in September 1914.

Phair began a whole new venture in Saanich on Vancouver Island, having been hired to oversee the building of the new summer resort at Brentwood Bay.[95] Mr. and Mrs. Phair had a son, H.J. Phair, who eventually opened the Queen Cigar Store on Baker Street in Nelson. The Phairs also had a daughter, Gretchen, who in 1915 married John Ayton ("Jock") Gibson, who was postmaster of Nelson for a time. John Gibson also landed a job that his father-in-law once held: manager of the Strathcona Hotel in Nelson.[96]

Over the next ten years, from 1915 to 1925, three proprietors came and went at the Strathcona Hotel, contributing their unique style to the historic establishment. In 1925, Armen and Mary Papazian bought the Strathcona Hotel and ran it for the next thirteen years.

Before coming to North America, Armanag ("Armen") D. Papazian, and his wife Marie ("Mary") Papazian, had lived and worked in an Armenian enclave in the troubled Ottoman Empire. It is not clear whether the couple were Turkish or Armenian, but the genesis of the surname "Papazian" may hold a clue, as papaz is Turkish for priest. The Papazians fled to the United States to escape the turmoil of war and slaughter when the genocide of 1909 saw mass murders of Armenians by the Ottoman Turks.[97] The Papazians arrived in New York City, glad to have left the war and misery behind, and planned for a bright future for themselves in a new land. By 1911, the Papazians were living in Nelson, BC, but may have come to the Kootenay town as early as 1910.[98]

Armen was a skilled watchmaker and jeweller, and Mary was an excellent seamstress. Within a few years of arriving in Nelson, they each had their own shop in town. Mary Papazian received high praise for her "hand-made laces of variety and beauty of workmanship not frequently seen in this country" on display in her shop window on Baker Street. But the piece that stole the show was a dress of hand-made lace that carried off first prize at the Turin exhibition. Mary was "herself a lace artist with marked ability."[99] Armen Papazian, who had been trained as a watchmaker, jeweller, and optometrist, had worked for Tiffany & Company in New York for a brief time before coming to BC. His new jewellery store was also on Baker Street, near his wife's shop.[100]

Armen and Mary Papazian were hard workers and both produced fine work that sold well to an appreciative public. Both were careful with their money, yet gave generously to charities and local fundraisers. Perhaps the couple were grateful to be in their adopted country, Canada, a land of plenty and opportunity, and relieved at their luck to have escaped the horrors of war in their troubled homeland. Over time, Armen and Mary invested in property, buying local Nelson businesses that included the Plaza Café and Starland Theatre building. One of the most significant purchases took place in 1924, when the Papazians submitted a sealed offer to buy the Strathcona Hotel, which was accepted.[101] Mary Papazian became manager of the hotel and ran it for the next twelve years.[102]

Shortly after the Papazians bought the Strathcona Hotel, a fire broke out in one of the buildings they owned that housed their extensive library. It was a total loss as what few books that didn't burn were unsalvageable due to water damage. In the same month as the fire, Armen Papazian received word that his uncle, also a jeweller, who worked in Constantinople (soon to become Istanbul), had died, leaving Armen and his brother $200,000 in his will. However, the Turkish government decreed the will invalid as Armen and his brother, who was living in Cairo at the time of his uncle's death, were no longer living in Turkey. While it would have been good to have the extra money for more possible investments, Armen and Mary were much more concerned with the loss of their library of precious books.[103]

The Papazians kept up to date with the disturbing events that continued to unfold in Turkey. In 1927, after hearing of the plight of Armenian refugees who were forced to flee and were streaming into Greece, they decided to act. The couple agreed to adopt two siblings through the Canadian Near East Relief Organization and Save the Children Fund. It was reported that there were 50,000 homeless waifs in the Near East, but the number was most likely much higher as the long campaign of genocide on the Armenians and the Kurds continued in the lands of the previous Ottoman Empire. Little Levon and his sister Satinik were brought from a refugee camp in Greece to the safety of Nelson, BC. After a few days in Nelson, Levon Papazian summed it up nicely when he was quoted saying, "This is a beautiful country with no soldiers to kill my daddy."[104] The following year, it was reported that over a "twelve-year period the Canadian-Armenian Near East Relief and Save the Children have rescued approximately one million refugees of which 132,532 were children."[105]

The Papazian family lived in comfortable quarters in the popular Strathcona Hotel. Levon and Satinik had a happy childhood, and, in time, both graduated from Nelson High School. Levon eventually continued his studies when he was accepted to medical school at McGill University in Montreal. Mary Papazian continued to operate her successful dressmaking business and to manage the hotel. In 1937, when Frank and Florence Manefroid took over the management duties at the Strathcona Hotel, the Papazian family still owned it but were considering selling it.

Fire has always been the biggest threat, not only to large wooden hotels like the Strathcona, but for all structures in the towns and cities of the BC Interior that traditionally had long, hot summers. The Strathcona Hotel had its fair share of small fires. Shortly before Mr. and Mrs. Papazian put in their offer to buy the Strathcona Hotel, a commercial traveller staying at the hotel in the summer of 1923 was arrested after it was discovered that he had attempted to light a number of fires inside the Strathcona Hotel. He was immediately arrested and appeared in court the following day.[106] The fire that destroyed the Papazian library and the building it was in was deemed suspicious. The most serious fire to date came in June 1938. The *Province* wrote the following day, "Nelson City Hotel Destroyed by Fire."[107] But it was not quite accurate. The fire began in a room in the attic on the fifth floor of the Strathcona Hotel where two elderly ladies and some children lived. All sixty occupants, including staff and families, got out safely, but the top floor was destroyed. Other than some water damage, the fourth floor down to the ground floor remained intact.[108] Armen Papazian assessed the damage, and repairs began soon afterward, but this was the last straw and the Papazians searched for a buyer of the Strathcona.

Mary Papazian was content to run her successful clothing and dressmaking shop while Armen invested in a couple of silver and gold mines near Nelson. In partnership with T.L. Paris, Armen Papazian owned and operated the King Solomon Mine Claim (Lot 14628), about ten miles northeast of Nelson, where they were mining for gold. He was also president of the Twilight Extension Mining operation west of Nelson that had four claims on Forty-nine Creek.[109] Armen thought it prudent for a jeweller to own a gold mine, and owning one could only enhance his already successful jewellery business in Nelson.

In 1939, the Papazians sold the Strathcona Hotel to Thomas J. Allan, who sold it to William D. Matthews. The Papazians retired to Los Angeles, where, in July 1949, seventy-year-old Armen Papazian died. He was survived by his wife Mary and his daughter Satinik.[110] Sadly, Levon Papazian predeceased his father when he took his own life by shooting himself on Christmas Day, 1942, in Montreal. He was twenty-three years old.[111]

Little did proprietor William ("Bill") D. Matthews and his wife Lucy Matthews know, when he bought the aging Strathcona Hotel in 1945, that they would be the last owners. The business still operated as a hotel, but it also provided apartments for a number of seniors who rented on a monthly basis. On a spring morning in 1955, a fire broke out.

Shortly after one in the morning on Friday, May 27, 1955, while most guests and residents of the Strathcona Hotel were asleep, someone smelled smoke and got up to investigate. They found that the halls were quickly filling up with smoke, and an alarm was turned on. Thirteen firefighters rushed to the scene and were met by smoke and flames and people screaming for help from the upper-floor windows, trapped by the choking smoke and heat of the fire. Ted Meyers was awoken by the sounds of screams and blaring sirens. The thirteen-year-old and his brothers, Pat (eleven) and Edward (fourteen), were in their apartment on the third floor when Ted realized the hotel was on fire and made a mad dash for the window. He escaped down to the landing level, where he found a man who helped him to the ground and away from danger. Back inside, Ed grabbed Pat and led him out the window and down a ladder that served as a fire escape between the bay windows of their apartment and the one across the hall. Pat went first. They'd used this ladder before to avoid walking down to the street, not realizing they were conducting their own fire drill. The bottom rung was a long way from the ground. Pat jumped and a firefighter caught him. Ed followed. All three boys made it to safety and were reunited with their frantic mother, who had been working late at the Cameo Café when she learned of the fire.[112]

Paul Franck, a twenty-eight-year-old typewriter serviceman, was awoken by the commotion and instantly smelled the smoke that was pouring into his room from under the door. He jumped up and quickly realized his life was in danger and that he could not escape the smoke and heat by going into the hall, so he went and opened the window and slid out until he was just hanging by his fingertips on the hot cement windowsill. "I remember screaming my lungs out, hollering for help. Then the fireman came with a ladder and took me off."[113] He was saved from serious injury or death by not having to jump from his third-floor room. It was estimated that twenty-five of the forty-five survivors of the fire were rescued by firefighters using their ladders. No nets were available for people to jump into, and firefighters only had one aerial ladder to reach those desperately waiting for rescue on the upper floors. Firefighter Don Cunningham worked the aerial ladder at a frantic pace, as so many lives were at stake.[114]

Nineteen-year-old rescuer Jim Peck, a volunteer firefighter, heard a cry down the hall but couldn't see a thing due to the thick black smoke that was everywhere. He managed to follow the sound and grabbed hold of a hysterical and frightened lady, whom he managed to pull to safety down the ladder. He went back into the black and heated hall where he found two more people. As he walked them to safety, he could hear the walls creaking and the floor shaking. He said he had no time to pray as he had to get them out before it was too late. His mask came off in the attempt to push a window open, and he blacked out. He woke up in the hospital suffering from smoke inhalation but made a full recovery.[115] Of the fifty-one people registered at the hotel, forty-five were saved, and sadly, six perished. The oldest was John Thomas Price, eighty-nine, and the youngest was Rudy Smington, ten.[116]

A new RCMP subdivision headquarters was eventually built on the site where the Strathcona Hotel had once stood. In 1992, the building served as the Nelson Police Department and Nelson Public Library.

HUME HOTEL

(1898-1979); Heritage Hotel (1980-2005);
Hume Hotel & Spa (2005-Present)
Vernon at Ward Street, Nelson

ON THURSDAY, March 17, 1898, insurance man Belville Perry, who worked for the Confederation Life Insurance Company, walked into the spanking-new lobby of the Hume Hotel and signed the hotel register, becoming the first guest in what would become the landmark hotel of Nelson.[117] One-hundred and twenty-four years later, the Hume Hotel & Spa is still in operation at the time of this writing, providing first-class service and amenities to its guests.

The late 1890s were a boom time for the burgeoning "Queen City of the Kootenays," initially built on the lucrative mines and sawmills that were working full tilt. Between 1892 and 1893, fifty buildings were erected in Nelson at a total cost of $94,150, and one of those new buildings was the residence for Mr. and Mrs. J. Fred Hume.[118] In 1897, when the city of Nelson was incorporated, John Fred Hume, together with Horace D. Hume and J.A. Kirkpatrick, commissioned contractors McLarty and Clayton to build their new hotel.[119] Citizens of Nelson couldn't miss the beehive of activity throughout the city as the buzz of handsaws and hammering of nails became a daily routine. They could not help but be impressed by the imposing wooden structure taking shape at the northeast corner of Ward and Vernon Streets. As building progressed, the five-storey hotel loomed over the street and quickly became the talk of the town even before it opened.[120]

Postcard of Hume Hotel, circa. 1907–12. GLEN A. MOFFORD COLLECTION

Alexander Charles Ewart, his wife Nettie, and their family moved to Nelson in 1897 from Victoria. Ewart designed a number of buildings in Nelson, including the McKillop block, Judge Forin's house, and the beautiful Hume Hotel. "Designed in the Queen Anne style, the Hume had a characteristic corner tower, oriel windows and recessed balconies as well as an ornate interior with modern amenities such as electricity and steam radiators."[121] The Hume Hotel was built for pioneer storekeeper John Fredrick Hume and his wife, Lydia Jane Hume (née Irvine). J. Fred Hume was also a miner, notary public, and political figure in British Columbia. He represented West Kootenay South in the Legislative Assembly of British Columbia from 1894 to 1898, serving as provincial secretary and then as minister of mines. Of Scottish descent, Hume was born in Jacksonville, New Brunswick, where he received his education. In 1891, Hume married Lydia J. Irvine and the couple moved to Nelson.[122]

The hotel was threatened by fire before construction was completed. A fire broke out in the Ward Street laundry building, perilously close to the unfinished Hume Hotel. The flame decimated the laundry, and if it weren't for the gallant effort of the

Nelson firefighters and a bucket brigade formed by a group of concerned citizens, the flames would have consumed the unfinished hotel. The fire was believed to have started in the drying room, where some pieces of washing became overheated and ignited. Portions of the Hume Hotel structure were singed, costing about $500 to replace.[123]

On opening day, March 17, 1898, the handsome new Hume Hotel opened with a grand celebration unlike any seen before in Nelson. The proud owners were elated, as was the public when they were permitted to finally get a closer view. The five-storey hotel, complete with a full basement, cost $60,000 and boasted a frontage of ninety-four feet on Vernon Street and seventy-five feet on Ward Street. Special features included fire appliances in every flat and fire escapes connected throughout. Beautifully carved and crafted oak could be found in the interior fittings and in the furnishings, lending to the sense of luxury and comfort. Imported in rough oak boards from Spokane, the wood was finished at Thomas Gray's mill. "The carving is elaborate and chaste, and the ideas well sustained throughout. A natural finish is given the fixtures, leaving the grain of the wood and the fineness of the work in bold relief. It is pronounced the most elaborate piece of work in the interior of the province and is the product of all home talent."[124]

Mr. Horace D. Hume, recently retired from ten years with the CPR dining car service, was the manager of the new Hume Hotel.[125] The goal was to open on St. Patrick's Day, but unfortunately the hotel wasn't quite finished on opening day, as the electric wiring and other essential internal fittings were still being installed. The great ball and supper had to be postponed but "it is only pleasure deferred."[126] It wasn't until March 23 that the palatial Hume Hotel was officially opened to the public, although guests had begun checking in six days earlier.[127]

Besides the usual meeting rooms, lush dining room, and regular amenities offered by most large hotels, the Hume had a large auditorium that served as an occasional sports venue. In December 1898, the boxing match to determine the Northwest Champion between Jerry Hall and all 133 pounds of his opponent,

Fred Ross, was held at the Hume auditorium. The boxers got to work in ten two-minute rounds, in which the exchanges were fast and furious, but "little science was displayed as the boxing tended to be of the windmill style." Hall was knocked down twice, but the condition of the floor may have played a part as it was not very even. There was no winner as the fight was declared a draw; but the spectators appeared to have enjoyed the live bout in their new surroundings.[128]

The Hume Hotel Company was incorporated in 1899 with capital totaling $50,000. The company was established for "facilitating traveling in the province by providing hotels and conveyances for the accommodation of travellers."[129] The stern-wheeler was the reliable mode of transportation, as roads were few, but there were well-worn trails. In March, the Hume Hotel bar received "the largest refrigerator ever," manufactured by McGee & Nichols.[130] It certainly got a lot of use as the hotel filled on a regular basis, as did the popular and ornate Hume bar.

A significant event for the city took place at the Hume Hotel when an enthusiastic gathering of hockey players and supporters formally reorganized the Nelson City Hockey Club. Officers were elected and prospects for the upcoming season were discussed.[131] A variety of different sports teams were active in the city, and they were not exclusive to men only. Women also had their hockey, baseball, lacrosse, and other teams that were highly competitive and popular.

A sad story came out of Nelson about a poor ex-school teacher, Mr. Goodrede, from Kuskonook (a village located on the eastern shore of south Kootenay Lake near Sirdar). Goodrede showed up at the police station in Nelson with several packages of cigarettes and insisted that the police take charge of them, claiming they were "doctored" by someone who would do him harm. The frantic man explained that the mirror in the Hume Hotel washroom had been arranged to cast a spell over him. He then rushed out of the police station to encounter fresh perils.[132]

In September 1901, Horace D. Hume stepped down from his job as manager of the Hume Hotel and was replaced by E.A. Edson.

Mr. and Mrs. Hume planned to spend two weeks vacationing in California and then return to Nelson to pursue other opportunities. The hotel staff presented Mr. Hume with a handsome opal-and-diamond scarf pin, and Mrs. Hume received a beautiful parasol inlaid with silver and mother of pearl.[133]

New manager Mr. Edson was on the job less than six months before he gave notice to depart to the town of Ferguson, where he purchased the Ferguson Hotel.[134] The changes in management did not affect the first-class service given to the guests of the hotel. J. Fred Hume saw to that. An example of that was when one of the guests, a Professor Foster, didn't care for the choices on the menu one evening in the dining room; the cook agreed to prepare anything Foster wanted, providing they had the appropriate meal items on hand.[135]

No matter how fine the service was at the Hume, one couldn't control the unpredictability of Mother Nature. One summer rainstorm was so prolific that it caused the main sewer to back up with such a force that it burst a hole in the pipe. Consequently, some basements in town, including at the Hume Hotel, become flooded with the sewer contents. It was reported that up to twelve feet of water with sand and silt caused damage to the Hume Hotel alone cost $2,000.[136]

First flood, then fire. Nelson was hit particularly hard by a lightning storm in the fall of 1905. Balls of fire rained down on the city as bolts of lightning hit houses and businesses. Guests at the Hume Hotel were astonished to see the lights go out and hear all the bells ringing in the big building. A bolt of lightning had turned the fuse box into a red-hot tangle of wires. "Another party in the Office Saloon down the street saw lightning play around the mirror and stand behind the bar. People on Ward Avenue saw lines of flame play along the wires. Mr. John Linebaugh was standing in the Nelson Transfer company office when a ball of fire hit him on the head and knocked him over."[137]

In 1907, J. Fred Hume sold his namesake hotel to George P. Wells, with the transfer of ownership taking effect on Dominion Day, July 1. The purchase price was not disclosed, but it was suspected to have sold in the neighbourhood of $50,000. Mr. Belville Tomkins, late of the Strathcona Hotel (previously profiled) would become the new manager. The signing of the contract of sale on June 22 marked the end of an era of sorts. The Hume family had owned the magnificent Hume Hotel in Nelson since it was first opened in 1898; J. Fred Hume had purchased his brother Horace's share in 1901.

No agent was used for the sale in 1907, and it marked one of the biggest transactions in the city for some time.[138] George Wells was the secretary of the Mountain Lumber Manufacturing Association and the son of philanthropist and millionaire Wilmer C. Wells.[139] Most likely, George's father, Wilmer Wells, backed up the purchase, treating it as just another of his many investments. Wilmer Wells had his two sons, George and James, operate the popular hotel. No major changes were planned, and the Hume name would remain.

Wilmer Cleveland Wells arrived in Alberta in 1886 from Montreal, where he had worked in the wholesale produce business. He purchased a ranch outside Cochrane, Alberta, before coming to British Columbia and building a large sawmill at Palliser. He ran and grew the business for twenty-two years and then sold it to American interests, reportedly for a half a million dollars. A town in the East Kootenay, Wilmer, is named after him. His main interests were real estate and politics, and by the time he bankrolled his two sons by purchasing the Hume Hotel, he was a bona fide millionaire. On one occasion, Wells was offered the position of lieutenant-governor of the province of British Columbia, but he respectfully refused the honour as it would have interfered with his many business interests.[140]

The Hume Hotel was only in the Wells family's control for five years, from 1907 to 1912. In that time, George Wells ran for election in Nelson's west ward.

Around this time, a visitor from Montreal, a Mr. H.W. Vaughan, attempted suicide in his room at the Hume. The gun he used to shoot himself misfired and caused a minor injury instead of ending his life.[141]

Postcard showing the new look of the Hume Hotel in 1929, mailed in 1930. GLEN A. MOFFORD COLLECTION

In October 1912, the Hume Hotel sold, for only the second time, to George Benwell of Brantford, Ontario, for $84,000.[142] The Wells family moved to Los Angeles, but before they left Nelson, the staff of the Hume Hotel presented W.C. Wells with a handsome suitcase and a Morocco leather dressing case.[143] A footnote regarding the senior Mr. Wells: He lived a good, long life continuing to dabble in business and politics until retiring at the age of ninety-four in 1933. He was, at the time, the oldest living ex-MLA in British Columbia.[144]

For the next thirty-four years, from 1912 to 1946, the Hume Hotel was managed by George Benwell. The first big project under Benwell's management was a $13,000, twenty-two-room extension to the back alley of the Hume. "Alex Carrier, architect expects the extension to be completed and opened sometime in mid-May 1913."[145] In November that year, improvements were completed when the British Columbia Plumbing Company added stationary washstands in thirty-six rooms.[146] One guest at the Hume remarked in a postcard home, "The [The Hume Hotel] is one of the leading hotels in Nelson, not so dusty for a town less than 30 years old. You'd be surprised at the size of some of the wooden buildings. There are five hotels [to] say nothing of saloons galore, when in the wet old days did a thriving business. In shifts of being 'dry' Nelson is still very much alive."[147]

A disturbing incident took place on the front stairs of the Hume Hotel in 1922, when Bobby Gale, young son of past Mayor R.H. Gale, was suddenly attacked by a large wolfhound. The dog seized the unsuspecting boy by his face and head but was saved from serious harm by the quick actions of the adults around him. The child escaped with minor cuts to the bridge of his nose.[148]

In May 1929, Benwell decided to make a radical change to the appearance of the Hume Hotel that would modernize it from the Queen Anne revival of the Victorian age to the Chicago style inspired by the likes of architect Frank Lloyd Wright. Benwell gambled that modernizing the Hume would be acceptable to his guests and locals alike, and hired John Burns and Sons as the sole contractor to make the change. The formal opening of the radically altered Hume Hotel took place on May 1, 1929. The hotel went from three storeys and a bit to four full storeys with stucco veneer. Gone was the magnificent cupola that once towered over Vernon and Ward Streets; the balconies were extended outward and incorporated into the exterior walls, and the entrance was moved. The number of rooms were slightly reduced to eighty from eighty-five but enlarged, with each containing a bathroom and shower room. A seven-passenger, electric-driven elevator was new to the hotel, and the new dining room capacity was extended to fit 150 guests comfortably. Manager Benwell, with his son G.M. Benwell as assistant manager, promised the same excellent service as before but now in a fully modern version of the Hume.[149] The Hume Hotel was so different in appearance that it was, as described in *The Daily News*, "hardly recognizable."[150] The newspaper devoted ten of eighteen pages in their May 1, 1929, issue to the opening of the Hume Hotel. The jury of public opinion was still out regarding the change at the Hume, but like it or not, Benwell irrevocably left his mark on the Hume Hotel forever.

The hotel carried on through the years and by the 1970s had become run down and dilapidated to the point where some considered demolishing it. New owners Dave and Sheila Martin, armed with a heritage grant, saved the magnificent hotel from a date with the wrecker's ball. They revamped the Hume and changed its name, which had been tarnished in recent years, to the Heritage Inn. It remained the Heritage Inn until 2005, when the familiar name the Hume Hotel once again was placed above the front entrance. Comedian Bob Hope once quipped about his stay at the Hume Hotel, "It's nice to actually stay in a hotel that is older than you are."[151] I would simply add that it's nice that the historic Hume Hotel has survived for the enjoyment of current and future generations to enjoy just as our ancestors did.

CHAPTER SIX

East Kootenay

MOUNT BAKER HOTEL

(1923–Present)
1017 Baker Street at
11th Avenue South, Cranbrook

THE CITY of Cranbrook is located on an ancient settlement of the Ktunaxa First Nation called A'qkis ga'ktleet. By the time Lieutenant-Colonel James Baker arrived in 1886, the village had long been abandoned, and he began clearing land for his ranch and home calling it the "Cranbrooke" Farm, after his hometown in Kent, England.[1] Baker was instrumental in convincing the CPR to establish their Crowsnest Pass line through Cranbrook, as opposed to Fort Steele.[2]

In 1923, the Mount Baker Hotel was under construction in Cranbrook, at the corner of Baker and Fenwick Streets, by its owner, Teddy Clauson. Theodore Iverson ("Teddy") Clauson was born in Mosjøen, Norway, in 1883. Clauson immigrated first to Seattle, Washington, before coming to Cranbrook in 1901.[3] By 1908, he was the proprietor of the Commercial Hotel in the East Kootenay logging town of Yahk, and in 1915 and 1916, he was the proprietor of the Kitchener Hotel in Kitchener, a small mining town eighteen kilometres east of Creston on today's Highway 3. Then from 1918 to 1919, Clauson was the proprietor of the Queens Hotel in Cranbrook and got himself in some hot water concerning an illegal bottle of liquor he had at a time of Prohibition. He fought the case in court and initially lost but later won on appeal.[4]

The Mount Baker Hotel, ca. 1924. GLEN A. MOFFORD COLLECTION

By April 1923, Mr. Parkins, working for Mr. Clauson, was "making rapid progress" having the foundation of the Mount Baker Hotel nearly completed.[5] By early October, carpenter J.H. Collins had completed the intricate and beautiful interior woodwork in the Mount Baker and was given a farewell party by friends, as the *Cranbrook Herald* reports: "There was an abundance of work and attractive wages in the land of the stars and stripes."[6] Two weeks later, the new furnishings, supplied by the Fink Mercantile Company, were moved into the hotel as opening day approached. The handsome, three-storey, red-brick Mount Baker Hotel opened on October 31, 1923, with the largest and finest rooms available in Cranbrook and was the peak of sophistication for the area.[7]

Teddy Clauson would occasionally have to leave town for business reasons and would have Fred Nelson fill in as manager for a couple of months while he was absent.[8] One sunny but cool Friday afternoon in February 1924, a crowd of people stood in a long line down Baker Street from the new Mount Baker Hotel to the Cranbrook Hotel. They were there for the anticipated inaugural Cranbrook Dog Derby, sponsored by local insurance man T.M. Roberts—"for the fun of the kiddies," Roberts exclaimed, although the majority of curious onlookers were adults who placed their bets on their favourite dog to win a place or the show. Only six dogs were entered in the race, with "Dinty," owned by Ernest Kennedy, as the favourite to win the not just one, but all three races that took place. In the first race, Dinty was the quickest off the mark and was out front for most of the race until he was distracted by another member of the canine family and darted off course, last seen heading for the tall timbers with tail a-wagging. The Dog Derby was a big hit and certainly entertained the crowd.[9]

On Saturday, July 6, 1946, a blue Cadillac convertible coupe arrived in town carrying popular crooner and actor Bing Crosby, accompanied by movie script writer Barney Dean and Hollywood advertising executive Vic Hunter. The trio checked into the Mount Baker Hotel and, once settled in, walked to Pat's Coffee Shop. I can only imagine the reception they may have had when folks learned who was having a coffee in the same room as them. For about twenty minutes, Bing Crosby was happy to sign autographs with his right hand while finishing up his meal with the left. Crosby was on his way to Jasper National Park to take part in the movie *The Emperor Waltz*, starring himself and Joan Fontaine.[10]

After twenty-four years, Teddy Clauson sold his thirty-room Mount Baker Hotel to Mr. and Mrs. W.N. Kennemann of Lethbridge, Alberta, in March 1947.[11] Clauson was sixty-four years old, but he did not go gently into that good night; instead, he built Teddy's Motel on Fernie Road in north Cranbrook, which he ran until he died in April 1962.[12] The Kennemanns ran the Mount Baker for a year and six months, with one minor incident worth mentioning. The hotel had a popular beer parlour where a fight or similar disruption would occasionally break out, as is typical whenever you have a large room filled with beer drinkers. One customer, Mr. Campbell, perhaps too far gone in his cups from celebrating the Jubilee weekend in May 1948, managed to break a large plate-glass window in the hotel and was remanded for sentence.[13]

The Kennemanns sold the hotel to Mrs. J. Waswick in October 1948 for $55,000.[14] They then purchased the Norbury Hotel on the west side of town from Mrs. William Ray after spending a year away in Victoria.

The Mount Baker Hotel saw a parade of owners come and go, from Mr. and Mrs. Coleman Reid in 1959 to Greg Eaton and partners, who in 2018 restored and revitalized the hotel to its former glory.[15] It stands today as The Baker, a handsome, revived historical landmark hotel in Cranbrook. Teddy Clauson would have been proud.

KING EDWARD HOTEL

(1905–1908, 1908–78)
172 Victoria Avenue at Hanson Street, Fernie

THE CITY OF Fernie was originally called Coal Creek as this was coal country and the community grew around coal mining. Fernie was named after William Fernie, an Englishman who travelled the world before arriving in British Columbia to prospect for gold in the Revelstoke area. He didn't find much gold, but he did find something that was just as precious and personally rewarding: coal. While prospecting on Michel Creek, Fernie discovered a vast coal seam and eventually had a lucrative association with the Crow's Nest Pass Coal Company that made him a wealthy man. The Fernie townsite was cleared and surveyed in 1898.[16]

John L. Gates was first mentioned in the 1902 Henderson BC Gazetteer and Directory for Fernie as the proprietor of the Victoria Hotel. He continued working there until 1904, the year the city of Fernie was incorporated, then ran the Alberta Hotel until the first of a series of fires destroyed a portion of town, including the hotel.[17] Gates rebuilt at a different location in town, the corner of Hanson Street and Victoria Avenue, opening the King Edward Hotel in 1905.[18]

The King Edward Hotel was a handsome, three-storey wooden structure with a half balcony on the second floor and a large hotel sign on the roof from which Gates ran the following advertisement: "The King Edward occupies a prominent position in Fernie

The King Edward Hotel, likely before the 1904 fire. IMAGE 00198 COURTESY OF THE FERNIE MUSEUM

only a step or two from the CPR depot and convenient to business houses in the city."[19] Gates didn't have a chance to enjoy his spanking-new hotel before it, too, was consumed by an even greater calamity in August 1908. The great Fernie fire began when smouldering embers from logging operations west of the city were brought to flame by gusty winds on August 1. The summer of 1908 had been a particularly hot and dry, perfect conditions for the firestorm that let loose on the city.[20] Very few structures were spared as the wall of fire, whipped up by strong winds, destroyed everything in sight in downtown Fernie, "cutting a swathe of destruction 30 miles in length," with fatalities estimated at over one hundred.[21]

As incredible as the disastrous fire was, the fortitude and determination of the saviours of Fernie to rebuild their town was equally as incredible. When the local Fernie newspaper, *The District Ledger*, was up and running again, some of the businesses were defiant in their advertising that they would not leave the devastated town but would build again. The fire would not defeat them, nor would it defeat the citizens of Fernie: J.D. Quail, hardware and furnishing store advertised, "Gee Wiz [sic], what's the matter with this town? Nothing can burn us out of business!" Whimster & Company Hardware echoed a similar sentiment: "We are burned out but we are NOT done out. Come right along, we can serve you." John Gates was not immune to the call to rebuild, stating in his hotel's first ad since the fire, "King Edward Hotel, We have some hot stuff—waiting for ice. J. Gates, proprietor."[22] Only a few days after the smouldering ruins cooled, Gates had the first (temporary) King Edward Hotel up and running on August 8. It was a makeshift restaurant-hotel that was the first to open in town. By August 19, less than three weeks after the great fire, shovels went into the ground for the permanent, three-storey, concrete-and-brick King Edward Hotel.[23]

John Gates estimated the loss of his hotel at approximately $15,000 but only had insurance for $8,000. Those who had no insurance or were under-insured lost everything. For weeks after the fire, the town was a tent city, with the occasional temporary wooden building rushed into use. The air was filled with the sounds of hammers and saws rebuilding Fernie—a town that had had its fair share of disasters from fire to mining disasters. Most of the residents stayed on to rebuild, while others left for a new life elsewhere. Relief came from every corner of the country—from the federal and provincial governments to cities and towns across the country, and from fundraising events that provided clothes, food, and money for the victims of the fire who had lost everything.[24]

In 1910, John Gates left the day-to-day routine of the King Edward Hotel to his head bartender, Paddy Hughes, while he pursued his varied investments and interests. Gates and Jacob Fleishman of the Fernie Lodge No. 31 represented the district at the Grand Lodge Meeting in Vancouver.[25] Gates also required the time off from the hotel to run for mayor of Fernie. The results of the March 1910 municipal elections saw the incumbent, Sherwood Herchmer, retain his seat as mayor with 212 votes; John L.

The temporary building until the new King Edward Hotel was completed, 1908. IMAGE 00199 COURTESY OF THE FERNIE MUSEUM

Gates had a very good showing for his first time out, managing to receive 174 votes, with nine spoiled ballots.[26] Gates would try again in 1913 and win. In all, Gates would win the mayor's seat four times through the years until he retired from politics.

While Gates was pursuing his political aims, Mrs. Hughes, managing the King Edward Hotel with her husband, Paddy, had a horrible accident that nearly ended her life. She was in bed when she heard her husband coming home and arose to unlock the door. She struck a match to find her way and the flame caught her nightgown on fire. "Before the flames could be extinguished, she had been badly burned from head to foot." Mrs. Hughes was rushed to hospital in dire pain with serious burns to her body.[27] The situation was more distressing in that the couple had a three-month-old baby boy and a toddler. Fortunately, Paddy Hughes found someone to care for them at this distressing time. Mrs. Hughes made a long and painful recovery.[28]

As mentioned earlier, John L. Gates had political ambitions and decided to run for mayor of Fernie in 1910 but went down

The rebuilt King Edward Hotel, Fernie, BC. IMAGE 00105 COURTESY OF THE FERNIE MUSEUM

to defeat. He tried again in January 1913 and this time won by a large majority of votes, 233 for Gates to 124 for C.E. Lyons, his opponent.[29] Mayor Gates juggled his duties in office with running a hotel, and after a brief absence from town to visit his brother in Moose Jaw, Saskatchewan, came back married. His new bride, formerly Miss Mary Brown, was at one time a resident of Fernie. She married John Gates in a small ceremony in the prairie town before the happy couple returned to Fernie.[30]

On April 1, 1925, the King Edward Hotel was granted a beer parlour licence. John Gates still owned the grand hotel and had no plans to leave. When Gates was not working or involved in his many other business activities, he did have one main hobby that helped him to relax: fishing. He was known as an expert angler and could be seen fishing for trout in the local rivers. The Crowsnest region was a lovely setting, surrounded by beautiful mountains and streams where hunting and fishing were very popular. One story was told about a time when a meeting of the mayor and city council was called but no quorum was reached as it was discovered that the mayor, the president of the council, and the chief of police had gone fishing.[31]

Some friends of Gates's arrived in Fernie for a twelve-day fishing and hunting trip in 1925, staying at the King Edward Hotel. Gates found time to host ten days of their trip by showing the visitors where the trout were biting. He had a very good reputation when it came to fishing and he earned the moniker "Champion wet fly fisherman of Fernie."[32]

In January 1929, Gates ran for the mayor of Fernie for a third time and won, outdistancing the incumbent by sixty-one votes.[33] The following January, he ran for office a fourth and final time, barely beating the second-place candidate by the slimmest of margins: only three votes.[34] This was the last kick at the can in local politics, as Mr. and Mrs. Gates planned to announce a big change in their lives once his term was over. In the spring of 1932, the couple announced that they sold the King Edward Hotel to J. William Kerr. If that wasn't shocking enough, the couple added that they were moving to Vancouver, where they had leased the Martinique Hotel at 1176 Granville Street from owner E.G. Johnson.[35] The Gateses remained in Vancouver, operating the Martinique Hotel until 1940, when they crossed the Strait of Georgia to run the Metropolis Hotel on Yates Street in Victoria.

The King Edward Hotel in Fernie saw four owners come and go between the years 1932 and 1949. Kerr sold the hotel to Jack Wilson and J.E. Dicks in 1935. Wilson was proprietor for the longest of the four short-term owners, operating the hotel for just under twelve years, from 1935 to 1947. He was followed by Adolph Sperka and his wife, who were from Calgary. They sold the King Edward two years later and bought the Waldorf Hotel in town. Dan Polomark and his two sons, Paul and Michael, were the next owners, in January 1949.[36]

The seventy-year-old historic, three-storey King Edward Hotel succumbed to fire on May 15, 1978. No injuries were reported in the early morning blaze, but firefighters believed they had the fire under control early, until it ignited a five-hundred-gallon oil tank inside the building.[37]

CORONATION HOTEL

(1907–69)
Athalmer

ORIGINALLY KNOWN AS Salmon Beds, the name for this community, nestled in the Columbia Valley at the head of navigation of the Columbia River, was changed to Athalmer in honour of civil engineer F.W. ("Fred") Aylmer.[38] ("Athalmer" is a combination of "Athel," meaning "noble" in Anglo-Saxon, and "mere," meaning "lake.") Athalmer is located a few miles north of Invermere at the foot of beautiful Windermere Lake. The village began as a mining camp extracting quartz, silver, and lead in the East Kootenay district and grew larger when the Kootenay Central railway, a branch of the CPR, arrived.

In 1899, George Stark, a successful miner and hotelier used his profits from the Delphine Mine to build the Delphine Hotel in Peterborough (a community in the Columbia Valley whose name was changed to Wilmer in 1902). The hotel, like the mine, was named after his wife.[39] In 1907, George and his brother, Robert Stark, seeing that there was a need for another hotel in the growing community of Athalmer, just south of Wilmer, built the Columbia House to compete with the established Windsor Hotel. Robert Stark also built the Coronation Hotel in 1908. George and Delphine sold the Delphine Hotel in 1909 and ran the Columbia (now a hotel), then moved on the following year, leasing the Columbia Hotel to manage the Canterbury Hotel in nearby Invermere.[40] Stark continued as manager when the Canterbury became the Invermere Hotel in 1911 and stayed on until 1918.

The Coronation Hotel. IMAGE COURTESY OF THE WINDERMERE DISTRICT HISTORICAL SOCIETY

An interesting article published in the *Vancouver Daily World* in May 1910 reported that George Stark had left a Vancouver hotel with a large sum of money and failed to return. It went on to say that police searched for days in vain and that "foul play [was] feared," as "friends of George Stark are frantic as to his whereabouts and condition as he hasn't been seen since leaving a Vancouver hotel six days ago."[41] It must have been a slow news week for the *Daily World* as it turned out that Mr. Stark had simply boarded a train to Golden and was quite unaware of the excitement stirred up by the Vancouver article. "George Stark has many friends among old-timers in the Golden district, who will be glad to know he is safe and sound."[42]

In 1910, Thomas Barry leased the Coronation Hotel from George Stark and came up with the idea to nail tin sheathing on the exterior of the hotel, which, when completed, made it come to life when "it did a lot of rattling as the wind whistled through the tin."[43] The Tin Man from the Wizard of Oz would feel at home in the Coronation Hotel, which was dubbed "Tommy's Tin House" by the regulars. I can't see that as a selling point for a hotel if one wished for a good night's sleep, but I imagine it must have looked amazing on a clear day as the rays of the sun reflected off the tin.

In March 1916, Robert Stark, George Stark's brother, who had built the Coronation Hotel, was walking down a street in Windermere when he suddenly collapsed and died. The cause of death was not revealed but I suspect it was from a heart attack. "Bob Stark was born in Farnham, Quebec, and is survived by a wife and five children in Newport, Vermont, USA."[44]

Less than two years later, on January 11, 1918, George Stark followed his brother to the grave when he passed away from heart failure while visiting Victoria, BC, with Delphine and their adopted daughter, May. Mr. Stark had not been feeling well for some time, and the thinking was that a visit to the coast might improve his health. "The late George Stark was born in Farnham, Quebec, in 1854 and came west in the early 1880s, arriving in a mining camp in 1882 that later became Golden, BC. George Stark loved the mountains and knew that he had found his forever home. Stark had operated hotels in Windermere, Wilmer, Invermere, and Athalmer. He also had investments in local mines. He had just recently resigned as manager of the Invermere Hotel [and was] succeeded by Bob Williams, late of the Columbia Hotel in Golden, BC"[45]

Thomas E. Barry, the person responsible for the inspired name "The Tin House" for the Coronation Hotel, sold the hotel to Joseph Davis in 1924. Davis had worked for the Columbia Lumber Company for years until a serious accident cost him one of his legs.[46] Davis had just gotten settled in when he died in the hospital in 1925, and the Coronation Hotel was purchased by Mr. and Mrs. W.G. Pennington. Perhaps it was just good timing, but the new owners applied for a beer parlour licence, which was granted; to accommodate the beverage room, the couple totally renovated the hotel, "putting it right" by painting, wallpapering, and cleaning it throughout.[47] The Penningtons operated the hotel until 1934. Over five and a half years, three owners came and went until the Ronacher family bought the hotel and ran it for the following fourteen years.

Simon Ronacher, who owned a sawmill and a logging company, was one of the chief lumber operators in the area. He added a portable sawmill unit to his expanding business interests that was put to work cutting railway ties for his big contract with the CPR.[48] His company was a major employer in the area, and many of the sawmill workers and loggers spent their free time at his beer parlour at the Coronation Hotel. But not all the employees had a choice to work for Ronacher's companies. "Sixteen Japanese [Canadian] internees were sent to Ronacher's Sawmill in Invermere by the Canadian Government."[49] Logging and sawmill work was a dangerous and risky occupation; this was especially true for the fallers, who were paid the most but who also experienced the most injuries and deaths. Alfred Davis, aged seventy-four, perhaps a bit too old to still be working in the woods, was fatally injured at one of Ronacher's camps when a tree fell and crushed the poor man's skull.[50] Called "widow-makers," branches falling on a faller cutting down a tree were, and still are, a common danger in the woods. All aspects of logging had their dangers, as demonstrated in January 1947, when John Droepfl cheated death after his ten-wheel truck carrying a heavy caterpillar crashed through icy Lake Windermere. The driver escaped sure death when he jumped out of the cab of the truck just before it sank beneath the ice, but he almost succumbed to a minor heart attack brought on by the shock. He ended up in Lady Elizabeth Bruce Memorial Hospital at Invermere but survived the ordeal. Meanwhile, the company attempted to fish the truck and the caterpillar out of the frigid waters.[51]

The Ronacher family greatly improved the cuisine at the Coronation Hotel to the point that word of mouth improved business substantially as well. With money coming in from the beer parlour and dining room, as well as from overnight guests, one could say this was the golden age (or, perhaps, the tin age?) for the Coronation Hotel. The Ronachers put money back into the hotel, keeping it up to date and making improvements as needed.[52] In December 1953, the hotel changed hands once more when Jack Klassen of Vancouver bought it, only to turn around four months later and sell it to Ivar Fossen from Victoria.[53] The next owners, Leon Walberg and Peter McKenzie, from Vancouver, bought the hotel in the summer of 1955. In spite of the short-term owners, the hotel continued to maintain a stellar reputation that had been built up through the years by the Ronachers and the Penningtons before them. In May 1959, the nineteen-room Coronation Hotel was again up for sale, with the asking price of $78,000.[54] Mr. Delesalle of Invermere bought the hotel but had it less than two years before he sold it in 1962.

Ed Steel, of Sandel Hotels Limited was the last owner of the "Tin House." Around one o'clock in the early morning of Sunday December 28, 1969, the sixty-two-year old-structure was destroyed by fire. The fire began in the back of the hotel, and enough warning was given that the fourteen guests and the owner escaped without injury into the cold early morning. The loss was estimated at around $125,000, of which Steel had insurance for $100,000.[55] The citizens of Athalmer lost their unique, historic tin hotel.

I leave the last word on the Coronation Hotel to Ron Ede who wrote the ballad of the history of the hotel and the stories of some who were there. It's called "The Night the Tin House Burned."[56]

> This old landmark is burning things just won't be the same.
>
> It's been here as long as memory; it measures the valley in years,
>
> It's echoed this Valley's laughter and it's drowned this Valley's tears;
>
> It was "Rest" at the end of the voyage for those who had left their home,
>
> And it was "Home" for the hardy pioneer, who wandered the hills alone.[57]

QUEEN'S HOTEL

(1883-1931; Golden Antlers Hotel (1931-33);
Queen's Hotel (1933-59)
North Third Avenue, Golden

GOLDEN CITY, now simply called Golden, would not have existed if it weren't for the Canadian Pacific Railway (CPR). A.B. Rogers, who worked for the CPR, was tasked to find a rail route through the Rocky Mountains between Lake Louise and Field, BC, in 1881. McMillan's Camp, named for the head man of the CPR survey crew, was the base camp for CPR workers. In 1884, when a nearby lumber camp named themselves Silver City, residents of the tiny settlement of McMillian, in a spirit of one-upmanship, renamed their settlement Golden City.[58]

In 1883, William and Mary Archer worked with a team of men to hew out raw logs to build the original Queen's Hotel. It contained five rooms with one shared bathroom and a large tent for the roof. The first guests were mainly men working on the railroad, miners, salesmen, and settlers.[59] From these humble beginnings, the Queen's Hotel would grow to become a major landmark hotel in Golden. In 1885, John Charles Green[60] arrived in Golden and was hired as manager of the Queen's Hotel. This freed the Archers to develop the ranch they had recently purchased north of Golden.[61] In 1888, the Archers sold the Queen's Hotel to John Gibson, who leased it to Green. Green began making major improvements and enlarging the popular hostelry. Gibson had his own ranch, where he spent most of his time, and he left his investment in the Queen's Hotel in the very capable hands of John Green.

Prime Minister Sir Wilfrid Laurier giving a speech from the balcony of the Queen's Hotel, August 5, 1910. IMAGE COURTESY OF THE GOLDEN MUSEUM AND ARCHIVES 39-P0496

Green patiently renovated and expanded the Queen's Hotel through the 1890s, taking the bulk of his proceeds earned in the hotel and putting it back into the business. The original log cabin gave way to a much larger building and expanded whenever Green could afford it. In 1893, he renovated the original small bar into an office and added considerably more space; he then put new lighting along the front entrance to the hotel, adding railings to the wooden sidewalk for the comfort and safety of his guests and those strolling by on an evening walk. By January 1894, a new addition to the hotel had "assumed vast proportions during the last week... showing his [Green's] unbounded faith in the prosperity of the town."[62] In April, his new furniture finally arrived, filling the additional rooms and the new bar. With all the changes, the Queen's Hotel attracted more business, not only from the travelling public but from other businesspeople as well. Miss Rocan, a milliner and dressmaker from Calgary, chose the Queen's Hotel to display her latest stock of millinery fashions, ready-made ladies' and children's underwear, and the latest styles in spring hats for "the woman of today."[63] Other commercial men and women followed with their wares for citizens of a growing community.

A minor setback came in July 1894 when the Kicking Horse River overflowed and businesses nearby like the Queen's Hotel experienced some water damage. It was quickly cleaned up with the aid of the CPR, who sent a work gang to fill up the channel and shore up the riverbank.[64] On occasion, Green would hold a raffle where the proceeds would go back into the costs of improving his hotel. In the summer of 1894, a magnificent "piano-cased organ," valued at $225, was available to the lucky person whose two-dollar ticket number was drawn. With the money from this raffle, Green added a sitting room next to the bar.[65] Sports were very important at the time. Various fledgling sports teams held their initial meetings at the Queen's, and the hotel even fielded their own soccer team, which took on their next-door rivals from the Kootenay Hotel. The game ended in a one-one tie.[66]

A sporting game of a different nature, and one close to Green's heart, was politics. Green was an ardent Liberal supporter and, in 1897, was elected president of the Liberal Association of Golden, whose purpose was to "look after the interest of the Liberal party," both provincially and federally.[67] Some years later, Green would be rewarded for his loyalty to the Liberal cause when a famous prime minister would visit the hotel and give a speech to the crowd that gathered in front of the Queen's. Regular meetings of the association took place at Green's hotel.

On December 23, 1896, John Gibson put the Queen's Hotel up for auction. He needed the money to pay off the mortgage on his ranch and to add more grazing land. There were few bidders, as most local folks felt that John Green was the best man for the job as owner and proprietor of the hotel.[68] Green won the auction and became the free and clear owner of the Queen's Hotel. To celebrate, Green renovated every room in the hotel, adding electric bells, and then turned the sitting room into a smoking room.[69] Green had big plans for his hotel. His next move was to purchase the vacant lot that sat between his hotel and the Kootenay Hotel for $800.[70]

The most significant and costly modification to the Queen's Hotel was completed in 1901, when the roof was lifted and two floors were added. The ground floor contained two conservatories, a sewing room, bathroom, large office, dining room, kitchen, bar, two sample rooms, and a large sitting room finished off with a grand fireplace. Totally gone were the trappings of the original hotel, and in their place was a grand mishmash containing various rooms. The first floor had twenty-two guest rooms with shared bathrooms. The third floor added another eighteen guest rooms, with three of those being self-contained with a complete bathroom and the other rooms sharing a bathroom. In October 1901, Green had a massive boiler installed in order to provide steam heat to his expanded hotel. It was the only steam-heated hotel in town at that time.[71] "The culmination of years of alterations and additions have turned the once small staid old hotel into an elaborate first-class house impressing those travellers disembarking from the nearby CPR train".[72]

The frenzy of expanding the Queen's Hotel didn't sit well with one neighbour. Green had given permission for Mr. Alexander to have his watch-repair shop in a modest building on land Green owned. In the summer of 1904, Green wanted to use the property to grow vegetables for his guests at the hotel, and it was mutually agreed between the two that the building would be removed from Green's property to an adjacent lot. Without permission, Alexander moved his business onto a lot belonging to a man who lived in Vancouver and directly across from C.A. Warren's store. Warren did not like the change as he said the building looked like an oversized outhouse. The local druggist, Mr. Buckham, didn't care for the building either, and when he overheard Warren say that someone should blow the place up, he quickly volunteered to do just that. Warren didn't take his offer seriously, but sure enough, one rainy night around midnight, guests of the Queen's Hotel, less than sixty feet away from Alexander's watch-repair shop, were jolted out of bed by a loud explosion. Buckham must have known what he was doing, as the concussion from the blast went across the Kicking Horse River and did little damage to nearby buildings. Alexander's watch-repair shop and everything that was in it was no more. A half-hearted investigation took place, but nothing became of it. The hat was passed around to compensate poor Mr. Alexander, to which Buckham donated twenty dollars. Enough money was raised to allow Alexander to start his business again, but he chose not to do it in Golden.[73]

One of the best days in John Green's life took place on August 5, 1910, when Prime Minister Sir Wilfrid Laurier and his entourage stepped off the train in Golden. For a few hours, they were special guests at the Queen's Hotel, where the Liberal prime minister gave a hearty speech to a large crowd from the second-floor balcony of the hotel. Laurier was in town for about an hour before boarding his special train, continuing his tour of Western Canada, but Green, a lifelong Liberal, surely must have been thrilled by his visit.[74]

One of Green's last major renovations to his Queen's Hotel took place in 1914, when he had electric lights installed, generated by his own pumping station. In 1922, Green was appointed official government liquor vendor for Golden as Prohibition gave way to provincial government control.[75] By 1926, John Charles Green had operated the Queen's Hotel for forty-one years and had owned it for thirty years. He died in June 1926,[76] and the Queen's Hotel sat dormant for two years. Six months after Green's death, two small cabins on his estate were demolished on orders from the fire marshal. They were the two oldest structures left in Golden, both built by Green in 1885.[77]

On June 1, 1928, the vacant Queen's Hotel was purchased by Ainsworth entrepreneur Mrs. Nelson. When she got the business up and running, she turned around and sold it to Mr. Ralph Blair, who was most interested in managing the beer parlour, so he leased the hotel portion to the Rocky Mountain Hotel Company in February 1931. The familiar name of the hotel changed from the Queen's to the Golden Antlers Hotel that April.[78] In 1933, the last of the short-term owners, Mrs. A.S. Clausen, purchased the aging hotel and hired Mr. and Mrs. Malcolm Morrison to manage it.

Mr. James Aitken bought the Queen's Hotel in 1936 and ran it for the next nine years until December 5, 1945. It was Aitken that added corrugated roofing and had the whole exterior stuccoed and painted. The interior of the hotel was modernized and cleaned up under his tenure. What didn't get cleaned up was some of the hijinks that went on when the miners came to stay and made regular visits to the Queen's beer parlour. "Golden in 1944 had only three stores at the time and one policeman... when the miners came to town to go on a drunk at the Queen's Hotel, there were no fire escapes, only a rope fastened inside the room that could be dropped out of the window. The miners took one man they didn't like, tied the rope to his ankles and hung him out the window upside down. He kept on screaming until someone finally pulled him back inside."[79]

The last owners of the Queen's Hotel were Stand and Dorothy LaRoy, who purchased it in May 1946. The couple opened up the dining room and advertised that the Queen's Hotel was back. The LaRoys ran the hotel until 1958, when they retired, selling it to the British American oil company (BA), which demolished the landmark and replaced it with a gas station.[80]

EMERALD LAKE CHALET

(1902–Present)
Emerald Lake

L EAVING GOLDEN, we travel approximately sixty-five kilometres northeast by CPR train (the same route as the Trans-Canada highway today) and turn down Snow Peak Avenue until we arrive at stunningly beautiful Emerald Lake in Yoho National Park. The first non-Indigenous person to discover Emerald Lake was packer and guide Tom Wilson, a CPR employee, who stumbled upon it by accident in 1882. The story goes that a string of his horses had gotten away and it was while tracking them that he first entered the valley. The lake made an impression on even the most seasoned of explorers: "For a few moments I sat [on] my horse and enjoyed the rare, peaceful beauty of the scene."[81] It was Wilson who gave the lake its name because of its remarkable emerald-green colour, caused by fine particles of glacial sediment (also referred to as rock flour) suspended in the water. Earlier that year, Wilson had come upon another spectacular lake that he also named Emerald Lake, but the name was later changed to Lake Louise.[82]

In 1901, the CPR decided to build a chalet at popular Emerald Lake, and in March 1902, after seeking tenders for the contract, a firm from Montreal was chosen to build it, beating out bids from across Canada, including from three Vancouver contractors.[83] The eleven-room Emerald Lake chalet borrowed the design of a rustic

The Emerald Lake Chalet. IMAGE COURTESY OF CANADIAN ROCKY MOUNTAIN RESORTS

Swiss lodge, using ten-inch, square-hewn cedar timber construction and details like stepped corbels that recalled Swiss carved roof brackets.[84] The two-storey interior was finished in hardwood, and, when completed, was the first log tourist lodge built by the CPR and quite a contrast to its grandiose hotels such as the Banff Springs Hotel or the Empress Hotel in Victoria.[85]

The location of the chalet could not have been better. Emerald Lake is the largest of the sixty-one lakes found in Yoho National Park in the Canadian Rockies and is approximately ten kilometres from today's Trans-Canada Highway. The lake is surrounded by Mount Burgess, Wapta Mountain, and the mountains of the President Range. The Emerald Lake chalet is perched high on the south edge of the lake, with an incredible view of the lake and mountain scenery. Tourists were attracted by the natural beauty and took advantage of all the chalet had to offer such as boating, swimming, hiking, horseback riding around the lake, and, of course, fishing. The peaceful beauty of Emerald Lake was excellent for those who just wished to get away and relax.

The CPR chalet was completed in time for their first summer season in 1902, which operated from June to October.[86] Guests disembarked in Field, a mining town seven miles from Emerald

Lake, and made the trip by carriage up Snow Peak Avenue, a forest road lined on either side by towering spruce and lodgepole pine. In the chalet, guests were entertained by a full orchestra, and electricity, hardwood floors, and wood stoves were in every room. From the menu to the amazing view, everything was first-class, and those that attended got their money's worth at the rate of five dollars per night.[87]

The number of visitors that first season was encouraging and continued to climb each subsequent season. At the beginning of the 1906 season, the CPR built lakeside cabins to accommodate the steady rise in seasonal tourists. A separate building was constructed for servants and guides' quarters, and the main chalet was remodelled throughout, with the exterior finished with kalsomine (a type of whitewash consisting of an inexpensive form of white paint that is simple to compound and is used on wooden surfaces such as picket fences or park benches as well as plaster surfaces).[88] The Emerald Lake Chalet opened for the summer season of 1906 from June 15 to September 30. The 1912 season saw over one thousand guests registered at the chalet and cabins, and the following year, 1913, saw that number double.[89]

The CPR developed the idea of constructing a series of camps based on the Emerald Lake Chalet model, calling them "bungalow camps," for tourists that wished to overnight or stay a few days with the option of visiting other nearby camps. The company believed the new camps would appeal to the elite sportsman on hunting and fishing trips and to those tourists who wished to hike on foot or ride horseback through the many trails developed around these bungalow camps. The camps could be easily accessed by car, and maps of other CPR bungalow camps would be available for tourists to explore. By 1923, the CPR had nine bungalow camps operating in the Canadian Rockies.[90]

Other regular customers to the Emerald Lake Chalet were alpinists. As early as 1905, the Alpine Club held annual meetings in Yoho National Park, for which some members chose to bus to Emerald Lake from Field and then trek twelve miles to the Yoho Valley. This was significant as the Mount Stephen Hotel in Field and the Emerald Lake Chalet and cabins would fill with members of the Alpine Club. In 1914, approximately two hundred members attended the ninth annual meeting, which included a ski outing.[91] The number of people going on ski trips to Yoho Park increased over the years and brought business to both hostelries.

At the end of the 1918 summer season, the CPR announced that the Mount Stephen Hotel, which had enjoyed a very successful tourist season, would be converted from hotel use into a YMCA for employees of the company. This rather shocking announcement was good news for the Emerald Lake Chalet, as they now had the only lodging available in this region of the Rockies.[92] In addition, the Alpine Club, which had suspended all major activity during the First World War, announced that it would revive the annual meetings and ski outings. The club held its first post-war camp at Summit, near Emerald Lake.[93]

In September 1919, the chalet extended its closing date to early October in order to accommodate a high-profile guest who came to visit. His Royal Highness Prince Edward, Prince of Wales, was on a two-month tour of Canada and spent a portion of his time in British Columbia. On September 19, the prince arrived for lunch at the Emerald Lake Chalet. The future king decided to walk the seven miles from Field up Snow Peak Avenue among the lodgepole pines. "The Prince of Wales trudged through rain and mud to Emerald Lake... He chose to walk the mountain roads for exercise and very much enjoyed the magnificent scenery of the district. Mrs. Costigan and her staff had prepared a pleasant meal in the comfortable inn parlour, festive with decorations of autumn foliage."[94]

In 1959, after countless visitors had enjoyed the chalet and cabins at Emerald Lake, the CPR sold the property to a private party. The chalet had been closed for some time and was in dire need of repair and upgrading. A succession of owners came and went until, in 1979, Pat and Connie O'Connor purchased the aging chalet and crumbling buildings and, many headaches and $8 million later, reopened Emerald Lake Lodge in 1986. In 2002, the *Globe and Mail* reported:

The original old log lodge is still there, brightly coloured canoes still bob by the boathouse, and the milky blue lake—nested like a robin's egg among the granite peaks of Mounts Burgess, Wapta, McArthur and Carnarvon—still makes arriving here feel like stumbling upon a hidden gem... Every room of the Emerald Lake Lodge has a fieldstone fireplace flanked by bent-willow armchairs, and a screen door that opens to the deck and the fresh mountain air.[95]

Aside from the chalet and the magnificence of Emerald Lake, the Burgess Shale deposit contains one of the most significant fossil beds in the world. While I am profiling the 120-year-old Emerald Lake Chalet, nearby there are fossils of the earliest proto-vertebrates that date as far back as 540 million years. The Burgess Shale site is a UNESCO World Heritage site that the public may view through guided tours.[96] Another good reason to visit Emerald Lake today is the chalet, much changed and updated through the years, but still in operation.

AFTERWORD

THE HISTORY of British Columbia over the past two hundred years is an interesting and colourful one, marked by the arrival of settlers from the east and the oceans beyond, who came with dreams of making a new life in a "new" land. Much has been written about the gold rushes and the arrival of the Canadian Pacific Railway, which paved the way for even greater settlement in the west, and this book provides a unique contribution to that canon of BC history by telling the stories of some of the province's earliest hotels and the people who operated or stayed in them. These early businesses were essential landmarks in their communities, serving not only as gathering places for residents and visitors alike, but also as symbols of the hopes and ambitions of the owners and the towns themselves. Thanks to Glen's dedicated research, the stories of these places and people are brought into the light, and the overarching history of the province is made all the richer.

Publishing a book is usually a highly collaborative process between author and publisher. With Glen's passing, we were sadly robbed of his insight and expertise during the editorial process; however, it was extremely important to us—and to his family—to see the project through and to honour Glen's vision. From the beginning, we were fortunate to have the full support of Glen's family, who facilitated the delivery of his final manuscript—which was days away from completion when he passed—and many of the images he had already selected for inclusion in the book. Even in their grief, the family was adamant that the book needed to be published. Glen's meticulous research and wealth of knowledge made what could have been an extremely daunting process into a relatively seamless one. Although we did not get the chance to work closely with him, we are grateful for all the work and passion he put into this project, and we hope that his family and his many supporters will be satisfied with his final contribution to BC history.

Glen was genuinely inspired by and passionate about the history of British Columbia's hospitality industry. He took great delight in his research and in sharing the real stories and anecdotes of the people and places that populated our province's history. His enthusiasm and curiosity for these stories truly shone in his writing and through his public interactions, whether he was reviewing other books and writing by peers, contributing to *BC History* magazine, presenting to an engaged audience in a crowded room, or moderating his Facebook groups, the Historic Hotels & Pubs of Vancouver Island and Historic Hotels & Pubs of British Columbia, which he started "to educate, entertain and to clear up any 'foggy' memories that members may have of a particular place. This is where the past comes alive." Glen was known to be kind, generous, and a lovely person to work with. He will continue to be missed.

NOTES

Chapter One: Similkameen, Nicola, Thompson, and Shuswap

1. "Keremeos Memories by Rita (Marguerite) Kirby Coleman as told to Eric Sismey." *Thirty-Fifth Annual Report of the Okanagan Historical Society*, November 1, 1971, pp. 28–32.
2. T.W. Paterson, *Okanagan-Similkameen*, British Columbia Ghost Town Series (Langley: Sunfire Publications, 1983), p. 115.
3. Ibid., p. 116.
4. "Keremeos Memories...", p. 30.
5. N.L. Barlee, "Gold Creeks and Ghost Towns" (*Canada West Magazine*, Summerland, BC: Fourth Printing, June 1972), p. 18.
6. *Keremeos Trumpet*, October 2, 1908, p. 1. Note that the funds raised at the dinner-charity dance and similar money-raising functions normally went to the widows and families of men who died or were seriously injured in the mines, as there was no compensation or social security net from the levels of government that we enjoy today.
7. Ibid., March 12, 1909, p. 1.
8. *Province*, March 29, 1910, p. 14.
9. *Hedley Gazette*, September 15, 1910, p. 4.
10. Ibid., May 15, 1913, p. 4.
11. *Vancouver Sun*, August 15, 1960, p. 12. See also: *Spokesman Review* (Spokane), August 6, 1960, p. 12.
12. N.L. (Bill) Barlee, *The Guide to Similkameen Treasure* (Hancock House Publishing, Big Country Books, 1987). And from the *Keremeos Review*, "Recalling the Keremeos Hotel," July 23, 2014: keremeosreview.com/our-town/recalling-the-keremeos-hotel/
13. *Vancouver Daily World*, June 21, 1918, p. 16. Mrs. Kirby ran Help Wanted ads from time to time over the next few years and especially during the busy summer season.

14 *Province*, "Keremeos Liquor Store Will Be Reopened," February 12, 1928, p. 20.
15 *Vancouver Sun*, May 1, 1930, p. 24.
16 *Province*, "Final Tribute Paid to BC Hotel Woman." September 6, 1944, p. 16.
17 "Keremeos Memories...", p. 30.
18 *Vancouver Sun*, February 9, 1946, p. 30.
19 *Vancouver Sun*, March 24, 1947, p. 3.
20 Ibid., November 2, 1951, p. 41.
21 G.P.V. and Helen B. Akrigg, *1001 British Columbia Place Names* (Vancouver: Discovery Press, 1970), p. 141.
22 "Memoirs of Hugh Hunter," *45th Annual Report of the Okanagan Historical Society* (Vernon: Wayside Press, 1981), pp. 102-8. See: granitecreekbc.ca/archive/Memoirs_of_Hugh_Hunter.pdf
23 N.L. Barlee, "Gold Creeks and Ghost Towns," *Canada West Magazine*, 1972, p. 10.
24 Ibid., p. 12.
25 *Vancouver Daily World*, January 1, 1896, p. 6.
26 *Province*, Obituary for Jas Wallace. March 20, 1928, p. 7.
27 *Similkameen Star*, March 15, 1911, p. 1.
28 Ibid., March 2, 1901, p. 1.
29 Ibid., August 4, 1900, p. 5. This was in reference to the Boxer Rebellion of 1899-1901, an anti-colonial uprising led by a northern Chinese political faction known as the Society of Righteous and Harmonious Fists, in opposition of the spread of foreign (European) influence and power as well as Christianity.
30 Ibid., March 15, 1911, p. 1.
31 Ibid., October 25, 1911, p. 1.
32 Ibid., September 22, 1906, 1.
33 Ibid., June 5, 1912, p. 1.
34 Ibid., August 6, 1912, p. 11.
35 Ibid., June 11, 1912, p. 3.
36 Jennifer Neil Bar, "Bresemann & Durfee Partnership, 1911-1913," in *Building the West: The Early Architects of British Columbia*, Donald Luxton, ed. (Vancouver: Talonbooks, 2007), p. 402.
37 *Vernon News*, August 6, 1914, p. 2.
38 Eric M. Goodfellow, "Princeton Hotel," *Seventy-First Report of the Okanagan Historical Society*, Kelowna, 2007, pp. 101-2.
39 *Province*, October 13, 1919, p. 3.
40 *Gazette* (Grand Forks), November 3, 1922, p. 2.

41 *Province*, May 12, 1925, p. 22.
42 Ibid., "Pioneer Prospector Dead at Princeton," March 20, 1928, p. 7.
43 Ibid., "Vancouver-Princeton Phone Service Complete," December 30, 1928, p. 13.
44 Ibid., July 14, 1929, p. 56.
45 Ibid., May 7, 1930, p. 3.
46 Ibid., June 16, 1932, p. 1.
47 *Vancouver Sun*, "Johnson Opens New Era for Interior," November 2, 1949, p. 1.
48 *Province*, March 13, 1945, p. 11.
49 *Vancouver Sun*, December 3, 1945, p. 1.
50 *Province*, June 27, 1956, p. 6.
51 Ibid., June 14, 1960, p. 10.
52 Lena Sin, "Landmark Hotel Burns to the Ground in Princeton," *Province*, April 9, 2006, p. 5.
53 N.L. Barlee, "Coalmont," "Gold Creeks and Ghost Towns," p. 9.
54 Diane Sterne, *White Gold and Black Diamonds: The History of Granite Creek and Coalmont* (Coalmont: Diane Sterne, 2011), p. 61.
55 *Similkameen Star*, May 10, 1911, p. 3.
56 Diane Sterne, *White Gold and Black Diamonds*, p. 101.
57 *Coalmont Courier*, "Coalmont Hotel Housewarming a Stunning Success," May 6, 1912, p. 1. Note: "Terpsichorean" describes something that has to do with dancing... The word "terpsichorean" comes from T*erpsikhore,* one of Greek mythology's nine muses. Terpsikhore literally means "enjoyment of dance," and she was the muse known for ruling over dance while playing her lyre.
58 Diane Sterne, *White Gold and Black Diamonds*, p. 101. See also: "Western Float," *Vancouver Sun*, September 20, 1912, p. 11.
59 Diane Sterne, *White Gold and Black Diamonds*, p. 103.
60 *Vancouver Sun*, December 21, 1912, p. 12.
61 *Similkameen Star*, December 19, 1913, p. 3.
62 Ibid., January 31, 1912, p. 2.
63 Ibid., January 24, 1912, p. 2.
64 Sterne, *White Gold and Black Diamonds*, p. 101.
65 Wrigley British Columbia Directory for 1918.
66 *Province*, "Big Raid Made By Liquor Board—More Than Score of Arrests In Similkameen Tuesday Morning," August 9, 1922, p. 1.
67 Sterne, *White Gold and Black Diamonds*, p. 101.
68 *Province*, "Brown-Miller," July 28, 1930, p. 18.
69 Sterne, *White Gold and Black Diamonds*, p. 103.

70 Ibid., p. 104.
71 T.W. Paterson, *Okanagan-Similkameen*, p. 34.
72 Sterne, p. 157.
73 *Province*, July 9, 1948, p. 43.
74 Sterne, p. 105. See also: "Service held for veteran hotel keeper," *Province*, August 10, 1960, p. 1.
75 Akrigg, p. 126.
76 *Merritt Herald*, "Gearing-Edge: Pioneer entrepreneur had many ventures," July 21, 2016. merrittherald.com/gearing-edge-pioneer-entrepreneur-had-many-ventures/.
77 L.E. Morrissey, "Romance and Adventure in Settlement of Beautiful Nicola Valley," *Province*, January 24, 1926, p. 41.
78 *Merritt Herald*, "Gearing-Edge...," July 21, 2016.
79 *Province*, "Anniversary is Celebrated," June 4, 1938, p. 13.
80 *Merritt Herald*, "Gearing-Edge:...", July 21, 2016.
81 *Vancouver Daily World*, November 18, 1892, p. 5.
82 *Manitoba Morning Free Press*, April 20, 1895, p. 1.
83 *Vancouver Daily World*, February 20, 1896, p. 7.
84 *Province*, February 28, 1901, p. 2.
85 *Victoria Daily Times*, "Railway to Tap Nicola Valley," November 13, 1903, p. 1.
86 *Nicola Herald*, July 13, 1905, p. 1.
87 Ibid., March 8, 1906, p. 1.
88 Ibid., May 21, 1908, p. 1.
89 *Vancouver Daily World*, May 28, 1908, p. 4.
90 *Nicola Valley News*, December 30, 1910, p. 7.
91 prabook.com/web/charles.goldman/2500410
92 *Province*, "Major Goldman Buys Town of Nicola, BC," May 25, 1921, p. 21.
93 *Vancouver Daily World*, June 25, 1921, 3.
94 *Province*, October 12, 1935, p. 6.
95 *Vancouver Sun*, "Nicola Pioneer A.E. Howse Dies, December 16, 1938, p. 2.
96 Akrigg, p. 161.
97 Barbara Roden, "Golden Century: A Canny Pioneering Businessman Links Spences Bridge and Marx Brothers," *Ashcroft–Cache Creek Journal*, April 17, 2019.
98 Ibid.
99 Glen A. Mofford, *Along the E&N: A Journey Back to the Historic Hotels of Vancouver Island* (Victoria: Touchwood Editions, 2019), p. 39.
100 *British Columbian*, June 26, 1886, p. 1.

101 *Vancouver Sun*, "BC's Oldest Auto Still Rarin' to Go," December 12, 1946, p. 5.
102 wikipedia.org/wiki/Wolseley_Motors https://www.oecc.ca/Spanners/Vol_1_SpannerJan06.pdf.
103 *Nicola Herald*, March 1, 1906, p. 1.
104 *Nicola Valley News*, February 18, 1910, p. 18.
105 Kamloops Museum and Archive online, Clemes Family fonds, 1979.
106 changingvancouver.wordpress.com/tag/art-clemes/.
107 en.wikipedia.org/wiki/Pantages_Theatre (Vancouver).
108 walkingoffthebigapple.com/2009/06/long-road-to-big-time-marx-brothers.html.
109 changingvancouver.wordpress.com/tag/art-clemes/.
110 *Daily Building Record*, January 2, 1913, p. 1.
111 Information taken from the first brochure published for the Regent Hotel in the author's collection, 1913.
112 *Province*, "Death of Mrs. Clemes." May 31, 1918, p. 14.
113 *Vancouver Sun*, "Arthur Clemes, Old-Timer, Dead." February 18, 1922, p. 7.
114 *Interior News* (Smithers), August 28, 1935, p. 1.
115 *Nanaimo Daily News*, "BC Woman Dies of Burns When Lamp Explodes. "June 10, 1939, p. 1.
116 Barbara Roden, "Golden Country: What's in a name? Who were the Brink, Barnes, and Evans that Ashcroft streets are named after?" *Ashcroft-Cache Creek Journal*, August 1, 2017. ashcroftcachecreekjournal.com/community/golden-country-whats-in-a-name/.
117 Akrigg, p. 20.
118 Roden, "Golden Country..." ashcroftcachecreekjournal.com/community/golden-country-whats-in-a-name/.
119 *Port Moody Gazette*, September 20, 1884, p. 2.
120 Kathy Paulos, *The Museum Corner* (monthly newsletter of the Ashcroft Museum), September 2017.
121 Barbara Roden, "Past, Present & Beyond—The Ill-fated Cargill Hotel," *Ashcroft-Cache Creek Journal*, March 24, 2015. ashcroftcachecreekjournal.com/community/past-present-beyond-the-ill-fated-cargile-hotel/
122 Barbara Roden, "Golden Country..." *Ashcroft-Cache Creek Journal*, November 28, 2017.
123 *Vancouver Daily World*, July 27, 1891, p. 2.
124 *Victoria Daily Times*, July 25, 1893, p. 8.
125 According to an email sent to the author from William Lynes's great-grand-daughter, Sharon Place.

126 *Vancouver Daily World*, March 31, 1898, p. 6.
127 *Victoria Daily Times*, June 5, 1900, p. 7.
128 *Province*, "Morphine Did It," November 14, 1901, p. 4.
129 *Victoria Daily Times*, April 13, 1903, p. 6.
130 Esther Darlington, "Canada's only train robber, Bill Miner: The Ashcroft Connection," The *Ashcroft-Cache Creek Journal*, March 21, 2011. Note: Bill Miner was not the only train robber to rob a train in Canada; follow this link to the *Canadian Encyclopedia* article on the history of "Bill" Miner: thecanadianencyclopedia.ca/en/article/william-miner.
131 *Vancouver Daily World*, "Train Robbers Captured after Sharp Encounter with Police. Leader of Gang Is Identified as "Old Bill Miner," May 15, 1906, headline, p. 1.
132 *Nanaimo Daily News*, "Train Robbers Take Heavy Sentences in Stoic Manner," June 2, 1906, p. 1.
133 *Calgary Herald*, "Business Portion of Ashcroft, BC, is Destroyed by Fire," July 6, 1916, p. 1.
134 *Lillooet Prospector*, "Rebuilding of Ashcroft," July 14, 1916, p. 3. In spite of losing two thousand sacks of recently arrived imported rice, Wing Wo Lung aided the rebuilding of Ashcroft after a personal loss of $30,000.
135 Barbara Roden, "Golden Country: Past, Present, and Beyond: Chinatown," *Ashcroft-Cache Creek Journal*, August 23, 2016.
136 ibid.
137 Wrigley-Henderson Amalgamated Directories for 1917 to 1928.
138 *The Ledge* (Greenwood), A humorous advertisement was worded, ""It is no longer necessary to sleep in a potato patch at Ashcroft; the Ashcroft hotel has built 15 more rooms," July 11, 1919, p. 1.
139 *Abbotsford Post*, April 20, 1917, p. 1.
140 *Times* (Nanaimo), "No Blame in Hotel Fire Deaths," February 6, 1975, p. 3.
141 Jay Morrison "The Little Town That Died of Snobbery," *Province*, May 9, 1982, p. 67.
142 Ibid.
143 Barbara Roden, "Golden Country: Past. Present, and Beyond— Walhachin, Part I," *Ashcroft-Cache Creek Journal*, December 27, 2016.
144 Joan Weir, *Walhachin, Catastrophe or Camelot?* (Surrey, BC: Hancock House, 1984), pp. 8-9.
145 Nelson A. Riis, "The Walhachin Myth: A Study in Settlement Abandonment," MA Thesis, in *Home Truths: Highlights from BC History*,

Richard Mackie and Graeme Wynn, eds., Madeira Park: Harbour Publishing, 2012, p. 313.
146   Roden, "Golden Country: Past. Present, and Beyond—Walhachin, Part I," *Ashcroft-Cache Creek Journal*, December 27, 2016.
147   Weir, *Walhachin, Catastrophe or Camelot?* p. 11.
148   Nelson A, Riis, "The Walhachin Myth: A Study in Settlement Abandonment," p. 315.
149   *Ashcroft Journal*, July 9, 1910, p. 1.
150   Riis, "The Walhachin Myth...," pp. 316-17.
151   Morrison "The Little Town That Died of Snobbery," p. 67.
152   Mark Zuehlke, *Scoundrels, Dreamers and Second Sons: British Remittance Men In The Canadian West* (Toronto: Dundurn Press, Second Edition, 2001), p. 126.
153   Weir, *Walhachin, Catastrophe or Camelot?*, p. 32.
154   Elsie G. Turnbull, "Ghost of Walhachin," *Pioneer Days in British Columbia*, Art Downs, ed. (Surrey: Foremost Publishing, 1973), p. 38. See also Larry Jacobson, *Walhachin, Birth of a Legend* (Walhachin Museum: Prolong Press, 2014), p. 111.
155   Graham Chandler, "The Short Season of High Society," legionmagazine.com/en/2009/06/the-short-season-of-high-society/.
156   Weir, *Walhachin, Catastrophe or Camelot?*, p. 43.
157   Morrison, "The Little Town...," p. 67. Note: The Commodore Ballroom had no ordinary dancefloor as it was engineered to absorb shocks and it bounced slightly. When the floor was being repaired in 1996, the secret to its bounce was revealed to be "a web of shiplap, two-by-three, and bats of horsehair and car tires." Source: Aaron Chapman, *Live at the Commodore, The Story of Vancouver's Historic Commodore Ballroom,* Vancouver: Arsenal Press, 2014, p. 156. It is unknown what they used in the Walhachin sprung floor.
158   Ibid., p. 67.
159   *Province*, May 20, 1912, p. 22.
160   Turnbull, "Ghost of Walhachin," p. 39.
161   Morrison, "The Little Town...," p. 67.
162   *Province*, June 15, 1916, p. 17.
163   Chandler, "The Short Season of High Society," *Legion Magazine*, June 4, 2009.
164   *Province*, November 20, 1918, p. 16.
165   *Province*, August 2, 1919, p. 23.
166   Weir, *Walhachin, Catastrophe or Camelot?*, p. 37.
167   Morrison, "The Little Town...," p. 67.

168 *Province*, November 4, 1919, p. 19.
169 Stephen Hume, "Ghosts of Walhachin, Ghosts of War," *Vancouver Sun*, August 4, 1989, p. 9.
170 Note: There are plenty of books and articles written about Walhachin. If you are interested in learning more, please refer to the bibliography at the end of this book.
171 Akrigg, pp. 93-94.
172 *Kootenay Star*, May 16, 1891, p. 4.
173 *Vancouver Semi-Weekly World*, September, 20, 1898, p. 3.
174 *Cumberland Island*, August 26, 1922, p. 3, quoting from the *Kamloops Standard-Sentinel*, 1902: "Napoleon Latremouille, always up to date, has ordered an automobile."
175 *Victoria Daily Times*, November 11, 1903, p. 2.
176 *Daily Advertiser* (Vancouver), September 9, 1904, p. 14.
177 *Province*, October 25, 1904, p. 5.
178 *Daily News Advertiser*, September 24, 1905, p. 13.
179 *Province*, February 13, 1906, p. 16.
180 *Vancouver Semi-Weekly News*, January 3, 1902, p. 7.
181 *Victoria Daily Times*, January 22, 1944, p. 15.
182 *Province*, February 13, 1906, p. 16.
183 *Nicola Valley News*, February 18, 1910, p. 2.
184 *Victoria Daily Times*, "Brown Jug Closes Doors Soon," November 27, 1917, p. 9.
185 *Victoria Daily Times*, January 13, 1944, p. 13.
186 *Kamloops Inland Sentinel*, August 11, 1911, p. 3.
187 Ibid., "Will Enlarge the Leland Hotel," November 28, 1911, p. 1.
188 *Vancouver Sun*, February 12, 1912, p. 4.
189 *Kamloops Inland Sentinel*, November 25, 1912, p. 5.
190 *Canadian Encyclopedia, Volume II* (Edmonton: Hurtig Publishers, 1985), p. 1116.
191 *Vancouver Sun*, July 24, 1946, p. 25.
192 *Kamloops Inland Sentinel*, "Exciting Runaway on Third Avenue," November 28, 1912, p. 1.
193 *Victoria Daily Times*, January 12, 1923, p. 1.
194 *Province*, January 19, 1925, p. 24.
195 *Victoria Daily Times*, January 16, 1928, p. 3.
196 BC Directories for the years 1930-1946. See also: The *Chilliwack Progress*, "Hotels Unite Under One Manager," March 20, 1930, p. 8.
197 *Vancouver Sun*, "Plaza and Leland Hotels," October 3, 1936, p. 30.
198 *Province*, "Interior Hotelmen Meet at Kamloops," October 30, 1936, p. 11.

199 *Vancouver Sun*, July 24, 1946, p. 25.
200 *Victoria Daily Times*, May 1, 1956, p. 3.
201 *Montreal Gazette*, "Landmark Destroyed," October 30, 1979, p. 70.
202 Akrigg, p. 152.
203 Denis Marshall, "Montebello Hotel," *Okanagan Historical Society Seventy-first Report*, 2007, pp. 104-5.
204 Ibid., p. 105.
205 "The Hyack Story," hyackfestival.com/our-story
206 Glen A. Mofford, *Aqua Vitae: A History of the Saloons and Hotel-Bars of Victoria, 1851-1917* (Victoria: TouchWood Editions, 2016), p. 114.
207 *Province*, "Old Time Hotelman Dead at Salmon Arm," October 8, 1926, p. 15.
208 Ibid., "Nicola," August 1, 1900, p. 2. Note: "Bornite (also known as peacock copper), is an important copper ore mineral and occurs widely in porphyry copper deposits along with the more common chalcopyrite." Source: en.wikipedia.org/wiki/Bornite
209 *Vancouver Daily World*, February 2, 1907, p. 3.
210 *Boundary Creek Times* (Greenwood), "The new Montebello Hotel at Salmon Arm has opened for business." September 18, 1908, p. 3.
211 *Province*, March 30, 1909, p. 9.
212 Eve Lazarus, "Every Place Has a Story: A blog about history, heritage, buildings and murder," "The Vancouver Heritage House Tour, Alvo von Alvensleben and the Old Residence," May 18, 2019. evelazarus.com/tag/alvo-von-alvensleben/.
213 *Province*, October 8, 1926, p. 15.
214 Ibid., September 30, 1928, p. 46.
215 Ibid., "Fire in Salmon Arm Hotel," April 6, 1936, p. 16.
216 Ibid., January 5, 1938, p. 26.
217 Ibid., July 26, 1941, p. 14.
218 Ibid., June 9, 1945, p. 29.
219 Marshall, "Montebello Hotel," p. 105.
220 Ibid.
221 *Victoria Daily Times*, "Victims Named in Hotel Blaze," August 9, 1967, p. 8.

Chapter Two: The Okanagan

1 *Edenograph*, "Enderby Wants Hotel," March 1, 1903, p. 1.
2 *Vancouver Daily World*, June 24, 1904, p. 3.
3 *Edenograph*, April 19, 1905, p. 1.

4   *Province*, March 20, 1905, p. 2.
5   *Armstrong Advance*, December 1, 1905, p. 3.
6   Robert Cowen, "Enderby's King Edward Hotel," *Seventy-first Report of the Okanagan Historical Society*, p. 93.
7   *Edenograph*, September 20, 1905, p. 1.
8   Robert Cowen, "Enderby's King Edward Hotel," p. 93.
9   *Edenograph*, July 5, 1905, p. 1.
10 *Walker's Weekly* (Enderby), August 27, 1908, p. 9.
11 *Province*, July 27, 1911, p. 13.
12 *Enderby Press and Walker's Weekly*, April 30, 1914, p. 1.
13 Ibid., July 23, 1914, p. 2.
14 Ibid., December 11, 1913, p. 1.
15 William J. Whitehead, "Clifford Hardwick," *Fifty-sixth Report of the Okanagan Historical Society*, 1992, p. 112.
16 Cowan "Enderby's King Edward Hotel," p. 94.
17 *Province*, June 4, 1933, 44.
18 Recollections of Bill Huffman.
19 Cowan, p. 94.
20 *Province*, "Enderby Hotel Razed, Blind Man Rescued," February 18, 1947, p. 8. Also sourced from the *Vancouver Sun*, "Hotel Burns at Enderby," February 17, 1947, p. 22.
21 *Vernon News*, March 17, 1949, p. 8.
22 *Province*, "Hotel Owner Pioneer Dies in Enderby," March 8, 1957, p. 10.
23 G.P.V. and Helen B. Akrigg, *1001 British Columbia Place Names* (Vancouver: Discovery Press, Second Edition, 1970), p. 18.
24 A brief history of the beginnings of Armstrong, BC and the role the railway played in its beginning can be found here: canadaehx.com/2021/09/28/the-history-of-armstrong/.
25 *Vancouver Daily World*, "It's Budding Fast, The Little Town of Armstrong Gives Promise of Great Things," January 29, 1892, p. 3.
26 Ibid., July 30, 1892, p. 3.
27 Quoted in the *Vernon News*, December 17, 1891, from the *Thirteenth Report of the Okanagan Historical Society*, 1966, p. 255.
28 *Pacific Canadian* (New Westminster) October 28, 1893, p. 8.
29 *Victoria Daily Times*, February 16, 1899, p. 7.
30 Ibid., August 5, 1901, p. 8.
31 *Hedley Gazette*, November 30, 1905, p. 3.
32 *Armstrong Advocate*, April 13, 1906, p. 1.
33 Devon L. Muhlert, "Armstrong Hotel Fits a Dowager's Role, *Sixty-First Report of the Okanagan Historical Society*, 1997, p. 86.

34 *Province*, "Fire Occurs at the Armstrong Hotel," February 8, 1909, p. 3.
35 *Vancouver Sun*, September 24 1912, p. 10.
36 *Mail Herald* (Revelstoke), April 20, p. 19.
37 Ibid., September 3, 1910, p. 6.
38 *Vancouver Sun*, "Marked Opposition to Prohibition Bill," June 21, 1916, p. 8.
39 *Weekly* (Victoria), July 29, 1916, p. 6.
40 *Sixty-first Report of the Okanagan Historical Society*, p. 86.
41 *Vancouver Sun*, "BC Pioneer G.C. Lembke Dies at 78," May 1, 1957, p. 11.
42 *Victoria Daily Times*, January 19, 1933, p. 1.
43 Devon L. Muhlert, "Armstrong Hotel Fits a Dowager's Role, p. 89.
44 Akrigg, p. 181
45 Ibid., p. 181.
46 Catherine Barford, "Charles Osborn Wickenden (1851-1934)" from *Building the West: Early Architects of British Columbia,* Donald Luxton, ed. (Vancouver: Talon Books, Revised Second Edition, 2007), p. 164.
47 Note that in the early years, the alternate spelling "Kalemalka" was used until George Raymond's time as proprietor, when his eldest daughter pointed out that the spelling of the hotel name was incorrect and that the "e" after "kal" should be dropped for an "a."
48 *Province*, July 24, 1927, p. 49.
49 Burt R. Campbell, "Vernon's Diamond Jubilee," *Sixteenth Report of the Okanagan Historical Society, 1952,* p. 49.
50 Jo Fraser Jones, ed., *Hobnobbing with a Countess and Other Okanagan Adventures: The Diaries of Alice Barrett Parke, 1891-1900* (Vancouver: UBC Press, 2002), p. 307, note 40.
51 *Vernon News*, June 16, 1892, p. 5.
52 *Weekly News-Advertiser*, May 31, 1893, p. 6.
53 *Nanaimo Daily Telegram*, February 6, 1894, p. 5.
54 *Vernon News*, September 9, 1893, p. 1.
55 Ibid., August 2, 1894, p. 1.
56 Fraser Jones, *Hobnobbing with a Countess,* "Diary entry by Alice Barrett Parke," p. 80.
57 *Vernon News*, August 6, 1896, p. 8.
58 Ibid., November 15, 1900, p. 5.
59 *Nanaimo Daily News*, August 29, 1902, p. 3.
60 *Province*, April 21, 1906, p. 3.
61 *Vernon News*, February 28, 1907, p. 8.
62 Ibid., August 18, 1910, p. 5.

63　Ibid., April 13, 1911, p. 5.
64　Ibid., June 6, 1912, p. 10.
65　Wrigley's BC Directory, 1920, p. 964. (With a photograph of the hotel.)
66　*Vernon News*, August 11, 1921, p. 10.
67　Ibid., April 12, 1923, p. 9.
68　Ibid., March 16, 1922, p. 5.
69　*Vancouver Sun*, May 2, 1929, p. 20.
70　*Chilliwack Progress*, August 19, 1936, p. 5.
71　*Province*, June 26, 1937, p. 25.
72　Ibid., November 7, 1949, p. 5.
73　Doug Currie, "Vernon's Historical Architecture," *Forty-fourth Annual Report of the Okanagan Historical Society, 1980*, p. 46.
74　T.W. Paterson, *Okanagan-Similkameen* (British Columbia Ghost Town Series) (Langley, BC: Sunfire Publications, 1983), p. 156.
75　Akrigg, p. 129.
76　Paterson, *Okanagan-Similkameen*, p. 165.
77　Ron Seymour, "Original Hotel Eldorado Built by Colourful Countess," *Daily Courier* (Kelowna), February 16, 2016, kelownadailycourier.ca/news/article_babe6366-d14a-11e5-b525-b33da050e7ee.html.
78　Ibid.
79　Cullin's many projects included designing Riverview Hospital in Coquitlam in 1919. Source: Donald Luxton, ed., *Building The West: Early Architects of British Columbia*, p. 496.
80　*Thirteenth Annual Report of the Okanagan Historical Society*, p. 245.
81　*Province*, June 18, 1926, p. 7.
82　Ibid., August 9, 1926, p. 7.
83　Ibid., August 3, 1927, p. 22.
84　Ibid., "Major Lloyd, Kelowna Hotel Manager Dies after Auto Accident," May 25, 1932, p. 11.
85　*Thirteenth Annual Report of the Okanagan Historical Society*, p. 245.
86　Sharron J. Simpson, *The Kelowna Story: An Okanagan History* (Madeira Park, BC: Harbour Publishing, 2011), pp. 136-38.
87　*Vancouver Sun*, "Local Tennis Players at Eldorado Arms," August 10, 1932, p. 8.
88　Ibid., June 11, 1932, p. 13.
89　*Province*, May 21, 1933, p. 42.
90　*Thirteenth Annual Report of the Okanagan Historical Society*, p. 245.
91　*Province*, "Countess Bubna Dies in Europe," August 14, 1935, p. 19.
92　Simpson, *The Kelowna Story*. p. 195.

93 John Armstrong, "Kelowna Landmark Lost to Fire Following Move," *Vancouver Sun*, April 20, 1989, p. 25.
94 *Okanagan Historical Society Annual Reports,* Nos. 24, 33, 35. OHS 97.
95 Kaye Benzer, "A brief history of the Lakeview Hotel," pp. 98-99; open.library.ubc.ca/collections/ohs/items/1.0132243#p97z-4r0f:hotel
96 Simpson, *The Kelowna Story*, p. 62.
97 Ibid, p. 62.
98 Ibid, chapter four, "And I thought we would be spared," pp. 139-42.
99 *Vancouver Sun*, "Kelowna Girl Feared Murdoch Would Slay Her, Jurors Told," January 20, 1932, p. 1.
100 *Vancouver Sun*, January 25, 1932, p. 1.
101 *Vernon News* September 25, 1906, p. 13.
102 Kaye Benzer, "The Royal Anne Hotel," *Seventy-first report of the Okanagan Historical Society*, 2007, pp. 82-83.
103 *Vernon News*, May 30, 1907, p. 3.
104 *Vernon News*, December 12, 1907, p. 8.
105 *Orchard City Record*, (Kelowna) April 8, 1909, p. 6.
106 Ibid., October 21, 1909, p. 1.
107 Ibid., January 12, 1911, p. 4.
108 *Vernon News*, November 16, 1911, p. 8.
109 *Kelowna Record*, "Hotelkeeper Fined," March 20, 1913, p. 1.
110 Ibid., September 27, 1917, p. 1.
111 Ibid., November 8, 1917, p. 4.
112 *Vernon News*, November 15, 1917, p. 7.
113 *Kelowna Record*, January 24, 1918, p. 4.
114 Ibid., April 25, 1918, p. 1.
115 *Vernon News*, July 27, 1922, p. 9.
116 *Province*, "Call Tenders for Hotel at Kelowna," September 21, 1927, p. 10.
117 Benzer, "The Royal Anne Hotel," p. 83.
118 *Vernon News*, March 15, 1928, p. 1.
119 Donald Luxton, ed., *Building the West*, p. 510.
120 *Province*, June 24, 1928, p. 15.
121 Benzer, p. 83.
122 *Vancouver Sun*, "New Hotel at Kelowna Opens," March 22, 1929, p. 15.
123 Wrigley's Directory for Kelowna, 1929, p. 384.
124 *Vernon News*, January 9, 1930, p. 8.
125 Ibid., July 17, 1930, p. 7.
126 Ibid., August 21, 1930, p. 9.

127 *Province*, October 19, 1930, p. 46.
128 *Vernon News*, February 19, 1931, p. 2.
129 Ibid., December 22, 1932, p. 7.
130 *Nanaimo Daily News*, October 27, 1943, p. 1.
131 *Vancouver Sun*, February 22, 1946, p. 4.
132 *Province*, November 2, 1949, p. 42.
133 *Vancouver Sun*, July 7, 1954, p. 12.
134 Ibid., December 14, 1971, p. 9.
135 David Gregory, "The Beginning of Summerland, 100 Years Ago," *Sixty-sixth Report of the Okanagan Historical Society* (Vernon, BC: Okanagan Historical Society, 2002), p. 59.
136 Ibid, p. 68.
137 Ibid.
138 Fredrick William Andrew, "Peachland, Summerland and Naramata," *Nineteenth report of the Okanagan Historical Society*, 1955, p. 67.
139 F. W. Andrew, "The Summerland Story." *Summerland Review* (Summerland, BC: Summerland Ladies Hospital Auxiliary, 1967, p. 11.
140 *Similkameen Star*, June 4, 1904, p. 1.
141 Gregory, "The Beginning of Summerland, p. 68
142 *Similkameen Star*, June 4, 1904, p. 1.
143 Andrew, "The Summerland Story," p. 14.
144 Note: In May 1892, the SS *Aberdeen* was constructed and launched from Okanagan Landing. It was a sternwheeler 146 feet long, net tonnage 350, registered in Vancouver and licensed to carry passengers and freight. This was an important mode of transportation, as many guests arrived at Summerland on these wonderful sternwheelers. The SS *Okanagan* (1907) and then the SS *Sicamous* were added to the fleet, CPR ships all.
145 *Vancouver Daily World*, September 18, 1906, p. 12.
146 Ibid., p. 17.
147 *Vancouver Daily World*, September 18, 1906, p. 13.
148 *Summerland Review*, December 19, 1912, p. 11.
149 *Penticton Herald*, "A Christmas Tragedy: Two Negroes Perish on Summerland Road." January 2, 1909, p. 1.
150 I researched three articles while learning the story of the unfortunate deaths of Wilson and Blair: the *Keremeos Trumpet*, "Death from Exposure," January 1, 1909, p. 1; *Vancouver Daily World*: "Negroes Met Death in Hills, Christmas Spree at Penticton Ends Fatally for Two," December 31, 1908, p. 12. The most complete version was the one cited in note 148.

151 *Province*, July 20, 1909, p. 11.
152 Henderson's BC Gazetteer and Directory for 1910.
153 *Enderby Press and Walker's Weekly*, October 9, 1913, p. 3.
154 The Dominion Experimental Farm static1.squarespace.com/static/5995f4e96b8f5b9ef7c7355f/t/5d13a00e93802d0001370720/1561567506854/11-History+of+the+Dominion+Experimental+Farm-combined.pdf.
155 John Arendt, "Summerland railway bridge was constructed in 1913," *Penticton Western News*, June 30, 2020, p. 1.
156 David Gregory, "Spanish Influenza Affected British Columbia," *Summerland Review*, May 17, 2020.
157 *Province*, May 25, 1921, p. 7.
158 *Province*, "Summerland Cars Collide Head-On," January 10, 1925, p. 30.
159 *Victoria Daily Times*, ""Hotel Burned in Summerland," November 16, 1925, p. 1.
160 R.N. Atkinson, *Penticton Pioneers in Story and Pictures*, Penticton: Okanagan Historical Society, 1967, pp. 95-96.
161 *Hedley Gazette*, "Penticton Notes," February 23, 1905, p. 5.
162 Atkinson, *Penticton Pioneers in Stories and Pictures*, Penticton: Penticton Museum, 1967, pp. 95.
164 Atkinson, p. 95.
165 *Penticton Press*, March 14, 1908, p. 1.
166 *Daily News* (Nelson), August 19, 1910, p. 4.
167 Atkinson, p. 95.
168 lakecountrymuseum.com/this-day-in-history-murder-on-okanagan-lake/.
169 *Vancouver Daily World*, March 25, 1912, p. 1.
170 Cecil Clark, "Murder on Okanagan Lake" in BC *Provincial Police Stories*, *Vol. 2* (Surrey: Heritage House Publishing, 2001), pp. 12-15
171 Atkinson, pp. 172-73.
172 Ibid., p. 173.
173 Ibid., p. 95.
174 *Vancouver Daily World*, "Wood Alcohol Fatal to Penticton Clerk," October 27, 1921, p. 3.
175 wordsense.eu/incolae/.
176 *Calgary Herald*, "Irrigation Banquet Marks the Opening of Penticton Hotel," August 19, 1912, p. 20.
177 Atkinson, p. 96.
178 *Vancouver Sun*, "Scaffold Gives Way and Carpenter Jumps Fracturing His Leg," December 4, 1912, p. 10.

179 *The Ledge* (Greenwood), "Lowery's Breezy Western Float—Odds and ends of BC News recorded in interesting paragraphs," June 6, 1912, p. 1. See also: *Vancouver Sun*, June 21, 1912, p. 10.
180 Elizabeth Pryce-Bork, "The Incola Hotel," *Sixty-third Report of the Okanagan Historical Society, 1999*, p. 119.
181 Atkinson, p. 96.
182 *Kelowna Record*, July 3, 1913, p. 3.
183 *Vancouver Sun*, January 7, 1913, p. 11
184 Atkinson, p. 96.
185 Ibid.
186 Pryce-Bork, p. 120.
187 Maggie Ricciardi, "Haven Hill Retirement Centre: A Short History," *Seventieth Report of the Okanagan Historical Society*, 2006, p. 122.
188 *Creston Review*, November 21, 1919, p. 5.
189 *Kelowna Record*, August 21, 1919, p. 1.
190 *Vancouver Sun*, January 25, 1920, p. 29.
191 Pryce-Bork, p. 120.
192 Ibid., p. 120.
193 *Province*, January 22, 1933, p. 46.
194 Ibid., August 16, 1941, p. 2.
195 Ibid., April 7, 1947, p. 25.
196 Ibid., "Bad Weather Holds Up Plane Search," October 20, 1947, p. 1.
197 *Vancouver Sun*, "Cloudy Sky Halts Hunt For Bomber," October 20, 1947, p. 2.
198 *Victoria Daily Times*, "Rescue Fleet Is Combing Arrow Lakes District," October 22, 1947, p. 1.
199 *Vancouver Sun*, August 24, 1951, p. 6.
200 Ibid., October 9, 1952, p. 14.
201 Ibid., "Beer Parlour Plans Readied At Penticton," April 22, 1950, p. 13.
202 Ibid., p. 13.
203 *Vancouver Sun*, "Incola Hotel Reported Sold," June 23, 1950, p. 29.
204 *Victoria Daily Times*, August 23, 1951, p. 21.
205 Glen A. Mofford, *Along the E&N: A Journey Back to the Historic Hotels of Vancouver Island*, Victoria: TouchWood Editions, 2019, p. 26.
206 *Nanaimo Daily News*, May 8, 1959, p. 2.
207 Pryce-Bork, p. 121.
208 John Aylward on Facebook, 2021.
209 *Victoria Daily Colonist*, December 6, 1978, p. 6.
210 Pryce-Bork, p. 121. Note: There are a number of YouTube videos regarding the Incola Hotel: youtube.com/watch?v=p655bQvXY1A.

211 Darryl MacKenzie, "Oliver's Historic Mesa Hotel," open.library.ubc.ca/collections/ohs/items/1.0132243#p77z-4r0f:hotel
212 *Vancouver Daily World*, January 11, 1922, p. 19.
213 Note: Shorty Knight and Slim Archibald drove the hotel pieces by truck from Penticton. However, because of the extremely poor condition of the road, the cargo may have been sent by York's barge to Okanagan Falls before being trucked into Oliver.
214 Katie Lacey, *Twenty-Second Report of the Okanagan Historical Society*
215 *Vancouver Sun*, August 15, 1936, p. 12.
216 MacKenzie, "Oliver's Historic Mesa Hotel," p. 78.
217 *Vancouver Sun*, "Liquor Board Closes Two Oliver Hotels," December 13, 1939, p. 2.
218 Ibid., "The Oliver Hotel has changed hands," March 25, 1947, p. 3.
219 *Province*, March 11, 1949, p. 8.
220 Claire Ogilvie, "Fire Destroys Oliver Heritage Hotel," the *Province*, May 25, 2010, p. 4.
221 Mackenzie, "Oliver's Historic Mesa Hotel," pp. 100-2
222 *Vancouver Sun*, "$20,000 Oliver Hotel," March 15, 1935, p. 12.
223 Ibid., "Building Activity in Oliver," April 27, 1935, p. 20.
224 Ibid., "New Hotel in Oliver." May 27, 1935, p. 12.
225 *Vancouver Sun*, March 23, 1937, 12.
226 Ibid., August 3, 1937, p. 10.
227 Ibid., "Liquor Board Closes Two Oliver Hotels.", December 13, 1939, p. 2.
228 *Province*, "Farris Quashes Liquor Conviction," September 15, 1942, p. 13.
229 Ibid., December 27, 1943, p. 1.
230 *Victoria Daily Times*, "Vernon Trial Ends in Acquittal," May 4, 1944, p. 2.
231 *Vancouver Sun*, "Arlington Hotel Sale Announced," September 20, 1944, p. 13.
232 *Province*, August 8, 1944, p. 11.
233 *Gazette* (Grand Forks), August 18, 1960, p. 7.
234 *Nanaimo Daily News*, May 5, 1961, p. 2.
235 *Province*, November 7, 1961, p. 2.
236 *Vancouver Sun*, July 8, 1938, p. 7.
237 *Province*, "New Beer Plebiscite," September 30, 1938, p. 3.
238 *Vancouver Sun*, December 11, 1939, p. 13.
239 *Province*, October 12, 1938, p. 10.
240 *Vancouver Sun*, June 26, 1939, p. 2.
241 Ibid., June 24, 1942, p. 22.
242 George J. Fraser, *The Story of Osoyoos: September 1811 to December 1952* (1952), p. 23.

243 *Province*, "Osoyoos," May 8, 1950, p. 33.
244 *Vancouver Sun*, September 9, 1992, p. 16.
245 *Calgary Herald*, "For Sale by Tender," January 21, 1995, p. 71.

Chapter Three: The Boundary Country

1. John Eck, "A Touch of the Boundary: Cowboy Poetry," *Fourteenth Report of the Boundary Country, 2001*, p. 157.
2. Alice Glanville, "Postal Service in the Boundary: 100 Years," *Eleventh Report of the Boundary Historical Society, 1988*, p. 12.
3. *Hedley Gazette*, June 14, 1906, p. 3.
4. Ibid., July 12, 1906, p. 3.
5. Ibid., November 29, 1906, p. 2.
6. Ibid., July 14, 1906, p. 3.
7. Ibid., August 23, 1906, p. 3.
8. Ibid., May 21, 1908, 3. Noted by Greg Nesteroff that Bridesville was unincorporated and that the title of "mayor" in this case was an honorary one.
9. *Boundary Creek Times*, June 4, 1909, p. 1.
10. *The Ledge* (Greenwood), June 2, 1910, p. 4.
11. Ibid., April 20, 1916.
12. *Grand Forks Gazette*, "Hotelman pioneer William Johns Dies in Vancouver," August 27, 1959, p. 1.
13. *Spokesman-Review* (Spokane, Washington), August 1, 1916, p. 12.
14. Ibid., August 7, 1916, p. 2.
15. *Lethbridge Herald*, "BC Hotelkeeper Is Murder Victim—Shot down in the kitchen of his hotel at Bridesville, near border." October 21, p. 1.
16. *Province*, October 23, 1922, p. 12.
17. *The Ledge* (Greenwood), December 9, 1926, p. 4.
18. *The Gazette*, "15 Years Ago," June 11, 1942, p. 2.
19. Ibid., April 28, 1933, p. 5.
20. Ibid., May 1, 1952, p. 9.
21. Ibid., October 16, 1952, p. 1.
22. Garnet Basque, "Rock Creek," *Ghost Towns & Mining Camps of the Boundary Country* (Surrey: Heritage House Publishing, 1999, reprinted, 2007, p. 3.
23. *The Ledge*, (Greenwood), October 16, 1913, p. 2.
24. Gladys Bell Burlton, "Early Days in Rock Creek: Riverside," *Third Annual Report of the Boundary Historical Society*, 1960, p. 30.

25 Basque, "Rock Creek," p. 10.
26 *Weekly News Advertiser*, May 17, 1899, p. 1.
27 *Boundary Times*, September 4, 1897, p. 8.
28 Burlton, "Early Days in Rock Creek," p. 30.
29 Basque, pp. 10-11.
30 *Greenwood Weekly Times*, "Bold Robbery, Sam Larsen's Hotel at Rock Creek Held Up," May 23, 1901, p. 23.
31 Burlton, pp. 31-32.
32 *Boundary Creek Times*, January 1, 1904, p. 4.
33 Basque, p. p. 11.
34 "International Harvester Auto Buggy & Wagon (1907 to 1917). The International Harvester Auto Buggy was the first automobile produced by the company. Introduced in 1907, the Auto Buggy was fitted with a flat two-cylinder engine and featured notable ground clearance as opposed to other early automobiles. In 1908, International Harvester introduced a variant known as the Auto Wagon that featured bench seating and a truck bed. Additional body styles for the Auto Wagon included a stake bed, panel delivery, and bus. Variants included the Model AA, Model AW, and Model MW. The Auto Buggy was discontinued in 1912 as the company focused on trucks, but the Auto Wagon remained in production until 1917." classic.com/m/international-harvester/auto-buggy-wagon/.
35 Burlton, p. 35.
36 Ibid.
37 *Calgary Herald*, March 8, 1919, p. 5.
38 The *Ledge* (Greenwood), "Death of Mrs. S.T. Larsen," September 16, 1920, p. 1.
39 *Gazette* (Grand Forks), "Friends Pay Tribute to Late Mrs. Larsen," September 24, 1920, p. 4.
40 Wrigley's British Columbia Directory, p. 656.
41 "Greenwood Hotel Has New Owner," Vancouver Sun, April 22, 1933, p. 10.
42 *Vancouver Sun*, June 23, 1934, p. 27.
43 en.wikipedia.org/wiki/Beaverdell.
44 Gary Trent, notes.
45 *Boundary Creek Times*, March 29, 1899 (thanks to Greg Nesteroff)
46 Michael Kluckner, *Vanishing British Columbia*.
47 Kluckner, "Boundary Country;" michaelkluckner.com/bciw, pp. 72-88.
48 *Gazette*, July 11, 1935, p. 4.
49 Ibid., August 21, 1947, p. 1.

50 Ibid., August 26, 1948, p. 9.
51 Ibid., September 11, 1951, p. 4.
52 *Province*, August 4, 1958, p. 25.
53 *Gazette*, September 23, 1964, p. 6.
54 Cheryl Weirda, *Kelowna Capital News*, March 29, 2911. Note: According to court documents, Daum had been fighting with the previous owners, Mary Ellen and Eugene Katchin, after a lease arrangement went south around the time Daum tried to purchase the property in what he characterized as a lease-to-own scenario. The court battle ended [in 2010] with Daum awarded title. The Katchins had taken out a mortgage in 2001, with Bryan and Leona Rosekrans acting as guarantors.
55 *Gazette*, "45 Years Ago," January 10, 1946, p. 5.
56 Cassandra Chin, "Weekender: A Short History of Grand Forks' Winnipeg Hotel," *Grand Forks Gazette*, December 1, 2012. grandforksgazette.ca/news/.dec-1-weekender-a-short-history-of-grand-forks-winnipeg-hotel/
57 *Evening Sun* (Grand Forks), January 28, 1902, p. 2.
58 *Victoria Daily Times*, November 18, 1908, p. 10.
59 *Evening Sun* (Grand Forks) February 19, 1909, p. 1.
60 Jim Glanville and Alice Glanville, *The Life and Times of Grand Forks: Where the Kettle River Flows: A Centennial History* (Kelowna: Blue Moose Publications, 1997), p. 80.
61 *Evening Sun* (Grand Forks), February 19, 1909, p. 1; See also: The *Gazette* (Grand Forks), April 8, 1909, p. 4.
62 *Gazette*, July 8, 1911, p. 2.
63 Ibid., June 1, 1912, p. 3.
64 Ibid., November 15, 1913, p. 1.
65 Ibid., July 15, 1916, p. 1.
66 *Vancouver Sun*, March 29, 1917, p. 8.
67 *The Grand Forks Sun and Kettle Valley Orchardist*, December 24, 1920, p. 1.
68 The *Ledge* (Greenwood), May 23, 1929, p. 1
69 Glanville, p. 61.
70 *Spokane Spokesman-Review*, "Dry Officer is Recovering," October 11, 1924, p. 7.
71 *Grand Forks Sun*, November 1, 1929, p. 4.
72 *Gazette*, August 2, 1945, p. 3.
73 Ibid., October 31, 1946, p. 7.
74 Ibid., April 15, 1948, p. 1.
75 Karl Yu for the *Grand Forks Gazette*, March 14, 2012, p. 1: issuu.com/blackpress/docs/i20120314070650924; See also: From CTV, March 7,

2012: bc.ctvnews.ca/historic-b-c-hotel-destroyed-in-suspected-arson-1.778396.

Chapter Four: West Kootenay, Part One

1. G.P.V. and Helen B. Akrigg, *1001 British Columbia Place Names* (Vancouver: Discovery Press, Second Edition, 1970), p. 171.
2. Elsie G. Turnbull, "Frontier Hotels in Kootenay Country," in *Pioneer Days in British Columbia: A Selection of Historical Articles From BC Outdoors Magazine, Vol. 3*, Art Downs, ed. (Surrey: Heritage House Publishing., 1977), p. 38.
3. Cited from waymarking.com/waymarks/WMFZM3_Crown_Point_Hotel_Trail_BC.
4. *Vancouver Daily World*, "Trail Tailings: The Peterson Brothers are planning some extensive improvements at the Crown Point Hotel," March 27, 1897, p. 3.
5. Elsie G. Turnbull, "Life In Trail, 1897," in *Pioneer Days In British Columbia: A Selection of Historical Articles From BC Outdoors Magazine, Volume Four*, Art Downs, ed. (Surrey: Heritage House Publishing, 1979), p. 35.
6. Ibid., p. 37.
7. *Daily News Advertiser*, "A Nefarious Attempt," August 31, 1900, p. 8.
8. "History of Trail," *The Trail Historical Society* online: trailhistory.com/history/.
9. *Victoria Daily Times*, "Two Injured In Fire at Trail," October 24, 1911, p. 1.
10. *Province*, August 7, 1907, p. 10.
11. *The Ledge*, January 25, 1912, p. 1.
12. *Vancouver Daily World*, November 11, 1915, p. 12.
13. *Hedley Gazette*, February 17, 1916, p. 3.
14. *Spokesman-Review* (Spokane, Washington), "Death Takes Hotel Man: Ambrose McDermott, Trail, Dies of Heart Failure," May 29, 1928, p. 3.
15. Ibid., "Republic," October 27, 1911, p. 8.
16. *Victoria Daily Times*, March 31, 1925, p. 2.
17. *Gazette*, May 18, 1928, p. 4.
18. *Province*, "New 100,000 Hotel to be Built at Trail," September 16, 1928, p. 15.
19. Ibid., September 23, 1928, p. 42.
20. "Ernest T. Brown, 1976-1950," in *Building The West: The Early Architects of British Columbia*, Donald Luxton, ed. (Vancouver: Talon Books, Revised Edition, 2007), pp. 455-56.

21 *Vancouver Sun*, "Contract Awarded For $80,000 Hotel," September 16, 1929, p. 7.
22 *Province*, "New Hotel at Trail Will Cost $150,000," October 20, 1929, p. 17.
23 *Daily News*," New Structure a Fine Addition to Trail's Facilities," October 11, 1930, p. 11.
24 Wrigley British Columbia Directories.
25 *Province*, January 18, 1940, p. 7.
26 Ibid., "Pioneer of Trail Dies at Age of 92," July 20, 1956, p. 6.
27 Ibid., September 29, 1948, p. 22.
28 *Nanaimo Daily News*, May 3, 1955, p. 1.
29 *Vancouver Sun*, "Police Rush To Steel Union Row," June 4, 1952, p. 1.
30 Ibid., March 22, 1956, p. 11.
31 Karen Robertson in a conversation with the author, 2021.
32 Akrigg, p. 151.
33 Mary Wagner, "St. Leon Hotel: Cedar Castle in the Bush," *The Valley Voice* (New Denver), June 26, 1997, p. 10.
34 *The Miner* (Nelson), June 25, 1892, p. 1.
35 *Nakusp Ledge* (New Denver), "The Mines," October 26, 1893, p. 2.
36 Rosemarie Parent, "St. Leon Hot Springs boomed at the turn of the century," *The Valley Voice* (New Denver), February 16, 2005, p. 8. British Columbia Regional Digitized History (BCRDH), Arrow Lakes Historical Society.
37 *Nelson Tribune*, May 31, 1901, p. 4.
38 Ibid., July 8, 1901, p. 4.
39 Elsie G. Turnbull, *Ghost Towns and Drowned Towns of West Kootenay* (Surrey: Heritage House Publishing, Third Printing, 1994), p. 47.
40 Parent, "St. Leon Hot Springs...," p. 8.
41 *Nelson Tribune*, February 15, 1902, p. 2; The hotel was advertised every day up until opening.
42 Parent, p. 8.
43 *Revelstoke Herald*, October 19, 1905, p. 8.
44 *Nelson Daily News*, October 15, 1912, p. 1.
45 *Victoria Daily Times*, May 18, 1911, p. 2.
46 Parent, p. 8.
47 Turnbull, *Ghost Towns and Drowned Towns*, p. 47.
48 Parent, p. 8.
49 Turnbull, *Ghost Towns*, p. 48.
50 *Vancouver Sun*, "Hotel Changes Hands," November 10, 1941, p. 8.
51 *Province*, June 3, 1944, p. 36.

52 *Arrow Lakes News*, August 23, 1945; August 20, 2015.
53 *Vancouver Sun*, August 6, 1946, p. 19.
54 *Vancouver Sun*, "Outdoors by Lee Straight," April 23, 1946, p. 8.
55 *Victoria Daily Times*, March 19, 1954, p. 4.
56 *Vancouver Sun*, May 10, 1966, p. 11.
57 *Gazette* (Grand Forks), March 15, 1967, p. 8.
58 *Province*, October 20, 1967, p. 9.
59 Ibid., November 2, 1968, p. 35.
60 *Vancouver Sun*, "Blaze Rips Doomed Hotel," November 12, 1968, p. 17.
61 Akrigg, *1001 British Columbia Place Names*, p. 77.
62 Rosemarie Parent, "The Story of Halcyon Hot Springs," Arrow Lake Historical Society: alhs-archives.com/articles/the-story-of-halcyon-hot-springs/.
63 Ibid.
64 "Halcyon" is said to be from the Greek myth in which the goddess Halcyon attempted to drown herself while grieving the loss of her husband. But, instead of drowning, she turned into a kingfisher. She was known to calm the wind and waves during the winter solstice. See: kelownanow.com/news/news/Sponsored/This_BC_attraction_has_a_surprisingly_interesting_history/.
65 Parent, "The Story of Halcyon Hot Springs."
66 *The Miner* (Nelson), July 20, 1895, p. 1. See also: The *Kootenay Mail* (Revelstoke), November 14, 1896, p. 1.
67 Parent, "The Story of Halcyon Hot Springs."
68 *Victoria Daily Times*, October 4, 1897, p. 7.
69 From an advertisement published in the *Province*, May 19, 1900, p. 12.
70 *Province*, May 25, 1900, p. 12.
71 *Nelson Economist*, July 20, 1898, p. 7.
72 *Vancouver Daily World*, May 8, 1900, p. 3.
73 *Calgary Herald*, "A Popular Health Resort," June 18, 1901, p. 7.
74 *Mail Herald*, September 28, 1910, p. 3.
75 Parent, "The Story of Halcyon Hot Springs."
76 Kayleigh Zinger, "This B.C. attraction has a surprisingly interesting history," *Kelowna Now*, July 5, 2019: kelownanow.com/news/news/Sponsored/This_BC_attraction_has_a_surprisingly_interesting_history/
77 *Province*, September 13, 1924, p. 32.
78 *Victoria Daily Times*, March 24, 1924, p. 3.
79 Mary Daem, "The General's Sanitarium: One Man Buttresses Halcyon Hot Springs," *Vancouver Sun*, July 26, 1952, p. 16.

80 Mary Davidson, "Balkans Hero Bears Torch of White Cross," *Province*, January 29, 1938, p. 46. Note: The White Cross of St. John is an ancient society dating back to the First Crusade, 1068, and is one of the oldest organizations for the alleviation of suffering, akin to the St. John Ambulance.
81 Ibid.
82 Ibid.
83 Turnbull, *Ghost Towns*, p. 46.
84 Ibid.
85 Davidson, "Balkans Hero..."
86 Turnbull, *Ghost Towns*, p. 46.
87 Parent, "The Story of Halcyon Hot Springs."
88 Ibid.
89 Tom Hazlitt, "Shrine to a Devoted Love, *Province*, July 6, 1964, p. 20.
90 *Victoria Daily Times*, March 19, 1954, p. 4.
91 Fern Pickering, "ss *Minto* Makes Her Farewell Cruise: Old Arrowhead Paddle Wheeler Whistles Goodbye to Living, Dead," *Vancouver Sun*, April 26, 1954, p. 17.
92 Turnbull, *Ghost Towns*, p. 47.
93 *Province*, "General Dies in Nakusp [sic] Hotel Fire, February 19, 1955, 1. See also: *Vancouver Sun*, February 21, 1955, p. 36.
94 Akrigg, *1001 British Columbia Place Names*, p. 146.
95 Williams' BC Directory for Revelstoke, p. 317.
96 *Revelstoke Herald*, August 25, 1897, p. 4.
97 *Daily Advertiser*, March 26, 1898.
98 *Vancouver Daily World*, January 16, 1907, p. 10
99 *Province*, "Conservatives of Revelstoke Meet," December 10, p. 1909.
100 *Building the West*, 508.
101 *Mail Herald*, April 6, 1910, p. 1.
102 *Saturday Sunset* (Vancouver), September 16, 1911, p. 2.
103 *Mail Herald*, October 5, 1910, p. 5.
104 Ibid., "The Enterprise Brewery," November 21, 1906, p. 4.
105 *Victoria Daily Times*, November 13, 1914, p. 14.
106 seerevelstoke.com/where-it-all-began-over-100-years-of-ski-history-in-revelstoke/.
107 *Victoria Daily Times*, "Compensation: another specific case," May 13, 1916, p. 15.
108 *Province*, January 31, 1919, p. 25.
109 Ibid., "King Edward Hotel, Revelstoke, Sold to Former Rival Owner," November 21, 1924, p. 3.

110 Ibid., November 29, 1927, p. 12.
111 Ibid., "Leave to Appeal Given In Revelstoke Hotel Case," June 6, 1928, p. 1.
112 Ibid., "Last Tribute Paid Pioneer at Revelstoke," March 24, 1939, p. 20.
113 King Edward Hotel, aka Hug n' Slug, facebook.com/King-Edward-Hotel-aka-Hug-n-Slug-172148099522.
114 Akrigg, p. 94.
115 Greg Nesteroff, "Kaslo, the place where blackberries grow," *Nelson Star*, May 31, 2015. nelsonstar.com/community/kaslo-the-place-where-blackberries-grow/.
116 *British Columbia News* (Kaslo), March 4, 1898, p. 8.
117 Ibid., August 20, 1898, p. 8.
118 *Vancouver Daily World*, August 6, 1902, p. 3.
119 *The Ledge* (Greenwood), June 22, 1911, p. 1.
120 Greg Nesteroff, "The King George Hotel," *The Weekender* (Nelson), December 2007, quoted from the *Kootenaian*, June 15, 1911.
121 en.wikipedia.org/wiki/Coronation_of_George_V_and_Mary.
122 *Province*, "Plans for Premier's Tour of Province," March 1, 1912, p. 34.
123 *Daily News* (Nelson), December 9, 1912, p. 2.
124 Nesteroff, "The King George Hotel," *The Weekender* (Nelson), December 2007.
125 *Province*, "Kaslo Girls Have Made Remarkable Contribution to the Empire's Cause," September 24, 1918, p. 8.
126 Elsie G. Turnbull, "Frontier Hotels in Kootenay Country," in *Pioneer Days in British Columbia, Vol. 3: A selection of historical articles from BC Outdoors magazine*, Art Downs, ed., (Surrey: Heritage House Publishing, 1977), p. 40.
127 *Province*, July 8 1928, p. 46.
128 Ibid., March 31, 1929, p. 24.
129 Ibid., September 9, 1933, 42.
130 Turnbull, "Frontier Hotels," p. 40.
131 *Calgary Herald*, April 14, 1945, p. 9.
132 Death certificate for Edward Herbert Latham, #50-09-011908, Kaslo.
133 *The Province*, "Fire Razes Landmark at Kaslo," September 28, p. 10.
134 Turnbull, "Frontier Hotels," p. 40.
135 *Province*, "Hotel for Kaslo," October 23, 1954, p. 7.
136 Greg Nesteroff and Eric Brighton, *Lost Kootenays: A History in Pictures* (Lunenburg, Nova Scotia: MacIntyre Purcell Publishing, 2021), p. 22.

Chapter Five: West Kootenay, Part Two

1. G.P.V. and Helen B. Akrigg, *1001 British Columbia Place Names*. (Vancouver: Discovery Press, Second Edition, 1970), p. 152.
2. N.L. Barlee, *Gold Creeks and Ghost Towns* (Summerland: Canada West Magazine, 4th printing, June 1972), p. 119, pp. 123-24.
3. Garnet Basque, *West Kootenay: The Pioneer Years* (Langley, BC: Sunfire Publications, 1990), p. 109.
4. Basque, p. 109, p. 117.
5. Basque, p. 113.
6. *Star-Tribune*, (Minneapolis, Minnesota) January 31, 1891, p. 4.
7. Greg Nesteroff, "Sandon founder's family visits," *Nelson Star*, August 24, 2014, nelsonstar.com/news/sandon-founders-family-visits/.
8. Veronika Pellowski, *Silver, Lead & Hell: The Story of Sandon* (Sandon: Prospectors' Pick Publishing, 2000), p. 21.
9. *The Paystreak* (Sandon), March 26, 1898, p. 1.
10. Ibid., "Reco Hotel Opening," May 14, 1898, p. 1.
11. N.L. Barlee, *Gold Creeks...*, p. 124.
12. Basque, *West Kootenay*, p. 117.
13. Ibid., p. 121.
14. *Similkameen Star*, May 12, 1900, p. 1.
15. Basque, *West Kootenay*, p. 128.
16. Ibid., p. 129.
17. George Stewart, "Sandon," in *Pioneer Days in British Columbia*, Art Downs. ed. (Surrey: Heritage House Publishing, 1979). See also: *BC Outdoors Magazine* (Surrey: Foremost Publishing), 1973, p. 21.
18. Clark Myers, grandson of William Bennett, posting on Facebook, 2021.
19. *Slocan Mining Review*, January 2, 1908, p. 4.
20. *District Ledge* (Fernie), "Sandon," May 9, 1908, p. 5.
21. *The Ledge* (Greenwood), June 18, 1908, p. 1.
22. *Daily News*, August 26, 1908, p. 4.
23. *The Ledge*, September 9, 1909, p. 1.
24. *Daily News Advertiser*, May 25, 1910, p. 10.
25. *Vancouver Daily World*, May 12, 1911, p. 5.
26. Ibid., "Hotelman Will Cast Vote For Prohibition," August 16, 1916, p. 1.
27. *Vancouver Daily World*, "Reco Mine Sold," May 17, 1919, p. 19.
28. Nesteroff, "Sandon founder's family visits," *Nelson Star*, August 24, 2014.
29. Basque, *West Kootenay*, p. 136.
30. *Daily News*, "Sandon Mad Man Taken to Coast by Police Escort," February 12, 1930, p. 10.

31 *Province*, April 13, 1935, p. 56.
32 Basque, p. 136. See also: Elsie G. Turnbull, *Ghost Towns and Drowned Towns of the West Kootenay* (Surrey: Heritage House Publishing, Third Printing, 1994), p. 78.
33 *Province*, June 26, 1955, p. 7.
34 N.L. Barlee, "New Denver," *Gold Creeks*..., pp. 111–13
35 Ibid., p. 113.
36 Akrigg, p. 124.
37 *Vancouver Daily World*, March 25, 1896, p. 6.
38 *Victoria Daily Times*, January 16, 1912, p. 5.
39 *Province*, May 25, 1930, p. 3.
40 *Vancouver Sun*, June 4, 1932, p. 12.
41 *Calgary Herald*, April 23, 1962, April 23, p. 5.
42 Akrigg, p. 142.
43 Greg Nesteroff and Eric Brighton, Lost Kootenays: A History in Pictures (Lunenburg, NS: MacIntyre-Purcell Publishing, 2021), p. 19.
44 Greg Nesteroff, "Place Names, Procter, Part I," in the *Nelson Star*, August 12, 2016. nelsonstar.com/community/place-names-procter-part-1/.
45 *The Miner* (Nelson), May 2, 1896, p. 3.
46 *The Tribune* (Nelson), May 8, 1897, p. 4.
47 *The Miner*, March 26, 1898, p. 6.
48 *The Tribune*, May 23, 1899, p. 4.
49 *The Miner*, July 3, 1898, p. 3.
50 Garnet Basque, *West Kootenay: The Pioneer Years* (Langley: Sunfire Publications Limited, 1990), p. 147.
51 *Daily News*, June 1, 1906, p. 2
52 Ibid., "Excursion to Procter," July 12, 1906, p. 5.
53 *The Ledge* (Greenwood), June 26, 1913, p. 1.
54 Tom Lymbery, *Tom's Gray Creek: A Kootenay Memoir, Part I: The Early Years* (Gray Creek, BC: Gray Creek Publishing, Third Printing, 2018), p. 36.
55 *Vancouver Daily World*, August 15, 1916, p. 8.
56 *Daily News*, April 5, 1917, p. 4.
57 Ibid., "W.A. Ward Takes Over Outlet Hotel," April 8, 1918, p. 5.
58 *The Miner*, June 21, 1890, p. 3.
59 *Nelson Daily News*, November 9, 1912, p. 2.
60 *Daily News*, June 12, 1929, p. 10.
61 *Nanaimo Daily News*, "Train Plunged Through Bridge, Two Killed," January 28, 1929, p. 1.

62 Lymbery, *Tom's Gray Creek*, p. 64
63 *Vancouver Sun*, January 23, 1941, p. 18.
64 *Daily Colonist* (Victoria), July 21, 1942, p. 15.
65 Conversation with Tom Lymbery on Facebook, 2021.
66 Greg Nesteroff, "Lost Kootenay Lake hotels remembered in postcards," *Today in BC*, September 17, 2012. todayinbc.com/news/lost-kootenay-lake-hotels-remembered-in-postcards/.
67 Note that the spelling of the resort is "beaches," not "beeches." This area of the New Brunswick coastline was famous for its sandy beaches from which the resort derived its name.
68 Sir Charles G.D. Roberts, *The Canadian Guide-Book*, 1891, p. 131.
69 *Vancouver Daily World*, April 15, 1891, p. 1.
70 Ibid., June 13, 1891, p. 2.
71 *The Miner* (Nelson), September 5, 1891, p. 12.
72 Patricia Rogers, BC *History Magazine*, Vol. 40, No. 2, p. 30.
73 *Vancouver Daily World*, May 7, 1892, p. 2.
74 *The Miner* (Nelson), October 3, 1891, p. 1.
75 *Vancouver Daily World*, November 14, 1891, p. 8.
76 *Nelson Economist*, July 20, 1898, p. 7.
77 *Province*, August 18, 1934, 19; from a story first appearing in the *Nelson Tribune* circa. 1899.
78 John English, *Robert Borden: His Life and World* (Toronto: McGraw-Hill Ryerson, 1977), p. 56.
79 *Victoria Daily Times*, September 17, 1902, p. 1.
80 *Nelson Tribune*, April 11, 1903, p. 3.
81 Note: To learn more about the history of the sternwheeler *Lytton*, follow this link: en.wikipedia.org/wiki/Lytton_(sternwheeler)
82 R. Edward Gosnell, *A History: British Columbia* (Victoria: Lewis Publishing, 1909), pp. 558–59.
83 *Similkameen Star* (Princeton), May 17, 1902, p. 2.
84 Gosnell, *A History: British Columbia*, p. 559.
85 *Nelson Daily News*, June 24, 1903, p. 2
86 *The Ledge* (New Denver), September 3, 1903, p. 1.
87 "Donald Alexander Smith, 1st Baron Strathcona and Mount Royal GCMG GCVO PC DL FRS (August 6, 1820–January 21, 1914), and known as Donald A. Smith from May 1886 to August 1897, was a Scottish-born Canadian businessman who became one of the British Empire's foremost builders and philanthropists." en.wikipedia.org/wiki/Donald_Smith,_1st_Baron_Strathcona_and_Mount_

Royal#:~:text=Donald%20Alexander%20Smith%2C%201st%20
Baron,s%20foremost%20builders%20and%20philanthropists.
88 *Nelson Tribune*, November 28, 1903, p. 4.
89 *Vancouver Daily World*, March 7, 1907, p. 3.
90 *Daily News* (Nelson), March 17, 1907, p. 1.
91 *Daily Canadian* (Nelson), June 22, 1907, p. 1.
92 *Province*, "Mortgage Sale," March 17, 1908, p. 19.
93 Ibid., August 17, 1911, p. 18.
94 *The Ledge* (Nelson), July 3, 1919, p. 1.
95 *Victoria Daily Times*, May 14, 1913, p. 18.
96 Greg Nesteroff, "Opulent hotel, witchcraft part of Nelson woman's past," in *Nelson Star*, March 21, 2012.
97 The Armenian minority in Turkey have been fighting to survive a genocide for over a hundred years.
98 *Daily News*, May 29, 1911, p. 1. The first mention of A.D. Papazian in Nelson, BC, was when he was with a team of other individuals raising money for the local YMCA.
99 *Nelson Daily News*, "Mrs. Papazian," March 18, 1912, p. 3.
100 Ibid., September 20, 1920, p. 8.
101 Ibid., March 29, 1924, p. 8.
102 BC Directory entries between 1925 and 1936 listed M. Papazian as manager of the Strathcona Hotel in Nelson.
103 *Victoria Daily Times*, "Loss of Library Was Greater Than Loss of Money," June 23, 1925, p. 12.
104 *Nanaimo Daily News*, May 4, 1927, p. 4.
105 *Victoria Daily Times*, May 26, 1928, p. 29.
106 *Nelson Daily News*, June 5, 1923, p. 3.
107 *Province*, June 20, 1938, p. 21.
108 *Vancouver Sun*, "Sixty Flee Blaze in Nelson Hotel," June 20, 1938, p. 12.
109 *Province*, "Twilight Extension Report Encouraging," September 10, 1940, p. 22.
110 Ibid., "Ex-Nelson Jeweler Dies in US," July 22, 1949, p. 8.
111 *Vancouver Sun*, "Nelson Medical Student Dead in Montreal," December 29, 1942, p. 3.
112 Greg Nesteroff, "Tied by tragedy and miracle: Survivors of 1955 Strathcona Hotel blaze thank Nelson firefighters," *Grand Forks Gazette*, June 27, 2019.
113 Don Stainsby, "It Looked Like The End of The World," *Vancouver Sun*, May 27, 1955, pp. 1–2.

114 Nesteroff, "Tied by tragedy and miracle..."
115 Stainsby, "It Looked Like The End...," p. 2.
116 *Vancouver Sun*, "Six Bodies Identified," May 28, 1955, p. 1.
117 *Nelson Economist*, March 23, 1898, p. 5.
118 John Norris, *Historic Nelson: The Early Years* (Lantzville, BC: Oolichan Books, 1995), pp. 259-60.
119 *Nelson Economist*, August 4, 1897, p. 6.
120 *Nelson Miner*, October 9, 1897, p. 3.
121 Carey Pallister and Dorothy Mindenhall, "Alexander Charles Ewart, 1854-1916," in *Building the West: The Early Architects of British Columbia*, Donald Luxton, ed. (Vancouver: Talon Books, 2007), p. 212.
122 wikipedia.org/wiki/John_Frederick_Hume
123 *Nelson Tribune*, "Nelson is a lucky city," November 20, 1897, p. 1.
124 Ibid., March 19, 1898, p. 1.
125 *Calgary Herald*, March 28, 1898, p. 2.
126 *Nelson Economist*, March 16, 1898, p. 1.
127 Ibid., March 23, 1898, p. 11.
128 *Province*, "Northwest Championship," December 7, 1898, p. 7.
129 *Weekly News Advertiser*, February 8, 1899, p. 12.
130 *Victoria Daily Times*, March 11, 1899, p. 7.
131 *Daily News*, December 22, 1899, p. 5.
132 *Daily News Advertiser*, May 24, 1900, p. 6.
133 *Vancouver Daily World*, September 21, 1901, p. 8.
134 *Nelson Tribune*, February 15, 1902, p. 1.
135 *Victoria Daily Times*, July 31, 1902, p. 6.
136 *Vancouver Daily World*, June 10, 1904, p. 1.
137 Ibid., September 1, 1905, p. 9.
138 *Daily Canadian* (Nelson), "Hume Hotel Sold... Changes Will be Few," June 22, 1907, p. 1.
139 *Daily News Advertiser*, "Hume Hotel, Nelson Sold," June 23, 1907, p. 1.
140 James McCredie Brown, "The Man Who Planned the New Westminster Bridge," *Province*, September 9, 1933, p. 43.
141 *Province*, "Attempted Suicide but Gun Misfired," May 18, 1909, p. 2.
142 *Vancouver Sun*, October 19, 1912, p. 8.
143 *Nelson Daily News*, October 16, 1912, p. 8.
144 Brown, "The Man Who Planned...," p. 43.
145 *Vancouver Sun*, April 26, 1913, p. 17.
146 *Daily News*, November 13, 1913, p. 6.
147 Author's postcard collection (unsent) showing Hume Hotel, circa. 1918.

148 *Vancouver Daily World*, September 22, 1922, p. 1.
149 *Province*, May 12, 1929, p. 56.
150 *Daily News*, May 1, 1929, p. 1.
151 *Nelson Daily Star*, April 17, 2015, p. 1. The story goes that Bob Hope was preforming in Nelson in 1991 and staying at the Heritage (Hume) Hotel. Hope was dressed as a bellhop and was in the elevator talking to future general manager Ryan Martin when he made the famous quote. Hope also quipped, "I got golf balls older than you, kid."

Chapter Six: East Kootenay

1 G.P.V. and Helen B. Akrigg, *1001 British Columbia Place Names*. (Vancouver: Discovery Press, Second Edition, 1970), p. 47.
2 en.wikipedia.org/wiki/Cranbrook,_British_Columbia. For more on the founding of Cranbrook and the railroad, visit this link: crowsnest-highway.ca/cgi-bin/citypage.pl?city=cranbrook.
3 *Calgary Herald*, April 19 1962, p. 22.
4 *Cranbrook Herald*, April 11, 1918, p. 1.
5 Ibid., April 27, 1923, p. 5.
6 Ibid., October 5, 1923, p. 6.
7 The Baker Hotel history: www.thebakerhotel.ca/history/.
8 *Vancouver Sun*, February 25, 1924, p. 2.
9 *Cranbrook Herald*, "Dog Races Attract Crowds on Street," February 1, 1924, p. 1.
10 *Fernie Free Press*, "Bing's In Town Was the Last Word Friday," July 20, 1946, p. 3.
11 *Province*, "Mt. Baker Hotel Sold at Cranbrook," March 17, 1947, p. 3.
12 *Courier* (Cranbrook), "Service for 'Teddy' Clauson on Thursday," April 18, 1962, p. 7.
13 *Calgary Albertan*, "Celebrants Pay Fines in Court," May 29, 1948, p. 11.
14 *Star-Phoenix* (Saskatoon, Saskatchewan), October 26, 1948, p. 15.
15 Barry Coulter, "Historic Cranbrook Hotel Gets New Life," *Cranbrook Daily Townsman*, July 11, 2018: cranbrooktownsman.com/news/historic-cranbrook-hotel-gets-new-life/.
16 Akrigg, p. 62.
17 *Province*, "Fernie Was Fire Swept," April 29, 1904, p. 1.
18 Henderson's BC Gazetteer and Directory for 1902, 1903, 1904, and 1905.
19 *Fernie Ledger*, August 9, 1905, p. 4.

20 Jim Cameron, "The Great Fernie Fire of 1908," *Cranbrook Daily Townsman*, November 8, 2012. cranbrooktownsman.com/opinion/the-great-fernie-fire-of-1908/.
21 *Victoria Daily Times*, August 3, 1908, p. 1. It was later determined that the actual number of lives lost was only ten, which is incredible, out of a population of nearly 5,000 and considering the ferocity of the rapid fire.
22 *District Ledger*, August 8, 1908 p. 4.
23 Ibid., August 22, 1908, p. 3.
24 David Scott and Edna Hanic, *East Kootenay Chronicle* (Langley: Antonson Publishing, A Mr. Paperback book, 1979), p. 146.
25 *District Ledger*, May 14, 1910, p. 1.
26 *Cranbrook Herald*, March 24, 1910, p. 1.
27 *Spokane Chronicle*, July 16, 1910, p. 5.
28 *District Ledger*, "Fernie Lady Painfully Burnt," July 16, 1910, p. 1.
29 Ibid., January 18, 1913, p. 1.
30 *Daily News*, February 2, 1913, p. 2.
31 *Spokesman-Review*, "Fernie is a Lovely Mountain Town," August 5, 1923, p. 38.
32 Ibid., July 26, 1925, p. 41.
33 *Fernie Free Press*, January 18, 1929, p. 1.
34 Ibid., "Gates Wins by Three at Fernie," January 17, 1930, p. 1.
35 *Vancouver Sun*, "J.L. Gates, Fernie, Leases Hotel Here," May 5, 1932, p. 12.
36 *Spokesman-Review* (Spokane, Washington), January 15, 1949, p. 5.
37 *Victoria Daily Times*, May 15, 1978, p. 10.
38 Akrigg, p. 20.
39 *The Golden Era*, "Local and General," October 27 1899, p. 4.
40 *Mail-Herald* (Revelstoke), April 23, 1910, p. 8.
41 *Vancouver Daily World*, "Man and Cash Disappear Together," May 5, 1910, p. 1.
42 *Cranbrook Herald*, May 19, 1910, p. 5.
43 *Vancouver Sun*, December 29, 1969, p. 14.
44 *Daily News* (Nelson), March 9, 1916, p. 5.
45 *Cranbrook Herald*, "Another Old Timer Passes to the Great Beyond," January 17, 1918, p. 1.
46 *Calgary Herald*, June 11, 1925, p. 6.
47 *Cranbrook Herald*, August 27, 1925, p. 2.
48 *Vancouver Sun*, November 23, 1943, 20.
49 *Province*, May 9, 1944, p. 10.

50   Ibid., November 22, 1946, p. 1.
51   Ibid., "Goes Through Ice on Lake," January 3, 1947, p. 24.
52   *Province*, April 27, 1948, p. 23.
53   *Calgary Herald*, March 25, 1954, p. 10.
54   Ibid., May 25, 1959, p. 30.
55   *Vancouver Sun*, "15 Escape as Fire Levels Colourful 'Tin House' Hotel," December 29, 1969.
56   For those who wish to learn more about the unique Coronation Hotel, Ron Ede has written a fine booklet entitled *The Night the Tin House Burned: A Ballad by Ron Ede* with illustrations by Kurt Reichel (Palliser Printing and Publishing, 1969). Contact the Windermere Museum, windermerevalleymuseum.ca/.
57   Ron Ede, *The Night the Tin House Burned*, no page numbers.
58   Tourism Golden: www.tourismgolden.com/about/golden-history.
59   The Golden Museum: www.goldenbcmuseums.com/queens-hotel-in-golden-bc/.
60   The surname was also spelled "Greene," but I have opted to use "Green."
61   Colleen Palumbo, "The Queen's Hotel Had a Long Life after Being Built in 1883," the *Golden Star*, February 5, 2014, p. A9.
62   *Golden Era*, January 20, 1894; open.library.ubc.ca/collections/bcnewspapers/goldenera/items/1.0227238.
63   Ibid., March 17, 1894, p. 1.
64   Ibid., July 14, 1894, p. 1.
65   Ibid., July 28, 1894, p. 1.
66   Ibid., June 22, 1895, p. 1.
67   Ibid., March 6, 1897, p. 4.
68   Ibid., December 19, 1896, p. 4.
69   Colleen Palumbo, "The Queen's Hotel Had a Long Life...," p. A9.
70   *Victoria Daily Times*, July 27, 1897, p. 3.
71   Palumbo, p. A9.
72   *Golden Era*, August 16, 1901, p. 14.
73   Thomas King, "The Story of Golden," *Golden Star*, June 10, 1965, p. 11.
74   The Golden Museum: goldenbcmuseums.com/queens-hotel-in-golden-bc/.
75   *Cranbrook Herald*, June 30, 1921, p. 6.
76   Palumbo, p. A9.
77   *Province*, "Link With Founding of Golden Severed in Demolition of Shacks," December 30, 1926, p. 11.
78   Palumbo, p. A9.

79 Judy Malone, "Nostalgia: A description of Golden," *Golden Star*, February 7, 1979, p. 6.
80 *Golden News*, "Queens Hotel for Wreckers," July 23, 1959, p. 1.
81 Don Beers, *The Wonder of Yoho: A trail guide* (Calgary: Rocky Mountain Books, 1989), p. 177.
82 Pierre Berton, *The Last Spike: The Great Railway, 1881–1885*, (Toronto: McClelland and Stewart, Twelfth Printing, 1977), p. 163.
83 *Province*, March 12, 1902, p. 1
84 Elsa Lam, "Rails, Trails, Roads and Lodgings: Networks of Mobility and the Touristic Development of the Canadian Pacific Rockies, 1885-1930," from *Moving Natures: Mobility and the Environment in Canadian History*, Ben Bradley, Jay Young, and Colin M. Coast, eds. (University of Calgary, 2016), p. 286, ucp.manifoldapp.org/read/moving-natures/section/3e74c74f-f60b-40fb-b451-ab2ee881a764.
85 Margaret A. Haapoja, "Summer Getaways: Three log resorts offer comfort and scenery," *Log Home Living Magazine*, June 2010, p. 24.
86 *Province*, September 23, 1902, p. 4.
87 Jane Levey, "Yoho Ho," *Washington Post*, December 6, 1987: washingtonpost.com/archive/lifestyle/travel/1987/12/06/yoho-ho/e1f18169-b175-4790-bb08-f0da59907e52/.
88 *Province*, "Railway Hotels Improve," May 2, 1906, p. 6.
89 Christine Barnes, *Great Lodges of the Canadian Rockies*, (Bend, Oregon: W.W. West, 1999), p. 79.
90 Elsa Lam, "Rails, Trails, Roads and Lodgings...," p. 291.
91 *Victoria Daily Times*, May 6, 1914, p. 14.
92 *Vancouver Sun*, October 15, 1918, p. 10.
93 *Province*, July 5, 1919, p. 8.
94 Ibid., September 20, 1919, p. 1.
95 Cinda Chavich, "Sleepover: Emerald Lake, Field, BC," October 9, 2002, theglobeandmail.com/life/sleepover-emerald-lake-lodge-field-bc/article4142624/.
96 Visit this site for information about the Burgess Shale site and some amazing photographs of the many fossils to be found there: field.ca/activities/burgess_shale/.

SELECTED BIBLIOGRAPHY

Akrigg, G.P.V. and Helen B. *1001 British Columbia Place Names*. Vancouver, BC: Discovery Press, 2nd Ed., 1970.

Bachusky, Johnny. *Ghost Town Stories III: Tales of Dreams, Tragedies and Heroism in British Columbia*. Cranmore, Alberta: Altitude Publishing Canada Ltd., 2004.

Barlee, N.L. *Gold Creeks and Ghost Towns*. Summerland, BC: Canada West Magazine, Fourth Printing, June 1972.

Basque, Garnet. *Ghost Towns and Mining Towns of the Boundary Country*. Surrey, BC: Heritage House Publishing Company Lt., Surefire Edition, Reprinted in 2007.

Basque, Garnet. West Kootenay, The Pioneer Years, Langley, BC: Sunfire Publications Ltd., 1990.

Basque, Garnet. *West Kootenays: The Pioneer Years*. Surrey, BC: Heritage House Publications, 1990.

Berton, Pierre. *Klondike: The Last Great Gold Rush, 1896-1899*. Toronto: McClelland & Stewart, 1972.

Bowen, Lynne. *Whoever Gives Us Bread: The Story of Italians in British Columbia*. Vancouver: Douglas & McIntyre, 2011.

Brown, Ron. *The Train Doesn't Stop Here Anymore: An Illustrated History of Railway Stations of Canada*. Toronto: Dundurn Press, 2008.

Clark, Cecil. *Tales of the British Columbia Provincial Police*. Sidney, BC: Gray's Publishing Ltd., 1971.

Downs, Art, ed. *Pioneer Days in British Columbia, Volume Two*. Surrey, BC: Heritage House Publishing Company Ltd., 1979.

Glanville, Jim & Alice. *The Life and Times of Grand Forks, Where the Kettle River Flows*. Kelowna, BC: Blue Moose Productions, 1997.

Hamilton, Douglas L., *Sobering Dilemma: A History of Prohibition in British Columbia*. Vancouver, BC: Ronsdale Press, 2004.

Heron, Craig. *Booze: A Distilled History*. Toronto: Between the Lines, 2003.

Jacobsen, Larry G. Walhachin, Birth of a Legend, Port Coquitlam, BC: Prolong Press, 2014.

Jones, Jo Fraser, ed. *Hobnobbing with a Countess and Other Okanagan Adventures: The Diaries of Alice Barrett Parke, 1891-1900*. Vancouver: UBC Press, 2001.

Kluckner, Michael, *Vanishing British Columbia*. Vancouver, BC: UBC Press, 2005.

Luxton, Donald, ed. *Building the West: The Early Architects of British Columbia*. Revised Second Edition. Vancouver, BC: Talonbooks, 2007.

Mofford, Glen A. Along the E&N: A Journey Back to the Historic Hotels of Vancouver Island, Victoria, BC: Touchwood Editions, 2019.

Nesteroff, Greg. A massive volume of work.

Norcross, Dave. "Granite Road Memories," written for the *Nelson Daily News*, Nelson, BC.

Norris, John, *Historic Nelson, The Early Years*. Lantzville, BC: Oolichan Books, 1995.

Ormsby, Margaret. *British Columbia: A History*. Toronto: Macmillan, 1958.

Paterson, T.W. *British Columbia: The Pioneer Years*. Langley, BC: Stagecoach Publishing Co. Ltd., 1977.

—— *Okanagan-Similkameen, British Columbia Ghost Town Series*. Langley, BC: Sunfire Publications Ltd., 1983.

Reksten, Terry. *The Illustrated History of British Columbia*. Vancouver and Toronto: Douglas & McIntyre, 2001.

Simpson, Sharron J. *The Kelowna Story, An Okanagan History*. Madeira Park, BC: Harbour Publishing, 2011.

Sterne, Diane. White Gold and Black Diamonds: The History of Granite Creek and Coalmont, Coalmont, BC: Mozey-on-inn Books, 2011.

Stonebanks, Roger. *Fighting for Dignity: The Ginger Goodwin Story*. St. John's, Newfoundland: Canadian Committee on Labour History, 2004.

Turnbull, Elsie G. *Ghost Towns and Drowned Towns of West Kootenay*. Surrey: Heritage House Publishing, 1995.

Turnbull, Elsie G. Ghost Towns and Drowned Towns of West Kootenay, Surrey, BC: Heritage House Publishing Co., Ltd., Third Printing, 1992.

Turner, Robert D. and Wilkie, J.S. David, *Steam Along the Boundary: Canadian Pacific, Great Northern and the Great Boundary Copper Boom*. Winlaw, BC: Sononis Press, 2007.

Webber, Jean. *A Rich and Fruitful Land: The History of the Valleys of the Okanagan, Similkameen and Shuswap*. Madeira Park, BC: Harbour Publishing, 1999.

Weir, Joan. Walhachin: Catastrophe or Camelot? Surrey, BC: Hancock House Publishers, 1984.

Zuehlke, Mark. *Scoundrels, Dreamers & Second Sons: British Remittance Men in the Canadian West*. Toronto: Dundurn Press, 2001.

Newspapers

(Title preceding newspaper name omitted, i.e. *The*)
Abbotsford Post
Armstrong Advance
Armstrong Advocate
Arrow Lakes News
Ashcroft Journal
Boundary Creek Times (Greenwood)
British Columbia News (Kaslo)
British Columbian
Calgary Albertan
Calgary Herald
Chilliwack Progress
Coalmont Courier
Courier (Cranbrook)
Cranbrook Herald
Creston Review
Daily Building Record (Vancouver)
Daily Canadian (Nelson)
District Ledger
Enderby Press and Walker's Weekly
Edenograph (Enderby)
Evening Sun (Grand Forks)
Fernie Free Press
Fernie Ledger
Gazette (Grand Forks)
Golden Era
Grand Forks Sun and Kettle Valley Orchardist
Hedley Gazette
Interior News (Smithers)
Kelowna Record
Keremeos Trumpet
Kootenaian (Nelson)
Ledge (Greenwood)
Ledge (Nelson)
Lethbridge Herald
Lillooet Prospector
Mail Herald (Revelstoke)
Manitoba Morning Free Press (Winnipeg)
Merritt Herald
Miner (Nelson)
Nakusp Ledge (New Denver)
Nanaimo Daily News
Nanaimo Daily Telegram
Nelson Economist
Nelson Tribune
Nicola Herald
Nicola Valley Times
Orchard City Record (Kelowna)
Pacific Canadian
Penticton Herald
Port Moody Gazette
Province
Star-Phoenix (Saskatoon, Sask.)
Similkameen Star
Spokane Chronicle (Washington State)
Spokesman-Review (Spokane, Washington)
Summerland Review
Times (Nanaimo)
Vancouver Daily World
Vancouver Sun
Vernon News
Victoria Daily Times
Walker's Weekly (Enderby)
Weekender (Nelson)
Weekly (Victoria)
Weekly News Advertiser

GLEN A. MOFFORD (1954–2022) was a historian and a writer with a passion for sharing the social history of British Columbia. He held a degree in history from Simon Fraser University and was the author of two previous books on BC's historical hotels and their drinking establishments: *Along the E&N* (TouchWood Editions, 2019) and *Aqua Vitae* (TouchWood Editions, 2016).

GREG NESTEROFF is the former editor of the Nelson Star, former news director of the Vista Radio stations in the West Kootenay, and the co-author of Lost Kootenays: A History in Photographs. He runs "The Kütne Reader," a blog about local history.